# Explainable AI (XAI)

# Explainable AI (XAI)

**Michael Ward**
**Sadie Graham**

Kruger Brentt
Publishers
2026

Kruger Brentt Publishers UK. LTD.
Company Number 9728962

Regd. Office: 68 St Margarets Road, Edgware, Middlesex HA8 9UU



ISBN: 978-1-78715-610-4



For information on all our publications visit our website at http://krugerbrentt.com/

# Preface

Artificial Intelligence (AI) has rapidly evolved into a transformative force across industries, shaping decision-making in healthcare, finance, agriculture, governance, and beyond. However, the opacity of many AI models—often referred to as "black-box" systems—has raised pressing concerns regarding accountability, fairness, and trust. As AI systems increasingly influence human lives, the need for transparency, interpretability, and ethical responsibility has never been greater.

Explainable AI (XAI) addresses these concerns by exploring the concepts, techniques, and real-world applications of explainable and interpretable machine learning. It delves into the foundations of XAI, examines current methods for model transparency, and highlights how organizations can balance performance with explainability. The text also discusses critical issues such as fairness, bias detection, and human–AI collaboration, offering readers a roadmap to responsible AI adoption.

The book is designed for students, researchers, and practitioners who wish to understand not only the technical aspects of XAI but also its societal and ethical implications. By bridging the gap between complex AI algorithms and human interpretability, this work aims to empower readers to build AI systems that inspire confidence, foster accountability, and enhance decision-making.

**Michael Ward**

**Sadie Graham**

# Contents

CHAPTER 1

# Introduction to Explainable AI (XAI)

## 1.1 WHAT IS EXPLAINABLE AI?

Artificial Intelligence (AI) is increasingly becoming a vital part of modern technology, influencing everything from healthcare and finance to autonomous vehicles and entertainment. However, many AI models, particularly those using deep learning and complex neural networks, function as "black boxes" — producing decisions without offering a clear explanation of how they arrived at them. This lack of transparency can lead to mistrust, ethical concerns, and challenges in regulatory compliance. Explainable AI (XAI) emerges as a crucial solution to these problems, aiming to make AI systems more interpretable, transparent, and accountable to human users.

Explainable AI is more than a technical innovation — it's a necessary step toward responsible and ethical AI deployment. By demystifying how AI systems make decisions, XAI fosters trust, supports regulatory compliance, and enables human oversight in critical applications. While challenges remain in balancing performance with interpretability, ongoing advancements promise a future where AI systems are both powerful and understandable, ensuring they serve humanity with transparency and integrity.

Explainable AI refers to a set of techniques and methods that allow humans to understand and trust the outcomes produced by AI systems. It seeks to answer key questions about an AI model's behavior: why a specific decision was made, why an alternative outcome wasn't chosen, what factors influenced the result, and whether the system will behave consistently in similar situations. The goal is to ensure that AI systems provide not just accurate predictions, but also understandable reasoning behind those predictions.

For example, in a healthcare setting, a black-box AI model might predict that a patient has a high likelihood of developing a disease. While this prediction could be clinically valuable, it's more beneficial if the AI also explains which factors — such as medical history, lifestyle, or genetic markers — contributed to that prediction. Explainable AI bridges this gap by making these contributing factors clear, empowering doctors to make better-informed decisions.

### 1.1.1 Why Explainability Matters

The importance of explainability in AI extends across various domains, driven by multiple factors including trust, accountability, and ethical considerations. In high-stakes environments like healthcare, finance, and criminal justice, decisions made by AI models can profoundly affect people's lives. Patients want to understand why they're recommended a specific treatment, loan applicants deserve to know why they were rejected, and defendants require clarity if an AI model influences sentencing. Without explanation, people are less likely to trust the technology, even if it consistently produces accurate results.

Explainability is also vital for debugging and improving AI models. When a system makes an incorrect or biased decision, transparency allows developers to trace the problem, identify biases, and retrain the model. This level of interpretability supports continuous learning and refinement of AI systems, making them more reliable and fair over time.

Regulatory and legal considerations further amplify the need for explainability. In regions like the European Union, the General Data Protection Regulation (GDPR) grants individuals the "right to explanation," meaning they can demand a clear rationale for automated decisions that affect them. This regulatory landscape is expanding globally, compelling companies to prioritize transparency in their AI-driven products and services.

### 1.1.2 Approaches to Explainable AI

Several methods have emerged to create more interpretable AI systems. These approaches generally fall into two categories: intrinsic explainability and post-hoc explainability.

- Intrinsic explainability involves designing models that are inherently interpretable. Simpler models like decision trees, linear regression, and rule-based systems are naturally easier to understand because their internal logic mirrors human reasoning. For example, a decision tree for loan approval may show a clear path — if income is above a certain threshold and debt is low, the loan is approved. However, these models may sacrifice accuracy when handling complex datasets, which is where more sophisticated techniques come into play.
- Post-hoc explainability methods apply to complex, already-trained models to interpret their behavior after the fact. Techniques like LIME (Local Interpretable Model-Agnostic Explanations) create simpler surrogate models that mimic the behavior of a complex AI for a specific prediction, offering insight into which features influenced the outcome. SHAP (Shapley Additive Explanations), based on cooperative game

theory, assigns each feature a value representing its contribution to the final decision. Visual methods like saliency maps highlight which parts of an image were most important to a convolutional neural network's classification, helping humans see what the AI "saw."

### 1.1.3 Challenges in Achieving Explainable AI

While XAI holds tremendous promise, it is not without challenges. One major issue is the accuracy-interpretability tradeoff. Complex models, such as deep neural networks, often achieve higher performance than simpler, interpretable models — but their complexity makes them less explainable. Striking a balance between performance and transparency remains an ongoing area of research.

Another challenge is the subjectivity of explanations. What one user finds clear and useful might seem confusing or insufficient to another. A radiologist, for example, might require a highly technical explanation of an AI-driven diagnosis, while a patient may need a more simplified version. Developing customizable explanations that adapt to different audiences is a key goal for XAI researchers.

Additionally, there's the risk of oversimplification. In efforts to make explanations accessible, developers might create interpretations that, while easy to understand, don't fully capture the underlying complexity of the model. This can lead to false reassurance — users believing they understand the system when they actually don't — undermining the goal of true transparency.

### 1.1.4 The Future of Explainable AI

As AI continues to integrate into critical areas of society, the push for explainability will only intensify. Future advancements in XAI are likely to focus on hybrid models that combine the accuracy of deep learning with the interpretability of simpler algorithms. Interactive explainability tools, allowing users to explore different outcomes and tweak inputs, may also become more prevalent. This "explanations-on-demand" approach can give users greater control over how they interact with AI systems, fostering a deeper understanding of the technology's behavior.

Moreover, AI systems may evolve to self-monitor and report when their confidence in a decision drops below a certain threshold — effectively knowing when they "don't know." This feature could improve safety in sensitive environments, ensuring human oversight is prioritized when the AI encounters unfamiliar scenarios.

In the long term, explainable AI is set to become a cornerstone of ethical AI development, promoting transparency, fairness, and accountability across industries. As researchers, engineers, and policymakers collaborate to refine XAI techniques, the ultimate vision is to create AI that not only performs at a high level but also earns and sustains human trust through clarity and openness.

## 1.2 IMPORTANCE OF EXPLAINABILITY IN AI

Artificial intelligence (AI) has rapidly transformed from a futuristic concept into an essential part of our everyday lives. From virtual assistants and recommendation algorithms to autonomous vehicles and advanced medical diagnostics, AI systems are now deeply embedded in critical decision-making processes. However, as AI grows more powerful and complex, its decision-making processes often become less transparent, leading to what is commonly known as the "black box" problem. This is where explainability becomes vital. Explainability in AI refers to the ability to understand, interpret, and trust how and why an AI system reaches a particular decision or prediction. It is essential for building trust, ensuring accountability, promoting ethical practices, and enabling collaboration between human experts and AI systems.

### 1.2.1 Building Trust in AI Systems

One of the most important reasons for making AI systems explainable is to build trust. Trust is the foundation for the widespread adoption of AI technologies across sectors such as healthcare, finance, transportation, and law enforcement. People are more likely to rely on AI decisions if they understand the reasoning behind them. For example, a patient may feel uneasy about an AI recommending a specific cancer treatment unless the system explains which factors — such as medical history, imaging data, and genetic markers — contributed to that recommendation. Similarly, financial clients are unlikely to trust an AI-based loan approval system without knowing why they were accepted or rejected.

Explainability fosters transparency, which helps demystify the decision-making process. When people see how an AI system arrives at a particular conclusion, they are more willing to trust that outcome — even if they might not initially agree with it. This trust is essential for AI to reach its full potential, particularly in high-stakes environments where human lives, finances, or freedoms are involved.

### 1.2.2 Ensuring Accountability and Responsibility

Accountability is crucial when AI systems influence decisions that affect people's lives. When an AI model makes an error — whether it's a misdiagnosis, an unfair credit rejection, or a wrongful criminal risk assessment — stakeholders need to determine where things went wrong. Explainability allows developers, regulators, and users to trace the decision-making process, understand what happened, and correct the system accordingly.

For example, if an AI model misclassifies a benign tumor as malignant, an explainable system could reveal whether the error was due to flawed training data, improper weightage of features, or a misinterpretation of medical images. This level of insight ensures that responsibility remains with the human creators and overseers of the system, rather than allowing mistakes to be dismissed as "AI errors." It also helps organizations defend their AI-based decisions in courts or regulatory investigations, ensuring compliance with legal frameworks like the General Data Protection Regulation (GDPR), which includes the "right to explanation" for individuals affected by automated decisions.

### 1.2.3 Promoting Ethical and Fair AI

AI models are only as unbiased as the data they are trained on — and the decisions made by the engineers who design them. Without explainability, biased or unethical behavior can easily go unnoticed, resulting in unfair outcomes that disproportionately harm certain groups of people. For instance, studies have shown that AI-based hiring systems trained on historical data may inadvertently favor male candidates over equally qualified female applicants due to embedded biases in past hiring practices.

Explainability helps identify and mitigate such biases. By revealing the key factors influencing an AI system's predictions, stakeholders can spot discriminatory patterns and adjust the model or data accordingly. This transparency also supports broader efforts to create ethical AI frameworks that prioritize fairness, inclusivity, and social responsibility. Without explainability, even well-intentioned AI systems could perpetuate or amplify harmful biases, undermining trust and leading to widespread ethical failures.

### 1.2.4 Supporting Human-AI Collaboration

In many fields, AI is designed not to replace human experts but to augment their abilities — creating a partnership where AI handles complex data analysis while humans provide judgment, experience, and empathy. However, this collaboration only works if humans can understand and validate the AI's reasoning.

Take healthcare as an example. An AI system might flag a patient as at high risk for sepsis, but without an explanation, doctors may be reluctant to act on the recommendation. If the system instead explains that the risk assessment was based on vital signs, lab results, and prior similar cases — all weighted and analyzed in a specific way — the medical team can evaluate that reasoning alongside their own clinical expertise. This empowers doctors to make more informed decisions, blending AI insights with human judgment for better patient outcomes.

Explainability is also crucial in cybersecurity, where AI systems must detect and respond to rapidly evolving threats. Security professionals need to understand why an AI flagged certain activities as malicious to ensure that the system isn't overreacting to benign behavior or, conversely, missing real threats. The same principle applies to industries like manufacturing, where AI-powered quality control systems must justify why they reject specific products on the assembly line.

### 1.2.5 Enabling Better Model Development and Improvement

From a technical standpoint, explainability plays a significant role in refining AI models. When an AI system performs poorly or unpredictably, developers need to understand why. Explainability helps pinpoint whether the issue stems from poor data quality, incorrect assumptions, or flawed model architecture. This accelerates the debugging and retraining process, enabling faster improvements and reducing the risk of persistent errors.

For example, an AI model designed to detect fraudulent credit card transactions may initially perform well, but over time, its accuracy might decline due to evolving fraud tactics. An explainable system can reveal which features (e.g., transaction location, frequency, or merchant type) are losing predictive power. Armed with this knowledge, developers can update the model to reflect new fraud patterns, keeping the system effective and adaptive.

### 1.2.6 Future-Proofing AI for Legal and Social Evolution

As governments and international bodies continue to develop regulations surrounding AI, explainability will likely become a legal requirement rather than an optional feature. Companies that prioritize explainability now will be better positioned to adapt to emerging policies and avoid costly re-engineering later.

Moreover, societal attitudes toward AI will continue evolving. Users and consumers may increasingly demand transparency in how AI systems influence their lives — from product recommendations to mortgage approvals to autonomous vehicle behavior. Organizations that proactively prioritize explainability will stand out as trustworthy leaders in their fields, gaining a competitive edge while promoting more responsible AI adoption.

## 1.3 ETHICAL AND LEGAL CONSIDERATIONS

### 1.3.1 The Ethical Imperative of Explainability

At the heart of AI ethics lies the principle of human autonomy and dignity. When AI systems make decisions that impact people's lives — such as determining creditworthiness, medical treatments, or job eligibility — individuals have a moral right to understand how these decisions are made. Without explainability, AI becomes an opaque force, stripping people of their ability to question or contest outcomes that may significantly affect their well-being.

An ethical AI system must prioritize transparency to ensure that users and stakeholders can grasp the reasoning behind its actions. For example, an AI model predicting loan approvals should explain whether factors like income, credit history, or location influenced its decision — and in what proportion. This clarity not only empowers individuals but also prevents AI from perpetuating hidden biases that could lead to discriminatory practices. Moreover, explainability aligns with the principle of beneficence — the obligation to act in the best interest of individuals and society. In healthcare, for instance, an explainable AI diagnosing diseases must allow doctors to understand its reasoning, ensuring that the technology supports, rather than undermines, medical expertise. Patients and healthcare providers alike deserve to know whether an AI's recommendation stems from genuine clinical insights or misleading patterns in data.

### 1.3.2 Accountability and the Need for Explainable Decision-Making

Explainability is crucial for holding AI systems — and their creators — accountable. When an AI model produces an incorrect or harmful outcome, explainability helps identify where things went wrong. Was the model trained on biased data? Did the algorithm prioritize the wrong features? Or was the decision the result of a technical malfunction?

Without a clear understanding of the decision-making process, responsibility becomes difficult to assign. This creates a dangerous gap in accountability, where developers, companies, or regulators may deflect blame by attributing errors to the "black box" nature of AI. Explainability mitigates this risk by offering a clear, traceable path from input to output, ensuring that human oversight remains intact.

In sectors like criminal justice, where AI increasingly influences sentencing recommendations or parole decisions, accountability is paramount. An opaque risk assessment model could unjustly categorize individuals as high-risk without revealing the rationale behind that classification — potentially leading to wrongful detentions. Explainability helps prevent such injustices by allowing defendants, lawyers, and judges to scrutinize AI-driven outcomes and challenge flawed reasoning.

### 1.3.3 Legal Frameworks and the Right to Explanation

Governments and regulatory bodies are recognizing the need for explainability in AI, embedding it into legal frameworks designed to protect individual rights and ensure ethical AI development. One of the most significant legislative moves in this direction is the European Union's General Data Protection Regulation (GDPR). Under Article 22 of the GDPR, individuals have the right not to be subject to purely automated decisions with legal or similarly significant effects — unless those decisions come with meaningful explanations. This "right to explanation" demands that organizations deploying AI systems provide transparency about how decisions are made, especially when those decisions affect personal rights, such as loan approvals or hiring processes.

In addition to the GDPR, the Artificial Intelligence Act proposed by the European Commission classifies certain AI applications — like those used in biometric surveillance, education, and law enforcement — as "high-risk." These systems face stricter requirements, including detailed documentation, traceability, and clear explanations of their functionality and decision-making processes.

The United States is also moving toward greater AI transparency. While federal regulations remain fragmented, agencies such as the Federal Trade Commission (FTC) are increasingly vocal about the need for explainable AI, particularly in consumer protection contexts. State-level initiatives, like New York City's AI hiring transparency law, are paving the way for local regulations mandating clearer disclosure of algorithmic decisions.

China, meanwhile, has introduced guidelines encouraging transparency in recommendation algorithms — particularly in social media and e-commerce — as part of a broader push to ensure AI development aligns with public welfare.

These evolving legal frameworks reflect a growing consensus: explainability is not merely an ethical aspiration but a legal necessity, especially when AI affects people's rights, opportunities, and freedoms.

### 1.3.4 Balancing Trade-offs: Explainability vs. Performance and Privacy

While explainability is undeniably crucial, it introduces practical challenges, particularly regarding the balance between transparency, model performance, and data privacy. Some of the most powerful AI models — like deep neural networks — are inherently complex, making them difficult to interpret. Simplifying these models for the sake of explainability can sometimes reduce their accuracy or efficiency.

For instance, in medical imaging, a highly complex AI might outperform simpler, more explainable models in detecting rare cancers. The ethical dilemma arises: should we prioritize transparency or raw performance, especially when lives are on the line? One potential solution involves hybrid models — combining interpretable components with high-performance black-box systems, ensuring both accuracy and a degree of explainability.

Privacy is another key consideration. Explainability often requires revealing how data influences decisions, but this transparency must not come at the cost of exposing sensitive personal information. Techniques like differential privacy and federated learning aim to balance these competing priorities, enabling AI systems to provide insights without compromising data security.

## 1.4 HISTORICAL BACKGROUND AND EVOLUTION OF XAI

The rise of artificial intelligence (AI) has brought about unprecedented advancements, reshaping industries, automating complex processes, and influencing human decision-making in ways once imagined only in science fiction.

However, the complexity of modern AI systems, especially those based on deep learning, has led to a significant challenge: the "black box" problem. This refers to the difficulty in understanding how AI systems make decisions, which has raised concerns about trust, accountability, and fairness. In response, the field of Explainable AI (XAI) emerged – aiming to create AI models whose workings are transparent and interpretable to humans. The journey of XAI is a fascinating blend of technological breakthroughs, evolving societal needs, and growing ethical considerations.

The evolution of XAI reflects the growing realization that AI systems must serve humanity responsibly and transparently. From the early days of rule-based expert systems to today's deep learning breakthroughs, the journey has been marked by a continuous push for balance – between performance and interpretability, innovation and accountability.

As AI becomes more embedded in daily life, the need for explainability will only intensify. Future advancements in XAI will likely focus on integrating explainability directly into model architectures, improving the clarity of complex models without sacrificing performance. The rise of self-explaining AI, where models not only provide decisions but also justify them in natural language, offers a glimpse of what lies ahead. Ultimately, XAI isn't just about understanding machines – it's about ensuring that AI systems remain aligned with human values, ethics, and rights. The pursuit of explainability is, at its core, a pursuit of trust – and trust is what will define AI's role in shaping our future.

### 1.4.1 Early Foundations: Rule-Based Systems and Expert Models

The roots of XAI can be traced back to the early days of artificial intelligence research in the 1950s and 1960s, when scientists began developing rule-based systems and symbolic AI. These early systems, often referred to as expert systems, relied on explicitly programmed rules and logical reasoning. They mimicked human decision-making by encoding knowledge from domain experts into "if-then" rules. For example, MYCIN, an AI system developed in the 1970s at Stanford University, diagnosed bacterial infections and recommended antibiotics based on a set of predefined rules. Because the reasoning process was encoded as human-readable rules, users could easily follow the system's decisions – an early form of explainability.

These systems, while interpretable, struggled to scale. As problems grew more complex, the number of rules exploded, leading to cumbersome, inefficient models. This challenge pushed researchers to explore more sophisticated techniques, eventually paving the way for machine learning – where models learn patterns directly from data rather than relying on handcrafted rules.

### 1.4.2 The Rise of Machine Learning and the Black Box Problem

By the 1980s and 1990s, machine learning began to overshadow rule-based systems. Algorithms like decision trees, support vector machines, and early neural networks became popular. Some models, like decision trees, retained an element of interpretability by visually representing decisions as branching paths. However, as neural networks evolved, they introduced layers of hidden units that performed complex transformations on data — making it nearly impossible to discern why a particular decision was made.

This shift reached a turning point in the 2010s with the explosion of deep learning. Convolutional neural networks (CNNs) revolutionized computer vision, while recurrent neural networks (RNNs) and transformers reshaped natural language processing. These deep models, trained on massive datasets, achieved remarkable performance. AI systems could now translate languages, diagnose diseases from medical scans, and even outperform humans in strategic games like Go.

Yet, this performance came at a cost: explainability. Even experts couldn't fully understand why a deep learning model reached a specific outcome. This opacity sparked concerns, especially in high-stakes fields like healthcare, finance, and criminal justice, where trust and accountability are paramount.

### 1.4.3 The Birth of XAI: A Formal Discipline Emerges

The growing demand for transparency led to the formal emergence of Explainable AI as a dedicated research field. The U.S. Defense Advanced Research Projects Agency (DARPA) launched its XAI program in 2016, aiming to develop AI systems that humans could trust and understand. DARPA's initiative marked a pivotal moment, driving research into techniques that balance performance with interpretability.

Around the same time, other organizations and academic institutions began prioritizing explainability. The European Union's General Data Protection Regulation (GDPR), introduced in 2018, underscored this need by granting individuals the "right to explanation" when subjected to automated decisions. This legal push further accelerated XAI research, encouraging companies to rethink how they design and deploy AI models.

### 1.4.4 Key Techniques and Breakthroughs in XAI

As XAI gained traction, researchers developed a range of techniques to interpret complex models. One approach focused on making models inherently interpretable — designing algorithms that produce human-understandable decisions from the start. Examples include linear regression, decision trees, and generalized additive models (GAMs), which maintain a straightforward decision structure. However, many cutting-edge applications require more complex, high-performing models that resist easy interpretation. To address this, scientists devised post-hoc methods – techniques that explain decisions after the model has made them. Notable breakthroughs include:

- **LIME (Local Interpretable Model-agnostic Explanations):** Introduced in 2016, LIME generates local approximations of a complex model's behavior. By perturbing input data and observing how predictions change, LIME constructs an interpretable, simplified explanation of how the model arrived at a specific output.
- **SHAP (Shapley Additive Explanations):** Based on cooperative game theory, SHAP values (introduced in 2017) assign credit to each input feature, showing how much it contributed to the final prediction. This technique offers both local (individual predictions) and global (overall model behavior) explanations.
- **Counterfactual Explanations:** This approach answers the question, "What would need to change for the AI to produce a different outcome?" For example, if an AI denies a loan application, a counterfactual explanation might reveal that a slightly higher income or improved credit score would have led to approval.

These innovations transformed XAI from a theoretical goal into a practical toolkit, empowering users to dissect even the most sophisticated models.

### 1.4.5 XAI in the Modern Era: Balancing Transparency, Performance, and Ethics

Today, XAI stands at the crossroads of technology, ethics, and regulation. Businesses increasingly recognize that explainability is not just a compliance requirement – it's a competitive advantage. Transparent AI fosters trust among customers, mitigates bias-related risks, and enhances accountability. In healthcare, explainable systems are helping doctors understand AI-generated diagnoses, ensuring they remain the ultimate decision-makers. Financial institutions are using XAI to explain credit decisions to customers and regulators alike. In autonomous vehicles, interpretability helps engineers diagnose malfunctions, improving safety and reliability.

However, challenges remain. Explainable models often sacrifice some performance compared to their "black box" counterparts. Researchers continue to explore ways to balance transparency with accuracy, ensuring that interpretable AI remains competitive. Additionally, the ethics of XAI are evolving. Transparency doesn't always equate to fairness – an explainable model can still reflect biased data. As a result, XAI is increasingly coupled with broader AI ethics initiatives, focusing on not just explaining decisions but ensuring those decisions are just and equitable.

CHAPTER

# 2 Key Concepts and Principles

## 2.1 INTERPRETABILITY VS. EXPLAINABILITY

There is a subtle difference between the terms explainability and interpretability in the context of AI.

| Term | Definition | Source |
|---|---|---|
| Interpretability | *"level of understanding how the underlying (AI) technology works"* | ISO/IEC TR 29119-11:2020(en), 3.1.42 |
| Explainability | *"level of understanding how the AI-based system ... came up with a given result"* | ISO/IEC TR 29119-11:2020(en), 3.1.31 |

### 2.1.1 Explainability

Explainability is useful for ensuring that AI models are not making decisions based on irrelevant or otherwise unfair criteria. For classification and regression models, several popular techniques exist:

- Partial dependency plots show the marginal effect of an input feature on the predicted outcome.
- SHAP (SHapley Additive exPlanations) enables visualization of the contribution of each input feature to the output. It works by calculating Shapley values, which measure the average marginal contribution of a feature across all possible combinations of features.
- Feature importance estimates how important a feature is for the model. It is usually done using permutation importance, which measures the performance decrease when it the feature value randomly shuffled across all samples.
- LIME approximates locally a model's outputs with a simpler, interpretable model.
- Multitask learning provides a large number of outputs in addition to the target classification. These other outputs can help developers deduce what the network has learned.

For images, saliency maps highlight the parts of an image that most influenced the result. Systems that are expert or knowledge based are software systems that are made by experts. This system consists of a knowledge based encoding for the domain knowledge. This system is usually modeled as production rules, and someone uses this knowledge base which the user can question the system for knowledge. In expert systems, the language and explanations are understood with an explanation for the reasoning or a problem solving activity.

However, these techniques are not very suitable for language models like generative pretrained transformers. Since these models generate language, they can provide an explanation, but which may not be reliable. Other techniques include attention analysis (examining how the model focuses on different parts of the input), probing methods (testing what information is captured in the model's representations), causal tracing (tracing the flow of information through the model) and circuit discovery (identifying specific subnetworks responsible for certain behaviors). Explainability research in this area overlaps significantly with interpretability and alignment research.

### 2.1.2 Interpretability

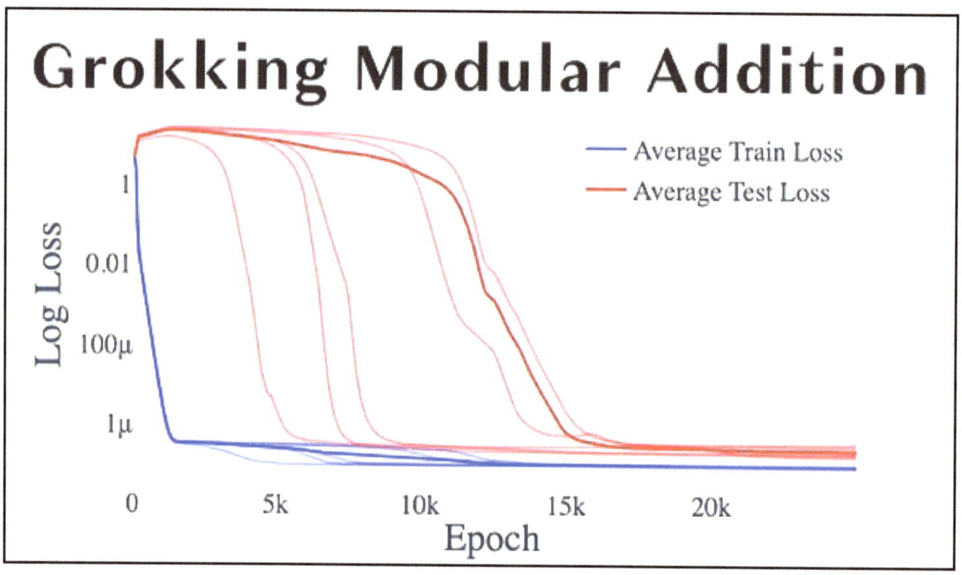


**Fig: Grokking is an Example of Phenomenon Studied in Interpretability. It Involves a Model that Initially Memorizes all the Answers (Overfitting), but Later Adopts an Algorithm that Generalizes to Unseen Data**

Scholars sometimes use the term "mechanistic interpretability" to refer to the process of reverse-engineering artificial neural networks to understand their internal decision-making mechanisms and components, similar to how one might analyze a complex machine or computer program.

Interpretability research often focuses on generative pretrained transformers. It is particularly relevant for AI safety and alignment, as it may enable to identify signs of undesired behaviors such as sycophancy, deceptiveness or bias, and to better steer AI models.

Studying the interpretability of the most advanced foundation models often involves searching for an automated way to identify "features" in generative pretrained transformers. In a neural network, a feature is a pattern of neuron activations that corresponds to a concept. A compute-intensive technique called "dictionary learning" makes it possible to identify features to some degree. Enhancing the ability to identify and edit features is expected to significantly improve the safety of frontier AI models.

For convolutional neural networks, DeepDream can generate images that strongly activate a particular neuron, providing a visual hint about what the neuron is trained to identify.

## 2.2 LEVELS OF EXPLAINABILITY: LOCAL VS. GLOBAL EXPLANATIONS

Explainable Artificial Intelligence (XAI) aims to bridge the gap between complex AI models and human understanding. As AI systems become more sophisticated — predicting disease outcomes, driving autonomous vehicles, or approving loans — the demand for transparency and interpretability grows louder. To make AI more interpretable, researchers have developed different types of explanations. Two primary levels of explainability dominate the field: local explanations and global explanations. Each serves a distinct purpose and helps stakeholders — from developers to end-users — grasp how AI systems work.

Local and global explanations represent two sides of the same coin in Explainable AI. While local explanations illuminate specific predictions, global explanations reveal overarching model behavior. Both are indispensable for building trust, ensuring accountability, and fostering transparency in AI systems.

As AI continues to permeate critical domains — from healthcare and finance to criminal justice and education — the demand for explainability will only grow. By combining local and global insights, XAI stands poised to make AI not only more powerful but also more understandable, ethical, and human-aligned. The future of AI depends not just on what models can achieve — but on how well we can explain their decisions.

### 2.2.1 Understanding Local Explanations

Local explanations focus on individual predictions rather than the overall model. The goal is to answer the question: "Why did the model make this specific decision?"

This is especially useful when users want to understand the outcome of a particular case rather than the entire system's behavior.

For example, in a medical AI system that predicts whether a patient has a high risk of developing heart disease, a local explanation would clarify why this specific patient received a high-risk score. It might highlight factors such as age, cholesterol levels, and smoking habits as the most influential contributors.

One of the most popular techniques for generating local explanations is LIME (Local Interpretable Model-agnostic Explanations). LIME works by creating a simplified, interpretable model — like a linear regression — that mimics the behavior of the original AI model within a small region around the data point of interest. This approach reveals which features (e.g., blood pressure or body mass index) mattered most for that specific prediction.

Another widely used method is SHAP (Shapley Additive Explanations). SHAP assigns each feature a Shapley value, representing its contribution to the prediction. Derived from cooperative game theory, Shapley values ensure a fair distribution of credit among features — showing how much each factor pushed the prediction higher or lower.

Local explanations are particularly valuable in fields like healthcare and finance, where users need to understand why a model reached a certain decision to ensure transparency and avoid harmful outcomes. However, local explanations have limitations. They don't provide insights into the model's overall behavior, making them less useful for debugging or improving the model's general performance.

### 2.2.2 Exploring Global Explanations

While local explanations zoom in on individual predictions, global explanations take a broader view. They aim to describe how the entire model behaves across all possible inputs. A global explanation answers questions like: "What patterns does the model rely on?" and "Which features are generally most important?"

For instance, imagine an AI model predicting housing prices. A global explanation might reveal that location and square footage consistently outweigh the number of bedrooms or age of the property in determining price. This insight helps developers, regulators, and businesses understand the model's overall logic and detect potential biases or errors.

Techniques for generating global explanations vary. Feature importance analysis is one of the most common methods, ranking features based on how much they influence the model's predictions. Permutation importance — where features are randomly shuffled to observe how model accuracy drops — is another powerful tool for understanding the model's reliance on specific variables.

Partial dependence plots (PDPs) are also widely used. They visualize how a feature impacts predictions while keeping other features constant, helping users see whether the relationship is linear, non-linear, or interaction-based. For example, a PDP might show that housing prices rise steadily with square footage — but plateau after a certain point, revealing a diminishing return.

Global explanations are essential for model developers, regulators, and businesses that need to ensure the AI system behaves responsibly. They help identify biases (e.g., does the model systematically favor certain groups?), overfitting (e.g., is the model too focused on irrelevant patterns?), and robustness (e.g., does the model perform consistently across different datasets?).

However, global explanations also come with challenges. They can oversimplify complex models, missing important nuances. Additionally, a globally interpretable model might still produce unintuitive or counterproductive predictions in specific cases — making local explanations necessary to complement the bigger picture.

### 2.2.3 Balancing Local and Global Explanations

For many AI applications, relying on just one type of explanation isn't enough. A comprehensive XAI strategy requires both local and global insights — combining the "what" with the "why."

Consider an AI system deployed in credit scoring. A global explanation might show that income and credit history are the two most influential factors driving decisions. This insight is crucial for regulators to ensure the model doesn't inadvertently discriminate against low-income applicants. But when a specific applicant is denied a loan, a local explanation is needed to clarify why — perhaps highlighting high debt levels or frequent late payments as key reasons.

Similarly, in healthcare, doctors may need both types of explanations. A global explanation can reassure medical professionals that the AI model prioritizes meaningful features like tumor size and patient age over irrelevant noise. Meanwhile, local explanations help doctors evaluate individual cases, understanding why one patient's tumor is classified as malignant while another's is benign — guiding personalized treatment decisions.

### 2.2.4 Challenges and Future Directions

Despite the progress in XAI, creating effective local and global explanations remains challenging. Many modern AI models, especially deep neural networks, are highly nonlinear and complex, making it difficult to extract faithful explanations without sacrificing performance.

Another challenge is the trade-off between simplicity and accuracy. A global explanation that oversimplifies a model's behavior may mislead users, creating a false sense of understanding. Conversely, overly detailed explanations may overwhelm non-expert users — defeating the purpose of explainability.

The future of XAI may involve hybrid approaches, blending local and global explanations into unified frameworks. Counterfactual explanations, for example, are gaining traction as a way to provide both perspectives — explaining why a certain outcome happened while also suggesting how to achieve a different one.

Moreover, researchers are exploring human-centric XAI, focusing on tailoring explanations to different audiences. A data scientist might need a mathematically rigorous global explanation, while an end-user might prefer a simple, intuitive local explanation. The ability to adapt explanations to various contexts will likely shape the next wave of XAI advancements.

## 2.3 TRUST, FAIRNESS, AND TRANSPARENCY IN AI

Trust, fairness, and transparency are not just ethical ideals — they are practical necessities for the future of AI. In an era where AI shapes critical decisions affecting millions of lives, ensuring these principles are embedded at every stage of development and deployment is imperative. By fostering trust, AI systems gain user confidence and acceptance. By ensuring fairness, they promote social equity and minimize harmful biases. And by embracing transparency, they empower users to understand, challenge, and improve the technology. The path to responsible AI is complex and evolving — but by prioritizing trust, fairness, and transparency, we can ensure that AI serves humanity, not the other way around.

### 2.3.1 The Foundation of Trust in AI

Trust is the cornerstone of any human-AI interaction. People are more likely to adopt and rely on AI systems when they feel confident in the technology's reliability, safety, and intentions. Building trust requires more than just technological sophistication — it demands that AI systems demonstrate consistent, accurate, and ethical behavior over time.

For trust to flourish, AI must first prove its reliability. Users need assurance that the system will perform as expected under various conditions. This involves rigorous testing, validation, and continuous monitoring to ensure the model behaves predictably — even when faced with new or unfamiliar data. In fields like medicine or autonomous driving, where mistakes can lead to life-or-death consequences, reliability is paramount.

Trust also hinges on accountability. People want to know that when an AI system fails or produces harmful outcomes, there's a clear path to determine what went wrong and who is responsible. This requires not only technical explanations but also legal and ethical frameworks that hold developers, companies, and institutions accountable for the AI's actions. Furthermore, user-centric design plays a critical role in fostering trust. When AI systems are designed with empathy and understanding of human behavior — offering clear explanations, intuitive interfaces, and adaptive learning — users feel more comfortable engaging with them. Trust is not built solely on performance but also on how the system communicates with and supports the user.

### 2.3.2 The Pursuit of Fairness in AI Systems

Fairness is crucial to ensure that AI systems do not reinforce or exacerbate societal inequalities. An unfair AI can lead to discriminatory outcomes, marginalizing certain groups or individuals. This is particularly concerning in areas like hiring, loan approvals, law enforcement, and healthcare, where biased decisions can have profound consequences.

AI systems learn from historical data — and if that data reflects existing biases, the model can unintentionally perpetuate those inequalities. For instance, if a recruitment AI is trained on resumes from a male-dominated workforce, it might undervalue applications from women, even if gender is not explicitly included as a feature. This phenomenon, known as proxy bias, occurs when the model learns to associate certain features — like education history or hobbies — with demographic groups.Ensuring fairness requires proactive strategies. Bias detection and mitigation should be embedded throughout the AI lifecycle, from data collection to model training and deployment. Techniques such as re-sampling data, re-weighting training examples, and fairness-aware algorithms can help reduce bias. Moreover, diverse development teams — representing different genders, races, and socio-economic backgrounds — are essential to identifying and correcting blind spots that a homogenous team might overlook.

Fairness also involves equitable outcomes. AI systems must not only treat people equally but also recognize that different groups may require different approaches to achieve similar results. In healthcare, for example, an AI diagnosing skin conditions must be trained on images from people with varying skin tones to avoid disproportionately inaccurate diagnoses for underrepresented populations.

However, fairness is not a one-size-fits-all concept. Context matters. In criminal justice, fairness may prioritize minimizing false accusations, while in healthcare, reducing false negatives (e.g., missed cancer diagnoses) might take precedence. Balancing these trade-offs is a complex ethical challenge that requires input from policymakers, ethicists, and affected communities.

### 2.3.3 Transparency: The Gateway to Understanding AI

Transparency ensures that AI systems are not black boxes, operating in secret without users or regulators understanding how they reach decisions. An opaque

AI system, no matter how accurate, can breed mistrust, fear, and resistance. Transparency involves making both the model and its decision-making process comprehensible to a wide range of stakeholders — from experts to everyday users.

One key aspect of transparency is algorithmic transparency, where the inner workings of the model are made visible. This doesn't necessarily mean exposing the raw code — which might be too complex for non-technical users — but instead offering clear explanations of how inputs are processed, which factors influence decisions, and why certain outcomes occur. For example, an AI-powered loan approval system should be able to explain why an application was denied, highlighting factors like credit score, income, or debt-to-income ratio.

Data transparency is equally vital. Users should know what data is being collected, how it's used, and whether it's shared with third parties. Misuse of personal data — as seen in high-profile scandals — can erode public trust and lead to calls for stricter regulations. By openly disclosing data practices, companies can foster a sense of control and reassurance among users.

Model interpretability is another facet of transparency. Some AI models, like decision trees or linear regressions, are naturally interpretable — their decisions can be traced back to specific inputs. Others, like deep neural networks, are more complex and require additional techniques to make them understandable. Methods such as LIME (Local Interpretable Model-agnostic Explanations) and SHAP (Shapley Additive Explanations) help break down complex models into human-readable insights, bridging the gap between performance and clarity.However, transparency doesn't mean oversharing. Too much technical detail can overwhelm users or reveal proprietary algorithms, leading to intellectual property concerns. Striking a balance between openness and simplicity is crucial — ensuring users understand the decisions without being bombarded with unnecessary complexity.

### 2.3.4 The Interplay between Trust, Fairness, and Transparency

Trust, fairness, and transparency are deeply interconnected. Transparency fosters trust by helping users understand and evaluate the system's behavior. Fairness enhances trust by ensuring the AI treats all individuals equitably, preventing discriminatory outcomes. Trust, in turn, supports the adoption and acceptance of AI technologies — driving innovation and unlocking their full potential.

However, achieving all three simultaneously is a delicate balancing act. Improving one may inadvertently weaken another. For example, enhancing transparency might expose sensitive data or proprietary methods, while prioritizing fairness might require sacrificing some level of model accuracy. Navigating these trade-offs requires collaboration across disciplines — from data scientists and engineers to ethicists, policymakers, and end-users.

## 2.4 TRADE-OFFS IN XAI: ACCURACY VS. INTERPRETABILITY

The trade-off between accuracy and interpretability remains one of the most pressing challenges in XAI. While highly accurate models promise exceptional performance, their lack of transparency can undermine trust, accountability, and fairness. On the other hand, interpretable models promote understanding and trust but may sacrifice predictive power. The key lies in context-driven balance — ensuring that AI systems are not only powerful and accurate but also understandable, accountable, and aligned with human values. By carefully navigating this trade-off, we can build AI systems that are both effective and explainable — unlocking their full potential while ensuring they remain responsible and human-centric.

### 2.4.1 The Meaning of Accuracy in AI Systems

Accuracy in AI refers to how precisely a model predicts outcomes or classifies data. In machine learning, accuracy is typically measured by comparing the model's predictions to the actual results in a dataset. High accuracy indicates that the model performs well in identifying patterns and generalizing from training data to new, unseen data.

For example, in a medical diagnosis system, a highly accurate AI model can correctly identify diseases with minimal false positives or false negatives. In financial systems, an accurate AI can reliably predict credit defaults, fraud, or stock price movements.

However, accuracy isn't the only measure of success. A model could achieve impressive accuracy but still be flawed or unreliable if it produces biased outcomes, fails to adapt to new data, or makes decisions that are incomprehensible to human users. This is where interpretability becomes crucial.

### 2.4.2 The Role of Interpretability in XAI

Interpretability refers to how easily humans can understand and trust an AI model's decisions. An interpretable model allows users to trace why a particular outcome was reached — making it clear what factors influenced the decision and how the data was processed. This is particularly vital in high-stakes domains like healthcare, criminal justice, and finance, where decision-making transparency can directly affect people's lives and livelihoods.

For example, a loan applicant denied credit by an AI system deserves to know whether the rejection was due to their income, credit history, or other factors. In healthcare, a doctor relying on AI for cancer diagnosis must understand why the system identified a tumor as malignant — whether it was based on tumor size, shape, color, or other characteristics. Interpretability also supports accountability and fairness. If a model produces biased or harmful outcomes, an interpretable system makes it easier to audit, correct, and improve the model. It also helps ensure that decisions comply with legal regulations and ethical standards, fostering greater trust among users and the wider public.

### 2.4.3 The Accuracy-Interpretability Trade-off

The core tension in XAI arises because the most interpretable models — like linear regression, decision trees, and rule-based systems — tend to be simpler and less powerful. They prioritize transparency over performance, which limits their ability to handle large, complex datasets. In contrast, highly accurate models — such as deep neural networks, gradient boosting machines, and ensemble models — are often "black boxes." Their complex internal structures, consisting of thousands or millions of parameters, make it nearly impossible to directly trace how they reach specific decisions.

This trade-off can be framed as a spectrum:

- On one end, **simple, interpretable models** are easy to understand but may sacrifice accuracy for complex tasks.
- On the other end, **highly accurate, complex models** offer superior performance but are harder to explain.

For example, a decision tree model predicting diabetes risk based on age, BMI, and family history might be easily interpretable but less accurate than a deep learning model trained on genomic data, lifestyle factors, and medical records. However, the deep learning model's decision-making process is far harder to unpack and justify — especially to a patient seeking reassurance.

### 2.4.4 When to Prioritize Accuracy

In some scenarios, accuracy is paramount. For example, autonomous vehicles rely on AI systems to detect pedestrians, navigate traffic, and avoid obstacles in real-time. A slight dip in accuracy could result in catastrophic failures. Similarly, fraud detection models need high precision to catch fraudulent transactions while minimizing false alarms that inconvenience customers.

In these cases, interpretability may be less critical — as long as the model is thoroughly tested, validated, and continuously monitored for errors. The emphasis is on performance, where even a small accuracy gain can lead to significant improvements in safety, efficiency, or profitability.

However, prioritizing accuracy over interpretability can backfire if the model's errors or biases go unnoticed. For example, a highly accurate recidivism prediction model used in criminal justice might disproportionately classify individuals from certain communities as high-risk — without offering an interpretable explanation for the decisions. This could perpetuate systemic bias and lead to public backlash.

### 2.4.5 When to Prioritize Interpretability

In many other situations, interpretability takes precedence — especially where accountability, fairness, and trust are critical. For example, in healthcare, doctors must understand and validate AI recommendations before making treatment decisions. An AI system suggesting aggressive chemotherapy must provide a clear rationale for its recommendation, especially when alternative treatments are available.

Legal and regulatory environments often demand interpretability. The General Data Protection Regulation (GDPR) in the European Union mandates a "right to explanation" for individuals affected by automated decisions. This means companies using AI for credit scoring, hiring, or medical diagnoses must explain how decisions were made — pushing interpretability to the forefront.

In public-facing systems, interpretability also supports user adoption. People are more likely to trust and engage with AI systems they understand. For example, an AI-powered fitness app that explains how it calculates personalized workout plans — based on factors like heart rate, sleep patterns, and previous workouts — may foster greater user satisfaction and long-term engagement than one that offers recommendations without explanation.

### 2.4.6 Striking the Right Balance

Achieving the optimal balance between accuracy and interpretability requires context-sensitive strategies. Several approaches help bridge the gap:

- **Hybrid Models**: Combining interpretable models with complex ones — for instance, using a deep neural network for feature extraction and a decision tree for final predictions — can provide both accuracy and transparency.
- **Post-Hoc Explanations**: Techniques like **LIME (Local Interpretable Model-agnostic Explanations)** and **SHAP (Shapley Additive Explanations)** create simplified, interpretable approximations of complex models, offering insight into individual decisions.
- **Domain-Specific Interpretability**: Tailoring explanations to specific industries or user groups can make even complex models more intuitive. For example, a healthcare AI might present explanations in clinical language familiar to doctors, while a credit scoring AI could translate factors into terms users understand.

CHAPTER

# Techniques for Explainable AI 3

## 3.1 MODEL-SPECIFIC VS. MODEL-AGNOSTIC METHODS

As Artificial Intelligence (AI) and Machine Learning (ML) continue to advance, the need for transparency and interpretability grows alongside them. Explainable AI (XAI) has emerged as a crucial field, helping to make complex models understandable to humans. Within XAI, two major categories of methods aim to provide this transparency: model-specific and model-agnostic methods. These approaches offer different ways to interpret AI models, each with its strengths and limitations.

Model-specific and model-agnostic methods each play a vital role in the growing field of explainable AI. Model-specific methods excel in providing detailed, accurate explanations tailored to the inner workings of a particular model, while model-agnostic methods offer versatility and adaptability across diverse models. The decision to use one over the other — or a combination of both — depends on the context, the type of model in question, and the desired balance between precision and flexibility. By understanding these methods and their trade-offs, AI practitioners can make better decisions about how to create trustworthy, transparent, and effective AI systems.

### 3.1.1 Defining Model-Specific Methods

Model-specific methods are techniques designed to explain a particular type of model. These methods leverage the internal structure and mathematical properties of the model to provide insights into how predictions are made. Each model type — such as decision trees, linear regression, or neural networks — has unique characteristics, which these methods exploit to offer tailored explanations.

For example, decision trees are inherently interpretable due to their branching structure, which breaks down decisions step by step. Similarly, linear regression models provide coefficients that indicate how much each feature influences the final prediction. Neural networks, on the other hand, require more sophisticated techniques like Layer-wise Relevance Propagation (LRP) or Saliency Maps to interpret the importance of neurons and connections.

Model-specific methods often deliver more detailed, accurate explanations because they directly interact with the model's architecture. However, they are limited in their versatility — they only work for the specific model they were built to interpret. This makes them less useful when comparing multiple model types or when the underlying model changes.

### 3.1.2 Examples of Model-Specific Methods

One of the most straightforward examples of a model-specific approach is the Gini Importance or Feature Importance in decision trees and random forests. This method calculates how much each feature reduces the overall impurity (e.g., Gini Index or entropy) in the tree's nodes, highlighting which features were most influential in driving predictions.

In neural networks, Integrated Gradients is another model-specific technique that works by examining the gradient of the model's output with respect to the input data, tracing back the contributions of each feature. This helps reveal which parts of an input — like pixels in an image or words in a text — had the greatest effect on the model's final decision.

While model-specific methods are powerful for gaining deep insights into a particular model's behavior, they are inherently restrictive. If an organization switches from a decision tree to a neural network, the interpretability methods would need to change as well, leading to more time and effort spent adapting the explanations to the new model.

### 3.1.3 Understanding Model-Agnostic Methods

Model-agnostic methods, on the other hand, are designed to work across any type of machine learning model. They treat the model as a "black box" — meaning they don't rely on the internal workings of the model. Instead, they analyze the inputs and outputs to derive explanations, making them versatile and adaptable.

These methods are particularly useful when dealing with complex ensembles, neural networks, or proprietary models where internal details might be inaccessible. By providing a consistent approach to interpretation across different models, they enable easier comparison and benchmarking.

However, model-agnostic methods tend to sacrifice some precision because they rely on approximations rather than the model's true structure. This trade-off between generality and accuracy is a key consideration when deciding which type of method to use.

### 3.1.4 Examples of Model-Agnostic Methods

One widely-used model-agnostic method is LIME (Local Interpretable Model-agnostic Explanations). LIME generates explanations by perturbing the input data — making slight modifications to the original input — and observing how the model's predictions change. It then trains an interpretable, local model (like a linear regression) on this perturbed data to approximate the behavior of the complex model around that specific instance. This approach is particularly useful when you need to explain individual predictions rather than the overall model behavior.

Another powerful model-agnostic technique is SHAP (Shapley Additive Explanations), which borrows from cooperative game theory to assign a "contribution value" to each feature. SHAP calculates how much each feature improves or worsens the prediction by considering all possible feature combinations. This provides a global view of feature importance while also offering local explanations for individual predictions — a balance few other methods achieve.

Partial dependence plots (PDPs) and permutation feature importance are additional model-agnostic approaches that help visualize the relationship between individual features and the model's output, offering insights into how changes in the input affect predictions. While model-agnostic methods are flexible and widely applicable, they come with their own challenges. They can be computationally expensive, especially for high-dimensional data or complex models, and may sometimes oversimplify explanations, leading to less accurate interpretations compared to model-specific methods.

### 3.1.5 Comparing Model-Specific and Model-Agnostic Methods

The choice between model-specific and model-agnostic methods hinges on several factors:

- **Model Type:** If you're working with a single, well-understood model type (e.g., a decision tree or linear regression), model-specific methods may provide more accurate and insightful explanations.
- **Flexibility Needs:** If you're comparing different models or using an ensemble of diverse models, model-agnostic methods offer greater versatility.
- **Computational Resources:** Model-specific methods are often faster and more efficient since they leverage the model's internal structure. Model-agnostic methods, especially perturbation-based ones like LIME, may require significant computational power.
- **Explainability Goals:** For deep insights into model behavior, model-specific methods may offer more detailed, technically precise explanations. However, if the goal is to communicate insights to non-technical stakeholders — like doctors, business leaders, or customers —

model-agnostic methods often provide more intuitive, human-friendly interpretations.

### 3.1.6 Finding the Right Balance

In practice, many organizations and researchers combine both approaches to maximize interpretability. For example, they might use model-specific methods to deeply understand the dominant model's behavior while employing model-agnostic techniques to validate that understanding and ensure consistency across alternative models. The future of XAI may bring hybrid methods that merge the strengths of both categories, offering tailored, accurate insights while remaining flexible enough for any model architecture.

## 3.2 POST-HOC EXPLANATION TECHNIQUES

Post hoc analysis consists of statistical analyses that were specified after the data were seen. They are usually used to uncover specific differences between three or more group means when an analysis of variance (ANOVA) test is significant. This typically creates a multiple testing problem because each potential analysis is effectively a statistical test. Multiple testing procedures are sometimes used to compensate, but that is often difficult or impossible to do precisely. Post hoc analysis that is conducted and interpreted without adequate consideration of this problem is sometimes called data dredging (p-hacking) by critics because the statistical associations that it finds are often spurious.

Post hoc analyses are not inherently bad or good; rather, the main requirement for their ethical use is simply that their results not be mispresented as the original hypothesis. Modern editions of scientific manuals have clarified this point; for example, APA style now specifies that "hypotheses should now be stated in three groupings: preplanned–primary, preplanned–secondary, and exploratory (post hoc). Exploratory hypotheses are allowable, and there should be no pressure to disguise them as if they were preplanned."

### 3.2.1 Causes

Sometimes the temptation to engage in post hoc analysis is motivated by a desire to produce positive results or see a project as successful. In the case of pharmaceutical research, there may be significant financial consequences to a failed trial.

### 3.2.2 Common Post Hoc Tests

#### Holm–Bonferroni Method

In statistics, the Holm–Bonferroni method, also called the Holm method or Bonferroni–Holm method, is used to counteract the problem of multiple comparisons. It is intended to control the family-wise error rate (FWER) and offers a simple test uniformly more powerful than the Bonferroni correction. It is named after Sture Holm, who codified the method, and Carlo Emilio Bonferroni.

### Motivation

When considering several hypotheses, the problem of multiplicity arises: the more hypotheses are tested, the higher the probability of obtaining Type I errors (false positives). The Holm–Bonferroni method is one of many approaches for controlling the FWER, i.e., the probability that one or more Type I errors will occur, by adjusting the rejection criterion for each of the individual hypotheses.

## Newman–Keuls Method

The Newman–Keuls or Student–Newman–Keuls (SNK) method is a stepwise multiple comparisons procedure used to identify sample means that are significantly different from each other. It was named after Student (1927), D. Newman, and M. Keuls. This procedure is often used as a post-hoc test whenever a significant difference between three or more sample means has been revealed by an analysis of variance (ANOVA). The Newman–Keuls method is similar to Tukey's range test as both procedures use studentized range statistics. Unlike Tukey's range test, the Newman–Keuls method uses different critical values for different pairs of mean comparisons. Thus, the procedure is more likely to reveal significant differences between group means and to commit type I errors by incorrectly rejecting a null hypothesis when it is true. In other words, the Neuman-Keuls procedure is more powerful but less conservative than Tukey's range test.

### History and type I error rate control

The Newman–Keuls method was introduced by Newman in 1939 and developed further by Keuls in 1952. This was before Tukey presented various definitions of error rates (1952a, 1952b, 1953). The Newman–Keuls method controls the Family-Wise Error Rate (FWER) in the weak sense but not the strong sense: the Newman–Keuls procedure controls the risk of rejecting the null hypothesis if all means are equal (global null hypothesis) but does not control the risk of rejecting partial null hypotheses. For instance, when four means are compared, under the partial null hypothesis that μ1=μ2 and μ3=μ4=μ+delta with a non-zero delta, the Newman–Keuls procedure has a probability greater than alpha of rejecting μ1=μ2 or μ3=μ4 or both.

In that example, if delta is very large, the Newman–Keuls procedure is almost equivalent to two Student t tests testing μ1=μ2 and μ3=μ4 at nominal type I error rate alpha, without multiple testing procedure; therefore the FWER is almost doubled. In the worst case, the FWER of Newman–Keuls procedure is 1-(1-alpha)^int(J/2) where int(J/2) represents the integer part of the total number of groups divided by 2. Therefore, with two or three groups, the Newman–Keuls procedure has strong control over the FWER but not for four groups or more. In 1995 Benjamini and

Hochberg presented a new, more liberal, and more powerful criterion for those types of problems: False discovery rate (FDR) control. In 2006, Shaffer showed (by extensive simulation) that the Newman–Keuls method controls the FDR with some constraints.

### Required assumptions

The assumptions of the Newman–Keuls test are essentially the same as for an independent groups t-test: normality, homogeneity of variance, and independent observations. The test is quite robust to violations of normality. Violating homogeneity of variance can be more problematic than in the two-sample case since the MSE is based on data from all groups. The assumption of independence of observations is important and should not be violated.

### Procedures

The Newman–Keuls method employs a stepwise approach when comparing sample means. Prior to any mean comparison, all sample means are rank-ordered in ascending or descending order, thereby producing an ordered range (p) of sample means. A comparison is then made between the largest and smallest sample means within the largest range.

Assuming that the largest range is four means (or p = 4), a significant difference between the largest and smallest means as revealed by the Newman–Keuls method would result in a rejection of the null hypothesis for that specific range of means. The next largest comparison of two sample means would then be made within a smaller range of three means (or p = 3). Unless there is no significant differences between two sample means within any given range, this stepwise comparison of sample means will continue until a final comparison is made with the smallest range of just two means. If there is no significant difference between the two sample means, then all the null hypotheses within that range would be retained and no further comparisons within smaller ranges are necessary.

**Table: Range of Sample Means**

| | $\bar{X}_1$ | $\bar{X}_2$ | $\bar{X}_3$ | $\bar{X}_4$ |
|---|---|---|---|---|
| **Mean values** | **2** | **4** | **6** | **8** |
| $\bar{X}_1 = 2$ | | 2 | 4 | 6 |
| $\bar{X}_2 = 4$ | | | 2 | 4 |
| $\bar{X}_3 = 6$ | | | | 2 |

To determine if there is a significant difference between two means with equal sample sizes, the Newman–Keuls method uses a formula that is identical to the one used in Tukey's range test, which calculates the q value by taking the difference between two sample means and dividing it by the standard error:

$$q = \frac{\overline{X}_A - \overline{X}_B}{\sqrt{\frac{MSE}{n}}},$$

where q represents the studentized range value, $\overline{X}_A$ and $\overline{X}_B$ are the largest and smallest sample means within a range, M S E MSE is the error variance taken from the ANOVA table, and n n is the sample size (number of observations within a sample). If comparisons are made with means of unequal sample sizes $(n_A \neq n_B)$, then the Newman–Keuls formula would be adjusted as follows:

$$q = \frac{\overline{X}_A - \overline{X}_B}{\sqrt{\frac{MSE}{2}(\frac{1}{n_A} + \frac{1}{n_B})}},$$

Once calculated, the computed q value can be compared to a q critical value (or $q_{\alpha\ v\ p}$), which can be found in a q distribution table based on the significance level ( $\alpha$ ), the error degrees of freedom ( $v$ ) from the ANOVA table, and the range ( $p$ ) of sample means to be tested. If the computed q value is equal to or greater than the q critical value, then the null hypothesis ($H_0$: $\mu_A = \mu_B$) for that specific range of means can be rejected. Because the number of means within a range changes with each successive pairwise comparison, the critical value of the q statistic also changes with each comparison, which makes the Neuman-Keuls method more lenient and hence more powerful than Tukey's range test. Thus, if a pairwise comparison was found to be significantly different using the Newman–Keuls method, it may not necessarily be significantly different when analyzed with Tukey's range test. Conversely, if the pairwise comparison was found not to be significantly different using the Newman–Keuls method, it cannot be significantly different with Tukey's range test either.

#### Limitations

The Newman–Keuls procedure cannot produce a confidence interval for each mean difference, or for multiplicity adjusted exact p-values due to its sequential nature. Results are somewhat difficult to interpret since it is difficult to articulate what are the null hypotheses that were tested.

### Rodger's Method

Rodger's method is a statistical procedure for examining research data post hoc following an 'omnibus' analysis (e.g., after an analysis of variance – anova). The various components of this methodology were fully worked out by R. S. Rodger in the 1960s and 70s, and seven of his articles about it were published in the British Journal of Mathematical and Statistical Psychology between 1967 and 1978.

Statistical procedures for finding differences between groups, along with interactions between the groups that were included in an experiment or study, can be classified along two dimensions: 1) were the statistical contrasts that will be evaluated decided upon prior to collecting the data (planned) or while trying to figure out what those data are trying to reveal (post hoc), and 2) does the procedure use a decision-based (i.e., per contrast) error rate or does it instead use an experiment-wise error rate. Rodger's method, and some others, are classified according to these dimensions in the table below.

**Table: Some Multiple Comparison Procedures**

| | Planned Contrasts | Post Hoc Contrasts |
|---|---|---|
| Decision-based error rate | *t* tests | Duncan's method<br>Rodger's method |
| Experiment-wise error rate | Bonferroni's inequality<br>Dunnett's method | Newman–Keuls method<br>Tukey's range method<br>Scheffé's method |

## Statistical Power

In early 1990s, one set of researchers made this statement about their decision to use Rodger's method: "We chose Rodger's method because it is the most powerful post hoc method available for detecting true differences among groups. This was an especially important consideration in the present experiments in which interesting conclusions could rest on null results" (Williams, Frame, & LoLordo, 1992, p. 43). The most definitive evidence for the statistical power advantage that Rodger's method possesses (as compared with eight other multiple comparison procedures) is provided in a 2013 article by Rodger and Roberts.

## Type 1 Error Rate

Statistical power is an important consideration when choosing what statistical procedure to use, but it isn't the only important one. All statistical procedures permit researchers to make statistical errors and they are not all equal in their ability to control the rate of occurrence of several important types of statistical error. As Table 1 shows, statisticians can't agree on how error rate ought to be defined, but particular attention has been traditionally paid to what are called 'type 1 errors' and whether or not a statistical procedure is susceptible to type 1 error rate inflation.

On this matter, the facts about Rodger's method are straightforward and unequivocal. Rodger's method permits an absolutely unlimited amount of post hoc data snooping and this is accompanied by a guarantee that the long run expectation of type 1 errors will never exceed the commonly used rates of either 5 or 1 percent. Whenever a researcher falsely rejects a true null contrast (whether it is a planned or post hoc one) the probability of that being a type 1 error is 100%. It is the average number of such errors over the long run that Rodger's method guarantees cannot exceed E$\alpha$ = 0.05 or 0.01. This statement is a logical tautology, a necessary truth, that follows from the manner in which Rodger's method was originally conceived and subsequently built. Type 1 error rate inflation is statistically impossible with Rodger's method, but every statistical decision a researcher makes that might be a type 1 error will either actually be one or it won't.

### Decision-Based Error Rate

The two features of Rodger's method that have been mentioned thus far, its increased statistical power and the impossibility of type 1 error rate inflation when using it, are direct by-products of the decision-based error rate that it utilizes. "An error occurs, in the statistical context, if and only if a decision is made that a specified relationship among population parameters either is, or is not, equal to some number (usually, zero), and the opposite is true. Rodger's very sensible, and cogently argued, position is that statistical error rate should be based exclusively on those things in which errors may occur, and that (necessarily, by definition) can only be the statistical decisions that researchers make" (Roberts, 2011, p. 69).

### Implied True Population Means

There is a unique aspect of Rodger's method that is statistically valuable and is not dependent on its decision-based error rate. As Bird stated: "Rodger (1965, 1967a, 1967b, 1974) explored the possibility of examining the logical implications of statistical inferences on a set of J - 1 linearly independent contrasts. Rodger's approach was formulated within the Neyman-Pearson hypothesis-testing framework [...] and required that the test of each contrast $\Psi_i$ (i = 1, ... , J - 1) should result in a 'decision' between the null hypothesis (${}_iH_0$: $\Psi_i = 0$) and a particular value $\delta_i$ specified a priori by the alternative hypothesis (${}_iH_1$: $\Psi_i = \delta_i$). Given the resulting set of decisions, it is possible to determine the implied values of all other contrasts" (Bird, 2011, p. 434).

The statistical value that Rodger derived from the 'implication equation' that he invented is prominently displayed in the form of 'implied means' that are logically implied, and mathematically entailed, by the J - 1 statistical decisions that the user of his method makes. These implied true population means constitute a very precise statement about the outcome of one›s research, and assist other researchers in determining the size of effect that their related research ought to seek.

### Whither Rodger's Method?

Since the inception of Rodger's method, some researchers who use it have had their work published in prestigious scientific journals, and this continues to happen. Nevertheless, it is fair to currently conclude that "Rodger's work on deduced inference has been largely ignored" (Bird, 2011, p. 434). Bird uses implication equations, similar to Rodger's, to deduce interval inferences concerning any contrasts not included in an analysis from the upper and lower limits of confidence intervals on J - 1 linearly independent planned contrasts; a procedure that Rodger himself opposes.

## Scheffé's Method

In statistics, Scheffé's method, named after American statistician Henry Scheffé, is a method for adjusting significance levels in a linear regression analysis to account for multiple comparisons. It is particularly useful in analysis of variance (a special case of regression analysis), and in constructing simultaneous confidence bands for regressions involving basis functions.

### Denoting Scheffé Significance in a Table

Frequently, subscript letters are used to indicate which values are significantly different using the Scheffé method. For example, when mean values of variables that have been analyzed using an ANOVA are presented in a table, they are assigned a different letter subscript based on a Scheffé contrast. Values that are not significantly different based on the post-hoc Scheffé contrast will have the same subscript and values that are significantly different will have different subscripts (i.e. $15_a$, $17_a$, $34_b$ would mean that the first and second variables both differ from the third variable but not each other because they are both assigned the subscript "a").

### Comparison with the Tukey–Kramer Method

If only a fixed number of pairwise comparisons are to be made, the Tukey–Kramer method will result in a more precise confidence interval. In the general case when many or all contrasts might be of interest, the Scheffé method is more appropriate and will give narrower confidence intervals in the case of a large number of comparisons.

## Tukey's Range Test

Tukey's range test, also known as Tukey's test, Tukey method, Tukey's honest significance test, or Tukey's HSD (honestly significant difference) test, is a single-step multiple comparison procedure and statistical test. It can be used to correctly interpret the statistical significance of the difference between means that have been selected for comparison because of their extreme values.

The method was initially developed and introduced by John Tukey for use in Analysis of Variance (ANOVA), and usually has only been taught in connection with ANOVA. However, the studentized range distribution used to determine the level of significance of the differences considered in Tukey's test has vastly broader application: It is useful for researchers who have searched their collected data for remarkable differences between groups, but then cannot validly determine how significant their discovered stand-out difference is using standard statistical distributions used for other conventional statistical tests, for which the data must have been selected at random. Since when stand-out data is compared it was by definition not selected at random, but rather specifically chosen because it was extreme, it needs a different, stricter interpretation provided by the likely frequency and size of the studentized range; the modern practice of "data mining" is an example where it is used.

### Development

The test is named after John Tukey, it compares all possible pairs of means, and is based on a studentized range distribution (q).

Tukey's test compares the means of every treatment to the means of every other treatment; that is, it applies simultaneously to the set of all pairwise comparisons,

$$\mu_i - \mu_j ,$$

and identifies any difference between two means that is greater than the expected standard error. The confidence coefficient for the set, when all sample sizes are equal, is exactly $1-\alpha$ for any $\alpha : 0 \leq \alpha \leq 1$. For unequal sample sizes, the confidence coefficient is greater than $1-\alpha$. In other words, the Tukey method is conservative when there are unequal sample sizes.

This test is often followed by the Compact Letter Display (CLD) statistical procedure to render the output of this test more transparent to non-statistician audiences.

### Assumptions

- The observations being tested are independent within and among the groups.
- The subgroups associated with each mean in the test are normally distributed.
- There is equal within-subgroup variance across the subgroups associated with each mean in the test (homogeneity of variance).

### The Test Statistic

Tukey's test is based on a formula very similar to that of the t-test. In fact, Tukey's test is essentially a t-test, except that it corrects for family-wise error rate.

The formula for Tukey's test is

$$q_s = \frac{|Y_A - Y_B|}{SE},$$

where $Y_A$ and $Y_B$ are the two means being compared, and SE is the standard error for the sum of the means. The value $q_s$ is the sample's test statistic. (The notation $|x|$ means the absolute value of x; the magnitude of x with the sign set to +, regardless of the original sign of x.)

This $q_s$ test statistic can then be compared to a q value for the chosen significance level α from a table of the studentized range distribution. If the $q_s$ value is larger than the critical value $q_\alpha$ obtained from the distribution, the two means are said to be significantly different at level $\alpha : 0 \le \alpha \le 1$.

Since the null hypothesis for Tukey's test states that all means being compared are from the same population (i.e. $\mu_1 = \mu_2 = \mu_3 = \ldots = \mu_k$ ), the means should be normally distributed (according to the central limit theorem) with the same model standard deviation σ, estimated by the merged standard error, SE, for all the samples. This gives rise to the normality assumption of Tukey's test.

### The Studentized Range (q) Distribution

The Tukey method uses the studentized range distribution. Suppose that we take a sample of size n from each of k populations with the same normal distribution N(μ, σ²) and suppose that $\bar{y}_{min}$ is the smallest of these sample means and $\bar{y}_{max}$ is the largest of these sample means, and suppose $S^2$ is the pooled sample variance from these samples. Then the following random variable has a Studentized range distribution:

$$q \equiv \frac{\bar{y}_{max} - \bar{y}_{min}}{S\sqrt{2/n}}$$

This definition of the statistic q given above is the basis of the critically significant value for $q_\alpha$ discussed below, and is based on these three factors:

- α the Type I error rate, or the probability of rejecting a true null hypothesis;
- κ the number of sub-populations being compared;
- df the number of degrees of freedom for each mean

( df = N - k ) where N is the total number of observations.)

The distribution of q has been tabulated and appears in many textbooks on statistics. In some tables the distribution of q has been tabulated without the $\sqrt{2}$ factor. To understand which table it is, we can compute the result for k = 2 and compare it to the result of the Student's t-distribution with the same degrees of freedom and the same α . In addition, R offers a cumulative distribution function (ptukey) and a quantile function (qtukey) for q .

### Confidence Limits

The Tukey confidence limits for all pairwise comparisons with confidence coefficient of at least 1 - α are

$$\bar{y}_{i\cdot} - \bar{y}_{j\cdot} \pm \frac{q_{\alpha;k;N-k}}{\sqrt{2}} \hat{\sigma}_\varepsilon \sqrt{\frac{2}{n}} \quad : \; i, j = 1, \ldots, k \quad i \neq j .$$

Notice that the point estimator and the estimated variance are the same as those for a single pairwise comparison. The only difference between the confidence limits for simultaneous comparisons and those for a single comparison is the multiple of the estimated standard deviation.

Also note that the sample sizes must be equal when using the studentized range approach. $\hat{\sigma}_\varepsilon$ is the standard deviation of the entire design, not just that of the two groups being compared. It is possible to work with unequal sample sizes. In this case, one has to calculate the estimated standard deviation for each pairwise comparison as formalized by Clyde Kramer in 1956, so the procedure for unequal sample sizes is sometimes referred to as the Tukey–Kramer method which is as follows:

$$\bar{y}_{i\cdot} - \bar{y}_{j\cdot} \pm \frac{q_{\alpha;k;N-k}}{\sqrt{2}} \hat{\sigma}_\varepsilon \sqrt{\frac{1}{n_i} + \frac{1}{n_j}}$$

where $n_i$ and $n_j$ are the sizes of groups i and j respectively. The degrees of freedom for the whole design is also applied.

### Comparing ANOVA and Tukey–Kramer Tests

Both ANOVA and Tukey–Kramer tests are based on the same assumptions. However, these two tests for k groups (i.e. $\mu_1 = \mu_2 = \ldots = \mu_k$) may result in logical contradictions when $k > 2$, even if the assumptions do hold.

It is possible to generate a set of pseudorandom samples of strictly negative measure such that hypothesis $\mu_1 = \mu_2$ is rejected at significance level $1-\alpha > 0.95$ while $\mu_1 = \mu_2 = \mu_3$ is not rejected even at $1-\alpha = 0.975$.

## 3.2.1 Feature Importance Methods (e.g., SHAP, LIME)

In machine learning, understanding how models make predictions is crucial for ensuring transparency, fairness, and reliability. One of the primary ways to achieve this is through feature importance methods, which help identify the contribution of each input feature to a model's predictions. These methods are critical in domains like healthcare, finance, and criminal justice, where decision-making must be explainable to stakeholders. Among the most widely used feature importance techniques are SHAP (Shapley Additive Explanations) and LIME (Local Interpretable Model-agnostic Explanations). Both of these methods offer insights into how a model makes decisions, but they do so in different ways and with unique strengths and limitations.

Feature importance methods like SHAP and LIME are essential for making machine learning models more transparent and interpretable. While SHAP provides rigorous, game-theoretic explanations with strong mathematical foundations, LIME offers a more computationally efficient, localized approach to explaining individual predictions. Both methods have their place in AI development, and choosing the right one depends on the balance between accuracy, interpretability, and computational efficiency. As AI continues to evolve, feature importance methods will play an increasingly critical role in building trust, fairness, and accountability in machine learning systems.

## The Need for Feature Importance Methods

Machine learning models, particularly complex ones like deep learning, gradient boosting machines, and ensemble methods, often function as "black boxes," meaning that their internal decision-making process is difficult to interpret. Without understanding which features contribute most to predictions, it becomes challenging to trust AI models, debug errors, and ensure fairness. Feature importance methods help address these challenges by providing transparency into which input variables play the most significant role in shaping outcomes. Feature importance techniques serve multiple purposes, including model debugging, where developers identify misleading correlations; regulatory compliance, where businesses must justify AI-driven decisions; and bias detection, where organizations need to ensure that models are not unfairly influenced by sensitive variables like race, gender, or socioeconomic status.

## SHAP (Shapley Additive Explanations)

### Introduction to SHAP

SHAP is a powerful, mathematically grounded method for explaining machine learning models. Based on game theory's Shapley values, SHAP provides a way to fairly distribute credit to input features based on their contribution to a model's predictions. The core idea is to analyze all possible combinations of input features and measure their impact on the model's output, thereby assigning a contribution value to each feature. Developed as a model-agnostic approach, SHAP works across various machine learning algorithms, including decision trees, support vector machines, and deep neural networks. Unlike some other feature importance techniques that offer only a high-level ranking, SHAP provides both local explanations (for individual predictions) and global explanations (for overall feature importance).

### How SHAP Works

SHAP calculates feature importance by evaluating how predictions change when different subsets of features are considered. The method assigns an average marginal contribution to each feature based on all possible feature combinations, ensuring a fair distribution of importance. This approach is based on three key principles:

- **Efficiency**: The total contribution of all features must sum up to the actual prediction.
- **Symmetry**: Features with identical contributions should receive the same importance score.
- **Dummy Feature Property**: Features that do not affect the prediction should receive zero importance.

These properties make SHAP one of the most theoretically sound feature attribution methods available.

### Advantages of SHAP

One of the key benefits of SHAP is its consistency and fairness in assigning importance scores. Additionally, SHAP provides global explanations through summary plots that visualize the overall impact of features on the model, as well as local explanations that offer insights into individual predictions. Moreover, SHAP generates force plots, which help illustrate how different features push a model's prediction higher or lower. This makes it particularly useful in applications like healthcare, where a doctor may need to understand why an AI system classified a patient as high-risk for a disease.

### Limitations of SHAP

Despite its strengths, SHAP has some challenges, primarily its computational complexity. Calculating exact Shapley values requires evaluating all feature combinations, which becomes infeasible for high-dimensional datasets. To address this, approximations like TreeSHAP (for tree-based models) and KernelSHAP (for arbitrary models) have been developed, but they can still be computationally expensive for large datasets.

## LIME (Local Interpretable Model-agnostic Explanations)

### Introduction to LIME

LIME is another widely used method for feature importance analysis, focusing on local interpretability. Unlike SHAP, which evaluates all possible feature combinations, LIME takes a more approximate approach by perturbing the input data and analyzing how the model's predictions change. This method is particularly effective for explaining individual predictions, rather than providing a holistic view of the model's behavior.

### How LIME Works

LIME works by generating a set of slightly modified versions of an input instance and observing how the model's prediction changes. By applying random perturbations to the input features and fitting a simple, interpretable model (such as linear regression) to approximate the black-box model's decision boundary, LIME determines which features have the most impact on a given prediction.

The steps in LIME include:

- Selecting a specific instance for explanation.
- Generating multiple perturbed samples around the instance.
- Obtaining model predictions for these perturbed samples.
- Training an interpretable model (e.g., linear regression) to approximate the local decision boundary.
- Extracting feature weights from the interpretable model to explain the original instance's prediction.

### Advantages of LIME

One of LIME's biggest strengths is its computational efficiency compared to SHAP. Since it does not require evaluating all feature combinations, it scales better for high-dimensional datasets. Moreover, its use of local surrogate models allows it to provide simple, interpretable explanations for individual predictions. LIME also supports explanations for various data types, including tabular data, images, and text, making it versatile for different machine learning applications. For example, in image classification, LIME can highlight which pixels contributed most to a model's decision, making it valuable in fields like medical imaging.

### Limitations of LIME

Despite its usefulness, LIME has some weaknesses. One major concern is stability—the explanations it provides can vary significantly depending on how perturbations are applied. This makes it less reliable for high-stakes applications where consistent explanations are needed. Additionally, LIME relies on simplified local models, which may not always faithfully represent the true decision boundaries of the original model. This can lead to misleading interpretations, especially for highly non-linear models like deep neural networks.

## Comparing SHAP and LIME

Both SHAP and LIME are valuable feature importance methods, but they have distinct trade-offs:

- **SHAP provides more theoretically grounded, consistent explanations**, making it ideal for applications requiring fairness and rigor. However, it is computationally expensive.

- **LIME is faster and more scalable**, making it more practical for real-time applications, but its explanations may lack stability.
- **SHAP excels in providing both global and local feature importance,** whereas **LIME is better suited for local explanations** of individual predictions.

The choice between SHAP and LIME depends on the specific requirements of a machine learning project. If accuracy and fairness are the priority, SHAP is preferable. If speed and efficiency are needed, LIME is a better choice.

### 3.2.2 Visualization Techniques (e.g., Heatmaps, Saliency Maps)

#### Understanding the Visualization

Visualization also known as graphics visualization, is any technique for creating images, diagrams, or animations to communicate a message. Visualization through visual imagery has been an effective way to communicate both abstract and concrete ideas since the dawn of humanity. from history include cave paintings, Egyptian hieroglyphs, Greek geometry, and Leonardo da Vinci's revolutionary methods of technical drawing for engineering purposes that actively involve scientific requirements.

Visualization today has ever-expanding applications in science, education, engineering (e.g., product visualization), interactive multimedia, medicine, etc. Typical of a visualization application is the field of computer graphics. The invention of computer graphics (and 3D computer graphics) may be the most important development in visualization since the invention of central perspective in the Renaissance period. The development of animation also helped advance visualization.

The use of visualization to present information is not a new phenomenon. It has been used in maps, scientific drawings, and data plots for over a thousand years. Examples from cartography include Ptolemy's Geographia (2nd century AD), a map of China (1137 AD), and Minard's map (1861) of Napoleon's invasion of Russia a century and a half ago.

Most of the concepts learned in devising these images carry over in a straightforward manner to computer visualization. Edward Tufte has written three critically acclaimed books that explain many of these principles.

Computer graphics has from its beginning been used to study scientific problems. However, in its early days the lack of graphics power often limited its usefulness. The recent emphasis on visualization started in 1987 with the publication of Visualization in Scientific Computing, a special issue of Computer Graphics. Since then, there have been several conferences and workshops, co-sponsored by the

IEEE Computer Society and ACM SIGGRAPH, devoted to the general topic, and special areas in the field, for example volume visualization.

Most people are familiar with the digital animations produced to present meteorological data during weather reports on television, though few can distinguish between those models of reality and the satellite photos that are also shown on such programs. TV also offers scientific visualizations when it shows computer drawn and animated reconstructions of road or airplane accidents. Some of the most popular examples of scientific visualizations are computer-generated images that show real spacecraft in action, out in the void far beyond Earth, or on other planets. Dynamic forms of visualization, such as educational animation or timelines, have the potential to enhance learning about systems that change over time.

Apart from the distinction between interactive visualizations and animation, the most useful categorization is probably between abstract and model-based scientific visualizations. The abstract visualizations show completely conceptual constructs in 2D or 3D. These generated shapes are completely arbitrary. The model-based visualizations either place overlays of data on real or digitally constructed images of reality or make a digital construction of a real object directly from the scientific data.

Scientific visualization is usually done with specialized software, though there are a few exceptions. Some of these specialized programs have been released as open source software, having very often its origins in universities, within an academic environment where sharing software tools and giving access to the source code is common. There are also many proprietary software packages of scientific visualization tools.

Models and frameworks for building visualizations include the data flow models popularized by systems such as AVS, IRIS Explorer, and VTK toolkit, and data state models in spreadsheet systems such as the Spreadsheet for Visualization and Spreadsheet for Images.

### Scientific Visualization

As a subject in computer science, scientific visualization is the use of interactive, sensory representations, typically visual, of abstract data to reinforce cognition, hypothesis building, and reasoning. Scientific visualization is the transformation, selection, or representation of data from simulations or experiments, with an implicit or explicit geometric structure, to allow the exploration, analysis, and understanding of the data. Scientific visualization focuses and emphasizes the representation of higher order data using primarily graphics and animation techniques. It is a very important part of visualization and maybe the first one, as the visualization of experiments and phenomena is as old as science itself. Traditional areas of scientific visualization are flow visualization, medical visualization, astrophysical visualization, and chemical visualization. There are several different techniques to visualize scientific data, with isosurface reconstruction and direct volume rendering being the more common.

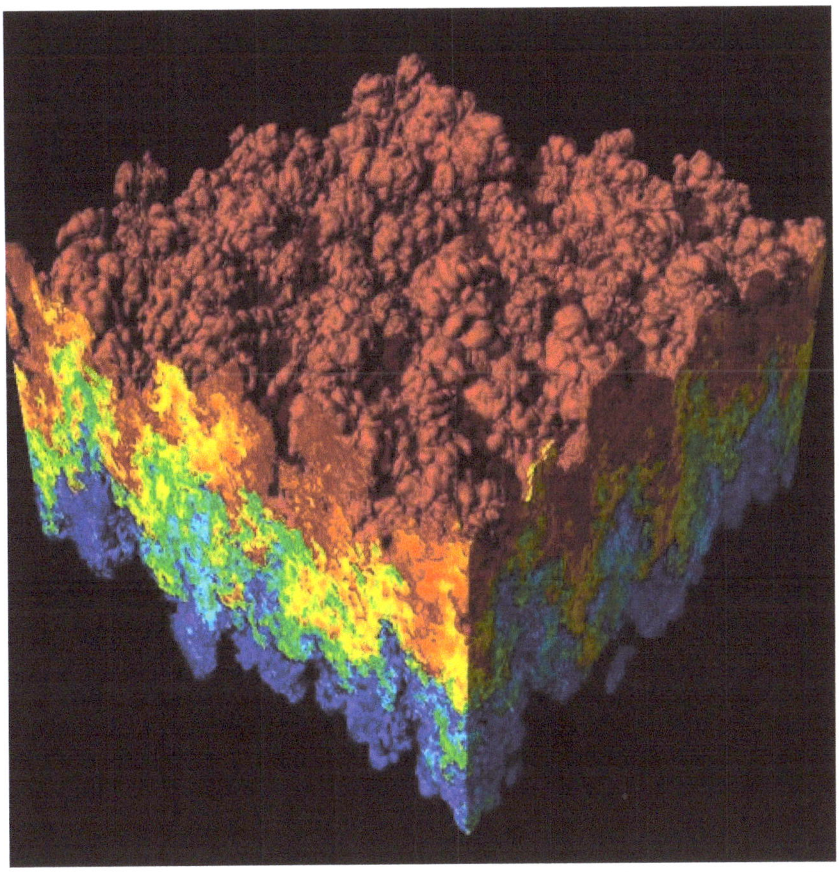

**Fig: Simulation of a Raleigh–Taylor Instability Caused by Two Mixing Fluids**

## Data and Information Visualization

Data visualization is a related subcategory of visualization dealing with statistical graphics and geospatial data (as in thematic cartography) that is abstracted in schematic form.

Information visualization concentrates on the use of computer-supported tools to explore large amount of abstract data. The term "information visualization" was originally coined by the User Interface Research Group at Xerox PARC and included Jock Mackinlay. Practical application of information visualization in computer programs involves selecting, transforming, and representing abstract data in a form that facilitates human interaction for exploration and understanding. Important aspects of information visualization are dynamics of visual representation and the interactivity. Strong techniques enable the user to modify the visualization in real-time, thus affording unparalleled perception of patterns and structural relations in the abstract data in question.

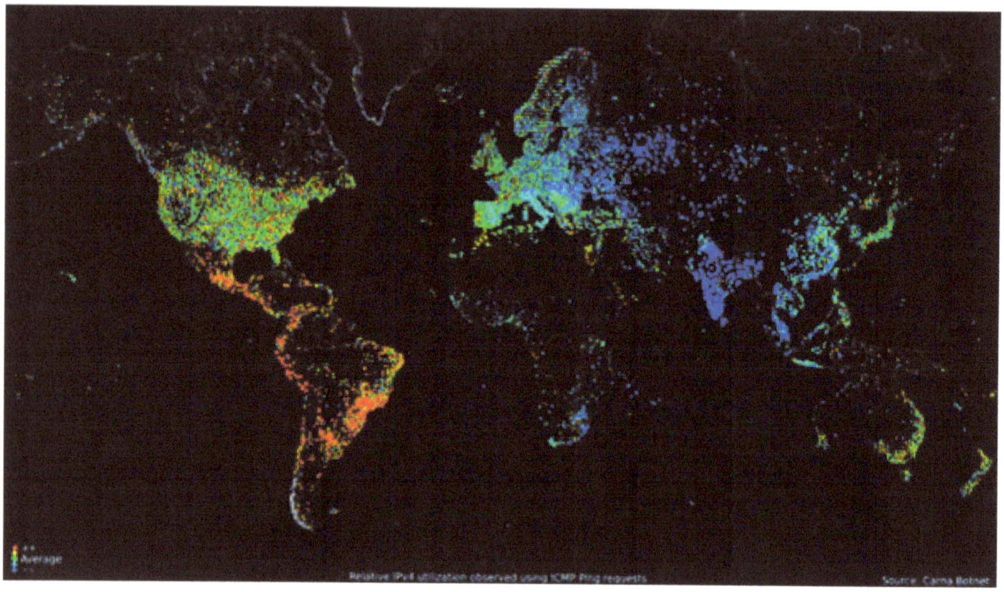


**Fig: Relative Average Utilization of IPv4**

## Educational Visualization

Educational visualization is using a simulation to create an image of something so it can be taught about. This is very useful when teaching about a topic that is difficult to otherwise see, for example, atomic structure, because atoms are far too small to be studied easily without expensive and difficult to use scientific equipment.

## Knowledge Visualization

The use of visual representations to transfer knowledge between at least two persons aims to improve the transfer of knowledge by using computer and non-computer-based visualization methods complementarily. Thus properly designed visualization is an important part of not only data analysis but knowledge transfer process, too. Knowledge transfer may be significantly improved using hybrid designs as it enhances information density but may decrease clarity as well. For example, visualization of a 3D scalar field may be implemented using iso-surfaces for field distribution and textures for the gradient of the field. Examples of such visual formats are sketches, diagrams, images, objects, interactive visualizations, information visualization applications, and imaginary visualizations as in stories. While information visualization concentrates on the use of computer-supported tools to derive new insights, knowledge visualization focuses on transferring insights and creating new knowledge in groups. Beyond the mere transfer of facts, knowledge visualization aims to further transfer insights, experiences, attitudes, values, expectations, perspectives, opinions, and estimates in different fields by using various complementary visualizations.

### Product Visualization

Product visualization involves visualization software technology for the viewing and manipulation of 3D models, technical drawing and other related documentation of manufactured components and large assemblies of products. It is a key part of product lifecycle management. Product visualization software typically provides high levels of photorealism so that a product can be viewed before it is actually manufactured. This supports functions ranging from design and styling to sales and marketing. Technical visualization is an important aspect of product development. Originally technical drawings were made by hand, but with the rise of advanced computer graphics the drawing board has been replaced by computer-aided design (CAD). CAD-drawings and models have several advantages over hand-made drawings such as the possibility of 3-D modeling, rapid prototyping, and simulation. 3D product visualization promises more interactive experiences for online shoppers, but also challenges retailers to overcome hurdles in the production of 3D content, as large-scale 3D content production can be extremely costly and time-consuming.

### Visual Communication

Visual communication is the communication of ideas through the visual display of information. Primarily associated with two dimensional images, it includes: alphanumerics, art, signs, and electronic resources. Recent research in the field has focused on web design and graphically oriented usability.

### Visual Analytics

Visual analytics focuses on human interaction with visualization systems as part of a larger process of data analysis. Visual analytics has been defined as "the science of analytical reasoning supported by the interactive visual interface". Its focus is on human information discourse (interaction) within massive, dynamically changing information spaces. Visual analytics research concentrates on support for perceptual and cognitive operations that enable users to detect the expected and discover the unexpected in complex information spaces. Technologies resulting from visual analytics find their application in almost all fields, but are being driven by critical needs (and funding) in biology and national security.

### Interactivity

Interactive visualization or interactive visualisation is a branch of graphic visualization in computer science that involves studying how humans interact with computers to create graphic illustrations of information and how this process can be made more efficient.

For a visualization to be considered interactive it must satisfy two criteria:

- **Human Input:** Control of some aspect of the visual representation of information, or of the information being represented, must be available to a human, and
- **Response Time:** Changes made by the human must be incorporated into the visualization in a timely manner. In general, interactive visualization is considered a soft real-time task.

One particular type of interactive visualization is virtual reality (VR), where the visual representation of information is presented using an immersive display device such as a stereo projector. VR is also characterized by the use of a spatial metaphor, where some aspect of the information is represented in three dimensions so that humans can explore the information as if it were present (where instead it was remote), sized appropriately (where instead it was on a much smaller or larger scale than humans can sense directly), or had shape (where instead it might be completely abstract).

Another type of interactive visualization is collaborative visualization, in which multiple people interact with the same computer visualization to communicate their ideas to each other or to explore information cooperatively. Frequently, collaborative visualization is used when people are physically separated. Using several networked computers, the same visualization can be presented to each person simultaneously. The people then make annotations to the visualization as well as communicate via audio (i.e., telephone), video (i.e., a video-conference), or text (i.e., IRC) messages.

### Human Control of Visualization

The Programmer's Hierarchical Interactive Graphics System (PHIGS) was one of the first programmatic efforts at interactive visualization and provided an enumeration of the types of input humans provide. People can:

- Pick some part of an existing visual representation;
- Locate a point of interest (which may not have an existing representation);
- Stroke a path;
- Choose an option from a list of options;
- Valuate by inputting a number; and
- Write by inputting text.

All of these actions require a physical device. Input devices range from the common – keyboards, mice, graphics tablets, trackballs, and touchpads – to the esoteric – wired gloves, boom arms, and even omnidirectional treadmills. These input actions can be used to control both the unique information being represented or the way that the information is presented. When the information being presented is altered, the visualization is usually part of a feedback loop. For example, consider an aircraft avionics system where the pilot inputs roll, pitch, and yaw and the visualization system provides a rendering of the aircraft's new attitude. Another example would be a scientist who changes a simulation while it is running in response to a visualization of its current progress. This is called computational steering. More frequently, the representation of the information is changed rather than the information itself.

### Rapid Response to Human Input

Experiments have shown that a delay of more than 20 ms between when input is provided and a visual representation is updated is noticeable by most people . Thus it is desirable for an interactive visualization to provide a rendering based on human input within this time frame.

However, when large amounts of data must be processed to create a visualization, this becomes hard or even impossible with current technology. Thus the term "interactive visualization" is usually applied to systems that provide feedback to users within several seconds of input. The term interactive framerate is often used to measure how interactive a visualization is. Framerates measure the frequency with which an image (a frame) can be generated by a visualization system.

A framerate of 50 frames per second (frame/s) is considered good while 0.1 frame/s would be considered poor. The use of framerates to characterize interactivity is slightly misleading however, since framerate is a measure of bandwidth while humans are more sensitive to latency. Specifically, it is possible to achieve a good framerate of 50 frame/s but if the images generated refer to changes to the visualization that a person made more than 1 second ago, it will not feel interactive to a person.

The rapid response time required for interactive visualization is a difficult constraint to meet and there are several approaches that have been explored to provide people with rapid visual feedback based on their input. Some include

- Parallel rendering – where more than one computer or video card is used simultaneously to render an image. Multiple frames can be rendered at the same time by different computers and the results transferred over the network for display on a single monitor. This requires each computer to hold a copy of all the information to be rendered and increases bandwidth, but also increases latency. Also, each computer can render a different region of a single frame and send the results over a network for display. This again requires each computer to hold all of the data and can lead to a load imbalance when one computer is responsible for rendering a region of the screen with more information than other computers. Finally, each computer can render an entire frame containing a subset of the information. The resulting images plus the associated depth buffer can then be sent across the network and merged with the images from other computers. The result is a single frame containing all the information to be rendered, even though no single computer's memory held all of the information. This is called parallel depth compositing and is used when large amounts of information must be rendered interactively.

- Progressive rendering – where a framerate is guaranteed by rendering some subset of the information to be presented and providing incremental (progressive) improvements to the rendering once the visualization is no longer changing.
- Level-of-detail (LOD) rendering – where simplified representations of information are rendered to achieve a desired framerate while a person is providing input and then the full representation is used to generate a still image once the person is through manipulating the visualization. One common variant of LOD rendering is subsampling. When the information being represented is stored in a topologically rectangular array (as is common with digital photos, MRI scans, and finite difference simulations), a lower resolution version can easily be generated by skipping n points for each 1 point rendered. Subsampling can also be used to accelerate rendering techniques such as volume visualization that require more than twice the computations for an image twice the size. By rendering a smaller image and then scaling the image to fill the requested screen space, much less time is required to render the same data.
- Frameless rendering – where the visualization is no longer presented as a time series of images, but as a single image where different regions are updated over time.

## Heat Map

A heat map (or heatmap) is a 2-dimensional data visualization technique that represents the magnitude of individual values within a dataset as a color. The variation in color may be by hue or intensity. In some applications such as crime analytics or website click-tracking, color is used to represent the density of data points rather than a value associated with each point. "Heat map" is a relatively new term, but the practice of shading matrices has existed for over a century.

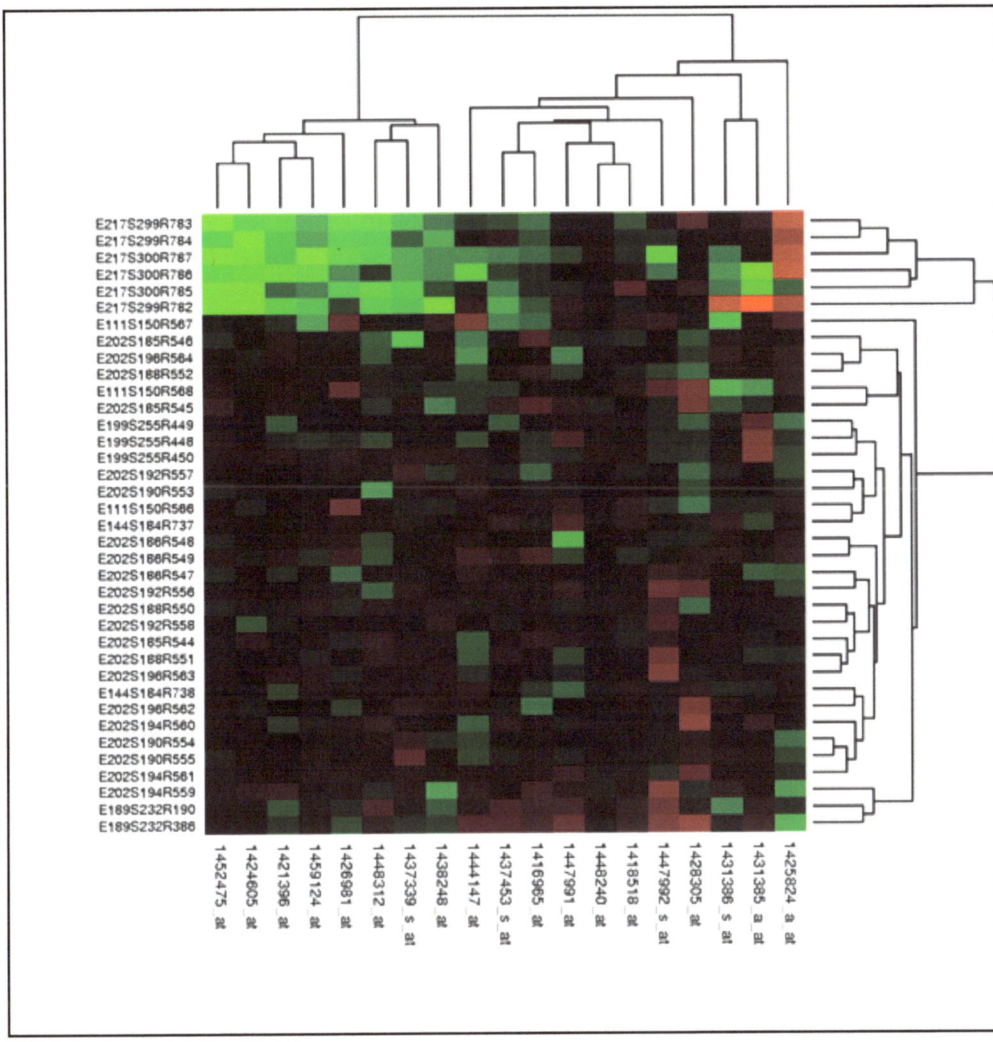


**Fig: Heat Map Generated from DNA Microarray Data Reflecting Gene Expression Values in Several Conditions**

## History

Heat maps originated in 2D displays of the values in a data matrix. Larger values were represented by small dark gray or black squares (pixels) and smaller values by lighter squares. Toussaint Loua (1873) used a shading matrix to visualize social statistics across the districts of Paris. Sneath (1957) displayed the results of a cluster analysis by permuting the rows and the columns of a matrix to place similar values near each other according to the clustering. Jacques Bertin used a similar representation to display data that conformed to a Guttman scale. The idea for joining cluster trees to the rows and columns of the data matrix originated with Robert Ling in 1973. Ling used overstruck printer characters to represent different shades of gray, one character-width per pixel. Leland Wilkinson developed the first computer program in 1994 (SYSTAT) to produce cluster heat maps with high-resolution color graphics. The Eisen et al. display shown in the figure is a replication of the earlier SYSTAT design.

Software designer Cormac Kinney trademarked the term 'heat map' in 1991 to describe a 2D display depicting financial market information. The company that acquired Kinney's invention in 2003 unintentionally allowed the trademark to lapse.

**Fig: Spatial Heat Map Example: Displays Temperature Across a World Image with Red being the Highest and Blue being the Lowest Degree in Temperatures (5 April 2019)**

## Types

There are two main type of heat maps: spatial, and grid. A spatial heat map displays the magnitude of a spatial phenomena as color, usually cast over a map. In the image labeled "Spatial Heat Map Example," temperature is displayed by color range across a map of the world. Color ranges from blue (cold) to red (hot).

A grid heat map displays magnitude as color in a two-dimensional matrix, with each dimension representing a category of trait and the color representing the magnitude of some measurement on the combined traits from each of the two categories. For example, one dimension might represent year, and the other dimension might represent month, and the value measured might be temperature. This heat map would show how temperature changed over the years in each month. Grid heat maps are further categorized into two different types of matrices: clustered, and correlogram.

- **Clustered Heat Map:** The example of the monthly temperature by year is a clustered heat map.
- **Correlogram:** A correlogram is a clustered heat map that has the same trait for each axis in order to display how the traits in the set of traits interact with each other. The correlogram is a triangle instead of a square because the combination of A-B is the same as the combination of B-A and so does not need to be expressed twice.

In a grid heat map, colors are presented in a grid of a fixed size, with every cell in the grid also being an equal size and shape. The goal is to detect clustering, or suggest the presence of clusters. A spatial heat map is often used on maps or satellite imagery, where there is no concept of cells, and instead the colours vary continuously.

### Uses

Heat maps have a wide range of possibilities amongst applications due to their ability to simplify data and make for visually appealing to read data analysis.

Business Analysis: Heat maps are used in business analytics to give a visual representation about a company's current functioning, performance, and the need for improvements. Heat maps are a way to analyze a company's existing data and update it to reflect growth and other specific efforts. Heat maps visually appeal to team members and clients of the business or company.

- **Websites:** There are many different ways heat maps are used within websites to determine a visiting users actions. Typically, there are multiple heat maps used together to determine insight to a website on what are the best and worst performing elements on the page.
- **Mouse Tracking:** Mouse tracking heat maps or hover maps, are used to visualize where the user of the site hovers their cursor.
- **Eye Tracking:** Eye tracking heat maps measure the eye position of the website's users and gathers measurements such as eye fixation volume, eye fixation duration, and areas of interest.
- **Click Tracking:** Click tracking heat maps or touch maps, are similar to mouse tracking heat maps, but instead of hover actions, these types of heat maps help visualize the users click actions. Click tracking heat maps not only allow for visual cues on clickable components on a webpage, such as buttons or dropdown menus, but these heat maps also allow for tracking on non-clickable objects anywhere on the page.
- **AI-Generation Attention:** AI-generated attention heat maps help visualize where the visiting user's attention will go on a certain section of a webpage. These types of heat maps are implemented using a created

software algorithm to determine and predict the attention actions of the user.

- **Scroll Tracking:** Scroll tracking heat maps are used to represent the scrolling behavior of the website's users. This helps produce visual cues to what section on the website the user spends the most time at.

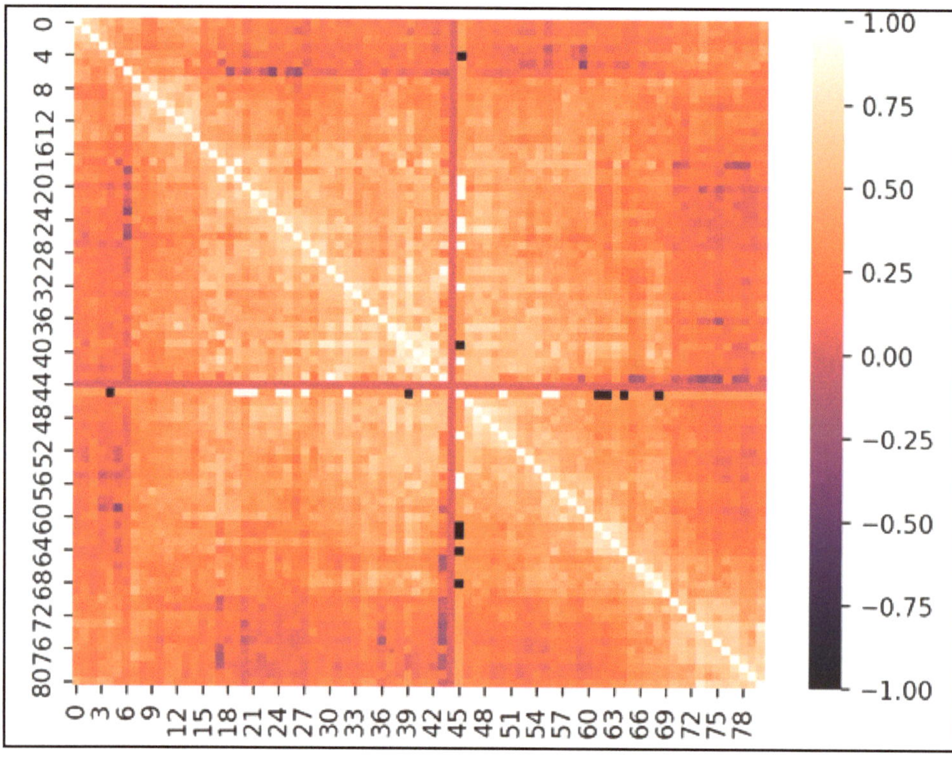


**Fig: Data Analysis Heat Map Example: Displays the Normalized Linkage Disequilibrium of Genomic Windows within the Hist1 Region of a Mouse**

Exploratory Data Analysis: Working with small and large data sets, data scientists and data analysts look at and determine essential relationships and characteristics amongst different points in a data set as well as features of those data points. Data scientists and analysts work with a team of others in different professions. The use of heat maps make for a visually easy way to summarize findings and main components. There are other ways to represent data, however heat maps can visualize these data points and their relationships in a high dimensional space without becoming too compact and visually unappealing. Heat maps in data analysis, allow for specific variables of rows and/or columns on the axes and even on the diagonal.

- **Biology:** In the biological field, heat maps are used to visually represent large and small sets of data. The focus is towards patterns and similarities in DNA, RNA, gene expression, etc. Working with these sets of data, data scientists in bioinformatics, focus on different concepts, some of which being community detection, association and correlation, and the concept of centrality, where heat maps are a compelling way to visually summarize results and to share amongst other professions not in the field of biology or bioinformatics. The two heat maps to the right, labeled "Data Analysis Heat Map Example," show different ways in which one may present genomic data over a specific region (Hist1 region) to someone outside the field of biology so they have a better understanding of the general concept a biologist or data scientist are trying to present.

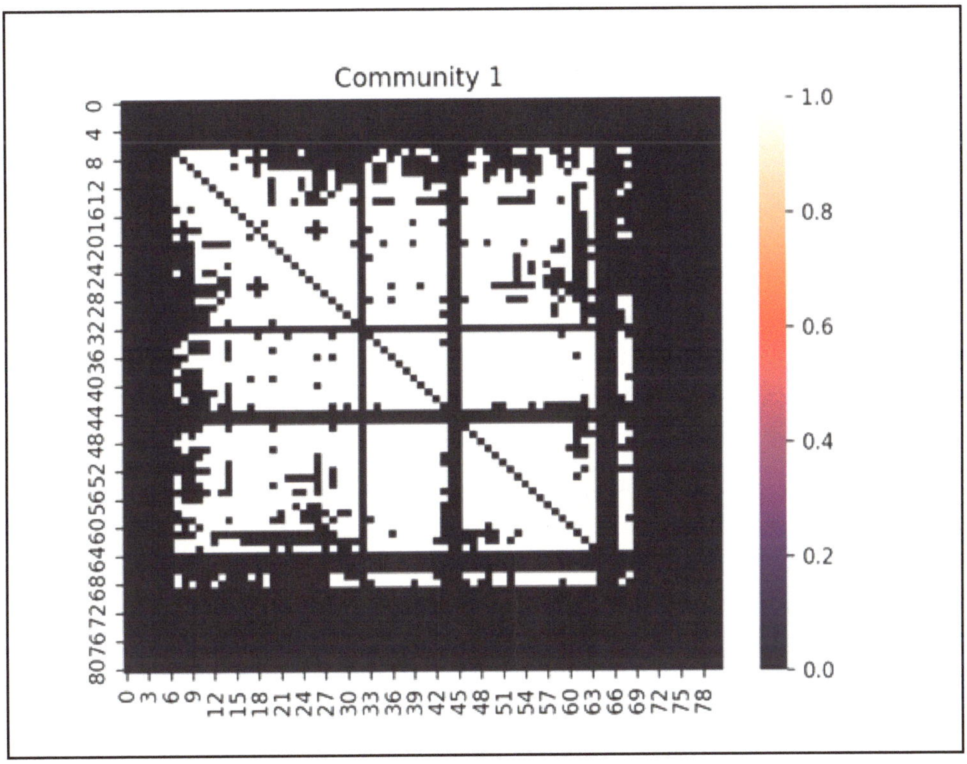


**Fig: Data Analysis Heat Map Example: Subgraph of One of Five Hub Nodes with a Large Degree of Centrality in a Genomic Region in Mice Called the Hist1 Region, where each Cell in the Graph Represents One Edge in the Genomic Network**

- **Financial Analysis:** The values of different product and assets fluctuate both rapidly and/or gradually over time. The need to log changes to the daily markets is imperative. It allows for the ability to draw predictions from patterns while being able to revisit past numerical data. Heat maps are able to remove the tedious process and enable the user to visualize data points and compare amongst the different performers.

- **Geographical Visualization:** Heat maps are used to visualize and display a geographic distribution of data. Heat maps represent different densities of data points on a geographical map to help users see the intensities of certain phenomena and to show items of most or least importance. Heat maps used in geographical visualization are sometimes confused with Choropleth maps, but the difference comes with how certain data is presented which differentiate the two.
- **Sports:** Heat maps can be used in many sports and can influence manager's and/or coaches decisions based on high and low densities of data displayed. Users can identify patterns within the game, the strategies of opponents and one's own team, make more informed decisions benefitting the player, team, and business, and can enhance performance in different areas by identifying enhancement is needed. Heat maps also visualize comparisons and relationships amongst different teams in the same sport or between different sports all together.

### Color Schemes

Many different color schemes can be used to illustrate the heat map, with perceptual advantages and disadvantages for each. Choosing a good color scheme is integral to accurately and effectively displaying data, whereas a poor color scheme can lead viewers to inaccurate conclusions or exclude those with color deficiencies from proper analysis of said data.

Rainbow color maps are a common choice, as humans can perceive more shades of color than they can of gray, and this would purportedly increase the amount of detail perceivable in the image. However, this is heavily discouraged in the scientific community for a number of reasons. Possibly the largest reason is that when there is a large number of colors involved, the visualization may give off the impression that there exist gradients in the data that are not really present. The more colors used in a visualization the more values begin to bleed together and color lacks the natural perceptual ordering found in grayscale or blackbody spectrum colormaps. Additionally, values represented by different shades of the same color can imply that the values are related when they are not.

An important consideration when choosing a color scheme is whether or not the data will be viewed by anyone with any form of color deficiency. If the audience contains individuals with any form of color blindness, it may be wise to avoid color schemes with prominent reds and greens or uneven color gradients.

In addition to audience considerations, it is also important to consider the form in which the data will be viewed. For example, if the data is to be printed in black and white or projected onto a large screen, it may be wise to adjust one's choice in color scheme. Common colormaps (like the "jet" colormap used as the default in many visualization software packages) have uncontrolled changes in luminance that prevent meaningful conversion to grayscale for display or printing. This also distracts from the actual data, arbitrarily making yellow and cyan regions appear more prominent than the regions of the data that are actually most important.

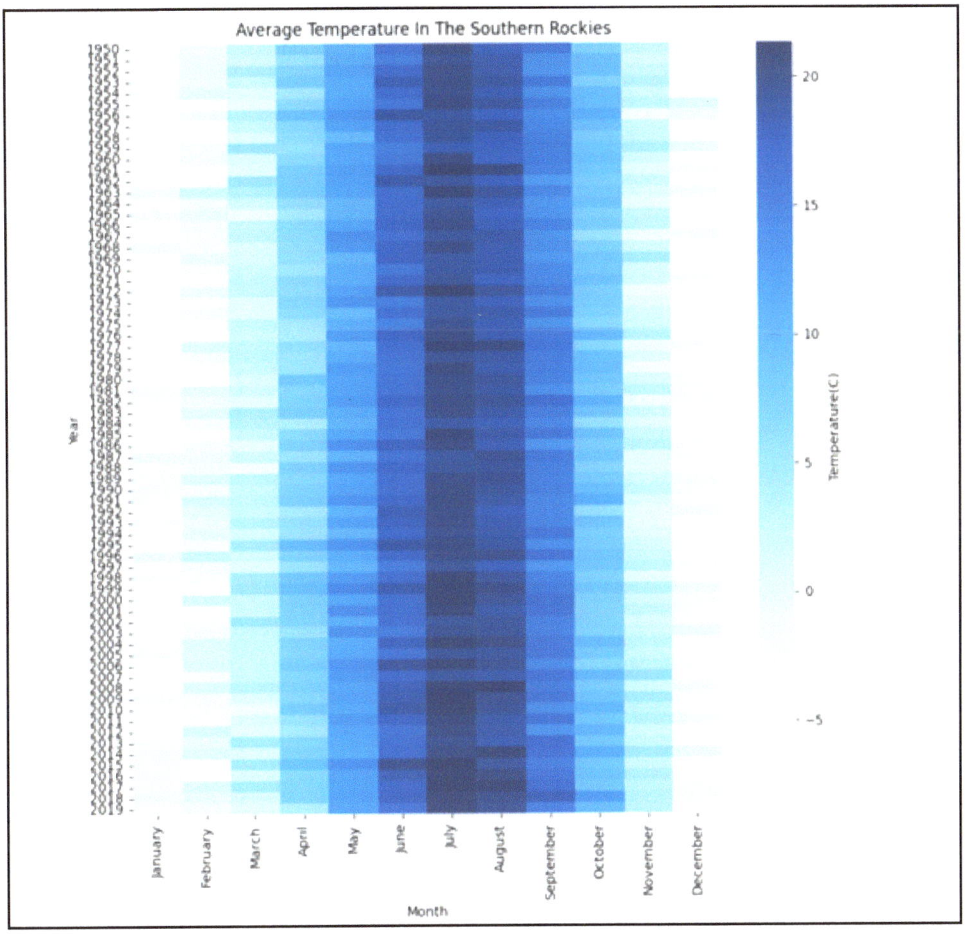


**Fig: A Heat Map Showing the Average Temperature in the Southern Rockies from 1950 to 2020 using the "Blues" Color Palette from the Color Brewer Library**

## Software Implementations

Several heat map software implementations are freely available:

- R, a free software environment for statistical computing and graphics, contains several functions to trace heat maps,
- Gnuplot, a universal and free command-line plotting program, can trace 2D and 3D heat maps.

- Google Fusion Tables can generate a heat map from a Google Sheets spreadsheet limited to 1000 points of geographic data.
- Dave Green's 'cubehelix' colour scheme provides resources for a colour scheme that prints as a monotonically increasing greyscale on black and white postscript devices.

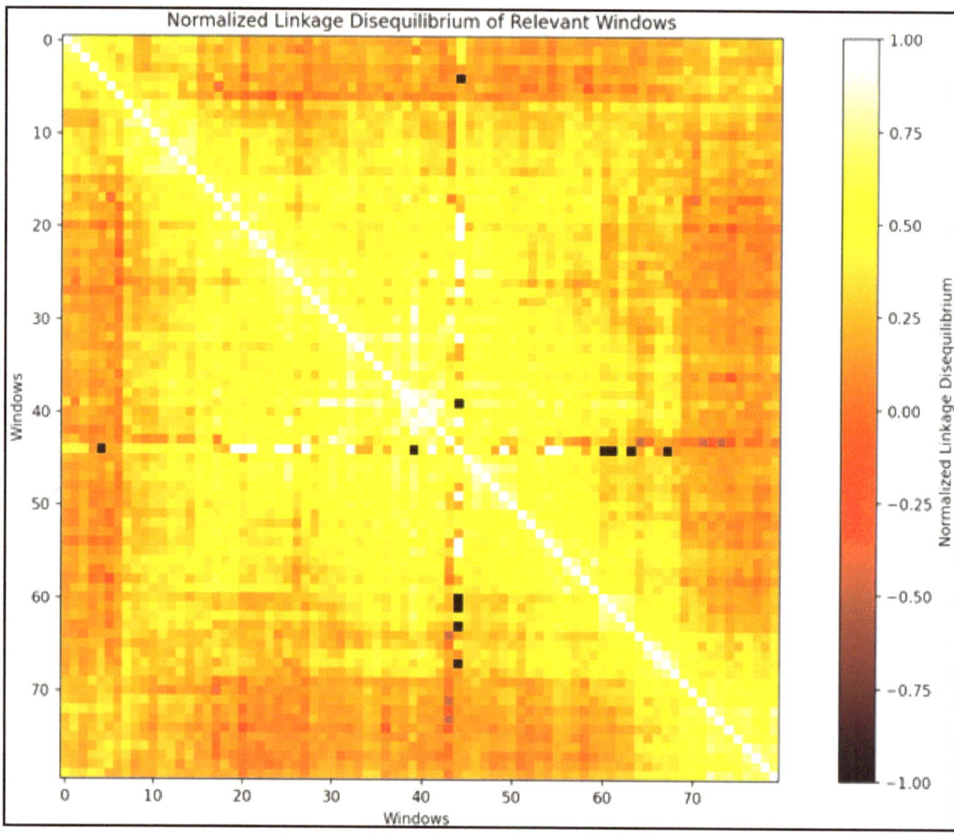


**FIg: This Heat Map Shows the Normalized Linkage Disequilibrium of Genomic Windows within the Hist1 Region of a Mouse**

- Openlayers3 can render a heat map layer of a selected property of all geographic features in a vector layer.
- D3.js, AnyChart and Highcharts are JavaScript libraries for data visualization that provide the ability to create interactive heat map charts, from basic to highly customized, as part of their solutions.

### Choropleth Maps versus Heat Maps

Choropleth maps and heat maps are often used in place of one another incorrectly when referring to data visualized geographically. Both techniques show the proportion of a variable of interest, but the two differ in how the boundaries for the variable's data aggregations are constructed. If the data were collected and aggregated using irregular boundaries, such as administrative units, then a heat map displaying that data will be the same as a choropleth map, encouraging confusion about how the two differ.

Choropleth maps show data grouped by geographic boundaries like countries, states, provinces or even floodplains. Each region has a singular value, visualized by color intensity, shading or pattern. The figure on the right displaying a choropleth map showing the United States' population density by state may be used as an example. The figure illustrates a singular value (population) denoted by blue color intensity proportionate to the state's value relative to all other states' values, bounded by each state's border.

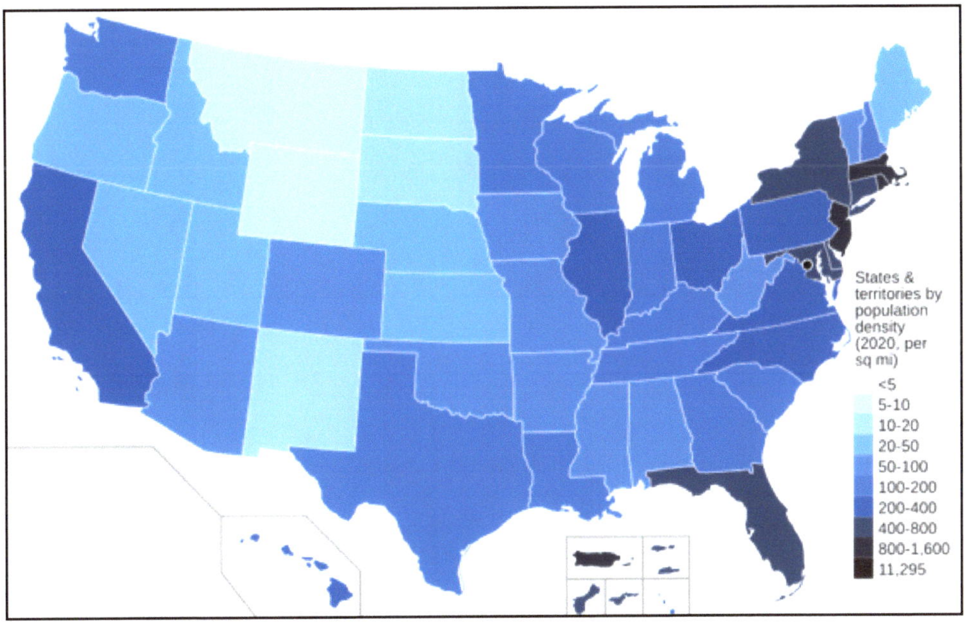


**Fig: A Choropleth Map Visualizing United States Population Density by State**

Similarly, heat maps may also visualize data over a geographic region. However, unlike choropleth maps, heat maps show the proportion of a variable over an arbitrary, but usually small grid size, independent of geographic boundaries. The figure on the right displaying a heat map of world population is an example. The figure illustrates a single value (population) bounded in an arbitrary grid (square kilometers) with each cell in the grid represented by a color intensity proportionate to the value of the cell relative to all other cells. Some heat maps that are created using approximated regional data may show familiar geographic borders in the visualization where none really exist. The illusion of geographic borders is due to the existence of patterns within the dataset rather than the visualization technique. The figure on the right displaying a heat map of world population also contains this occurrence. Areas in rural parts of the United States and South America may closely resemble familiar geographic borders in those regions.

## Saliency Map

A saliency map is an image that highlights either the region on which people's eyes focus first or the most relevant regions for machine learning models. The goal of a saliency map is to reflect the degree of importance of a pixel to the human visual system or an otherwise opaque ML model. For example, in this image, a person first looks at the fort and light clouds, so they should be highlighted on the saliency map. Saliency maps engineered in artificial or computer vision are typically not the same as the actual saliency map constructed by biological or natural vision.

**Fig: A View of the Fort of Marburg (Germany) and the Saliency Map of the Image Using Color, Intensity and Orientation**

## Application

Saliency maps have applications in a variety of different problems. Some general applications:

Human Eye:

- **Image and Video Compression:** The human eye focuses only on a small region of interest in the frame. Therefore, it is not necessary to compress the entire frame with uniform quality. According to the authors, using a salience map reduces the final size of the video with the same visual perception.
- **Image and Video Euality Assessment:** The main task for an image or video quality metric is a high correlation with user opinions. Differences in salient regions are given more importance and thus contribute more to the quality score.
- **Image Retargeting:** It aims at resizing an image by expanding or shrinking the noninformative regions. Therefore, retargeting algorithms rely on the availability of saliency maps that accurately estimate all the salient image details.

- **Object Detection and Recognition:** Instead of applying a computationally complex algorithm to the whole image, we can use it to the most salient regions of an image most likely to contain an object.

Explainable Artificial Intelligence:

- Explainable Artificial Intelligence in the context of black box machine learning models: Saliency maps are a prominent tool in XAI, providing visual explanations of the decision-making process of machine learning models, particularly deep neural networks. These maps highlight the regions in input images, text, or other types of data that are most influential in the model's output, effectively indicating where the model is "looking" when making a prediction. By illustrating which parts of the input are deemed important, saliency maps help in understanding the internal workings of otherwise black box models, thereby fostering trust and transparency. In image classification tasks, for example, saliency maps can identify pixels or regions that contribute most to a specific class decision. There are multiple methods of creating saliency maps, ranging from simply taking the gradient of the class score output to much more complex algorithms, such as integrated gradients, XRAI, Grad-CAM, and SmoothGrad.

### Saliency as a Segmentation Problem

Saliency estimation may be viewed as an instance of image segmentation. In computer vision, image segmentation is the process of partitioning a digital image into multiple segments (sets of pixels, also known as superpixels). The goal of segmentation is to simplify and/or change the representation of an image into something that is more meaningful and easier to analyze. Image segmentation is typically used to locate objects and boundaries (lines, curves, etc.) in images. More precisely, image segmentation is the process of assigning a label to every pixel in an image such that pixels with the same label share certain characteristics.

### Algorithms

There are three forms of classic saliency estimation algorithms implemented in OpenCV:

- **Static Saliency:** Relies on image features and statistics to localize the regions of interest of an image.
- **Motion Saliency:** Relies on motion in a video, detected by optical flow. Objects that move are considered salient.
- **Objectness:** Objectness reflects how likely an image window covers an object. These algorithms generate a set of bounding boxes of where an object may lie in an image.

In addition to classic approaches, neural-network-based are also popular. There are examples of neural networks for motion saliency estimation:

- **TASED-Net:** It consists of two building blocks. First, the encoder network extracts low-resolution spatiotemporal features, and then the following prediction network decodes the spatially encoded features while aggregating all the temporal information.
- **STRA-Net:** It emphasizes two essential issues. First, spatiotemporal features integrated via appearance and optical flow coupling, and then multi-scale saliency learned via attention mechanism.
- **STAViS:** It combines spatiotemporal visual and auditory information. This approach employs a single network that learns to localize sound sources and to fuse the two saliencies to obtain a final saliency map.

There's a new static saliency in the literature with name visual distortion sensitivity. It is based on the idea that the true edges, i.e. object contours, are more salient than the other complex textured regions. It detects edges in a different way from the classic edge detection algorithms. It uses a fairly small threshold for the gradient magnitudes to consider the mere presence of the gradients. So, it obtains 4 binary maps for vertical, horizontal and two diagonal directions. The morphological closing and opening are applied to the binary images to close the small gaps. To clear the blob-like shapes, it utilizes the distance transform. After all, the connected pixel groups are individual edges (or contours). A threshold of size of connected pixel set is used to determine whether an image block contains a perceivable edge (salient region) or not.

### Difference in Algorithms

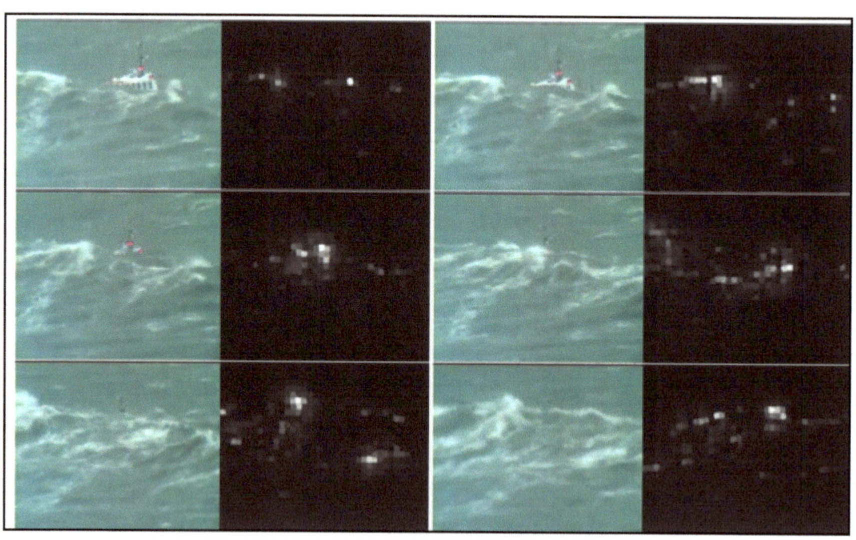

**Fig: Saliency Result**

The major difference between function one and two is the difference of contract function. If spnum1 and spnum2 both represent the current frame's pixel number, then this contract function is for the first saliency function. If spnum1 is the current frame's pixel number and spnum2 represent the previous frame's pixel number, then this contract function is for second saliency function.

If we use the second contract function which using the pixel of the same frame to get center distance to get a saliency map, then we apply this saliency function to each frame and use current frame's saliency map minus previous frame's saliency map to get a new image which is the new saliency result of the third saliency function.

### Datasets

The saliency dataset usually contains human eye movements on some image sequences. It is valuable for new saliency algorithm creation or benchmarking the existing one. The most valuable dataset parameters are spatial resolution, size, and eye-tracking equipment. Here is part of the large datasets table from MIT/Tübingen Saliency Benchmark datasets, for example.

**Table: Saliency datasets**

| Dataset | Resolution | Size | Observers | Durations | Eyetracker |
|---|---|---|---|---|---|
| CAT2000 | 1920×1080px | 4000 images | 24 | 5 sec | EyeLink 1000 (1000Hz) |
| EyeTrackUAV2 | 1280×720px | 43 videos | 30 | 33 sec | EyeLink 1000 Plus (1000 Hz, binocular) |
| CrowdFix | 1280×720px | 434 videos | 26 | 1-3 sec | The Eyetribe Eyetracker (60 Hz) |
| SAVAM | 1920×1080px | 43 videos | 50 | 20 sec | SMI iViewXTM Hi-Speed 1250 (500Hz) |

To collect a saliency dataset, image or video sequences and eye-tracking equipment must be prepared, and observers must be invited. Observers must have normal or corrected to normal vision and must be at the same distance from the screen. At the beginning of each recording session, the eye-tracker recalibrates. To do this, the observer fixates his gaze on the screen center. Then the session started, and saliency data are collected by showing sequences and recording eye gazes. The eye-tracking device is a high-speed camera, capable of recording eye movements at least 250 frames per second. Images from the camera are processed by the software, running on a dedicated computer returning gaze data.

### 3.2.3 Counterfactual Explanations

As artificial intelligence (AI) systems continue to shape critical decisions in areas such as finance, healthcare, criminal justice, and hiring, the demand for transparency and accountability has grown. One of the most compelling techniques for making AI systems more interpretable is counterfactual explanations. Unlike traditional feature importance methods, counterfactual explanations focus on providing insights into how an outcome would have changed if specific input conditions were different. By doing so, they help users understand the decision-making process of AI models and offer actionable insights for individuals affected by AI-driven decisions.

Counterfactual explanations serve as a bridge between complex AI models and human comprehension. They allow individuals to ask "what-if" questions regarding AI decisions, making it easier to identify biases, correct errors, and improve user trust in automated systems. As AI permeates regulatory environments, counterfactual explanations have become a preferred method for explaining decisions in compliance-driven industries, ensuring alignment with ethical and legal guidelines.

Counterfactual explanations are a powerful tool in explainable artificial intelligence, offering clear, actionable insights into AI decisions. Unlike traditional interpretability methods that focus on ranking feature importance, counterfactual explanations provide concrete modifications that could lead to different outcomes. This makes them particularly useful in high-stakes applications where understanding and influencing AI decisions is crucial. While challenges remain in ensuring feasibility, stability, and computational efficiency, counterfactual explanations represent a promising approach to making AI more transparent and accountable. As research advances and regulatory pressures increase, counterfactual explanations will play an increasingly vital role in ensuring that AI systems are both fair and comprehensible to human users.

#### Understanding the Concept of Counterfactual Explanations

Counterfactual explanations revolve around the idea of presenting alternative scenarios that could have led to different outcomes. For example, if an AI system rejects a loan application, a counterfactual explanation might suggest that the loan would have been approved if the applicant's income had been slightly higher or their debt-to-income ratio had been lower. This type of explanation helps the affected individual understand how they can alter their circumstances to achieve a different result in the future.

Counterfactual explanations differ from traditional feature importance techniques in that they do not merely rank features based on their impact but rather provide direct modifications to input variables that would result in an alternate prediction. This makes them particularly useful in high-stakes applications where understanding the pathway to a different outcome is crucial.

## The Role of Counterfactuals in Explainable AI

Explainable artificial intelligence (XAI) aims to make AI decision-making processes transparent, interpretable, and trustworthy. Counterfactual explanations align with this goal by offering human-centric justifications for model predictions. Rather than simply stating why a decision was made, counterfactual explanations emphasize how a different decision could have been reached, offering practical and intuitive insights.

Counterfactuals are especially valuable in applications requiring personalized decision support. In credit scoring, they can help applicants understand why they were denied a loan and what changes they need to make to secure approval. In hiring, they can assist candidates in understanding which qualifications they need to improve to be considered for a job. In healthcare, they provide insights into how a patient's condition might change under different treatment regimens.

## Generating Counterfactual Explanations

The process of generating counterfactual explanations involves identifying the smallest set of changes to input variables that would lead to a different decision from the AI system. Several computational approaches exist to derive counterfactual explanations, including optimization-based methods, nearest neighbor search, and generative models.

Optimization-based methods rely on mathematical techniques to minimize the distance between the original instance and a modified version that leads to a different prediction. These methods ensure that counterfactual explanations remain realistic and achievable. Nearest neighbor approaches identify similar instances in the dataset that have different outcomes, providing real-world examples as counterfactual explanations. Generative models, such as variational autoencoders and generative adversarial networks, can synthesize realistic counterfactual examples that adhere to data distributions.

The effectiveness of counterfactual explanations depends on their feasibility and validity. Ideally, counterfactual scenarios should be actionable, meaning that users can realistically implement the suggested changes. Additionally, they should be sparse, meaning that only a minimal number of features are altered, making the explanation more comprehensible.

### Counterfactual Explanations vs. Other Explainability Methods

Counterfactual explanations offer distinct advantages over other explainability methods such as SHAP (Shapley Additive Explanations) and LIME (Local Interpretable Model-agnostic Explanations). While SHAP assigns importance scores to individual features and LIME constructs interpretable local models, counterfactual explanations focus on actionable insights by answering how a decision could have been different under modified conditions.

One of the key strengths of counterfactual explanations is their user-centric approach. Unlike global interpretability methods that provide an overall understanding of model behavior, counterfactuals tailor explanations to specific instances, making them highly relevant to individuals affected by AI decisions. This makes them more aligned with legal and ethical standards that require AI systems to offer meaningful explanations to users.

However, counterfactual explanations also have limitations. They require sophisticated computational techniques to ensure that suggested modifications remain realistic. Additionally, they may not always capture the broader trends in model behavior, making them less useful for debugging AI models at a system-wide level.

### Ethical and Legal Implications of Counterfactual Explanations

The increasing use of AI in decision-making has led to growing concerns about fairness, bias, and accountability. Counterfactual explanations can play a crucial role in addressing these concerns by making AI decisions more interpretable and justifiable. By revealing what changes are necessary to achieve a different outcome, counterfactuals help ensure that AI systems do not systematically discriminate against certain groups.From a legal perspective, counterfactual explanations align with transparency requirements set forth in regulations such as the European Union's General Data Protection Regulation (GDPR). The "right to explanation" provision in GDPR mandates that AI-driven decisions, especially in high-impact domains like credit scoring and hiring, must be explainable to affected individuals. Counterfactual explanations fulfill this requirement by offering clear, actionable insights into AI decisions.

Ethically, counterfactual explanations promote autonomy by empowering individuals to understand and influence decisions that affect them. They also enhance accountability by enabling AI developers to identify and correct biased decision-making patterns in machine learning models.

### Challenges in Implementing Counterfactual Explanations

Despite their advantages, counterfactual explanations present several challenges in practical implementation. One of the primary difficulties is ensuring the feasibility of the suggested modifications. Some counterfactual explanations might suggest changes that are impossible or unrealistic, such as altering immutable characteristics like age or gender. Researchers are actively working on refining counterfactual generation methods to ensure that explanations remain both actionable and ethical.

Another challenge is the computational complexity of generating counterfactual explanations. Since they require identifying minimal and realistic changes in input variables, counterfactual explanations often involve solving optimization problems that can be computationally intensive. Efficient algorithms and heuristics are being developed to improve the scalability of counterfactual methods.

A further concern is the stability of counterfactual explanations. Small variations in input data should not lead to drastically different counterfactuals. Ensuring consistency in counterfactual explanations across similar instances remains an active area of research.

#### Future Directions and Applications

The future of counterfactual explanations in XAI is promising, with ongoing research focusing on improving their robustness and applicability. One area of development is integrating counterfactual explanations with causality-based approaches to provide deeper insights into decision-making. By incorporating causal reasoning, counterfactual explanations can become more aligned with real-world dependencies and constraints.

Another exciting application is in interactive AI systems, where users can query AI models with counterfactual scenarios in real time. This capability could enhance decision support in domains such as medicine and law, allowing experts to explore alternative scenarios and make informed judgments.

As AI continues to evolve, counterfactual explanations will likely become a standard component of explainable AI frameworks. They provide an intuitive, human-centric way of understanding machine learning models and fostering trust in automated decision-making systems.

## 3.3 INTRINSICALLY INTERPRETABLE MODELS

### 3.3.1 Decision Trees and Rule-Based Models

#### Decision Tree

A decision tree is a decision support recursive partitioning structure that uses a tree-like model of decisions and their possible consequences, including chance event outcomes, resource costs, and utility. It is one way to display an algorithm that only contains conditional control statements. Decision trees are commonly used in operations research, specifically in decision analysis, to help identify a strategy most likely to reach a goal, but are also a popular tool in machine learning.

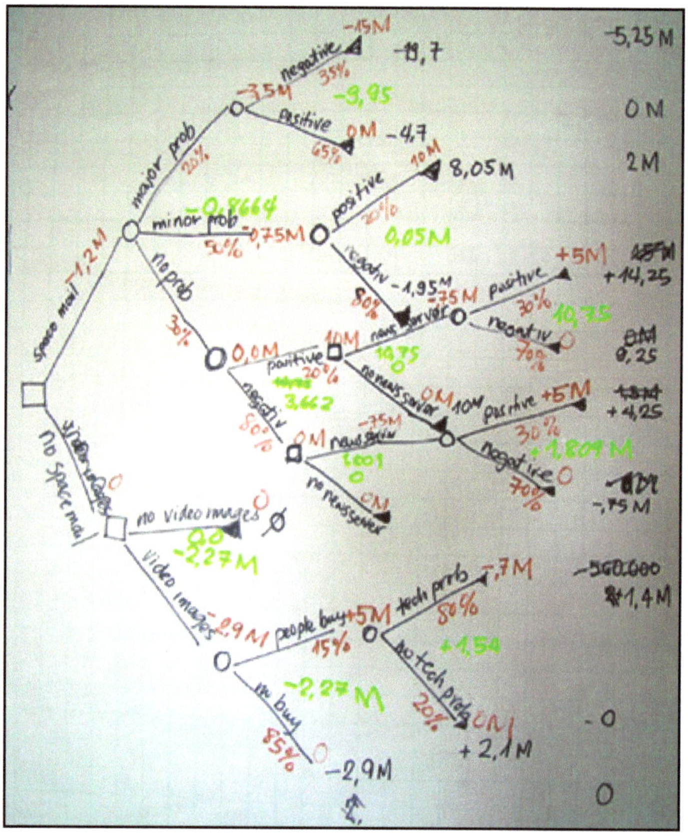


Fig: Traditionally, Decision Trees have been Created Manually

A decision tree is a flowchart-like structure in which each internal node represents a test on an attribute (e.g. whether a coin flip comes up heads or tails), each branch represents the outcome of the test, and each leaf node represents a class label (decision taken after computing all attributes). The paths from root to leaf represent classification rules.

In decision analysis, a decision tree and the closely related influence diagram are used as a visual and analytical decision support tool, where the expected values (or expected utility) of competing alternatives are calculated.

A decision tree consists of three types of nodes:

- Decision nodes – typically represented by squares.
- Chance nodes – typically represented by circles.
- End nodes – typically represented by triangles.

Decision trees are commonly used in operations research and operations management. If, in practice, decisions have to be taken online with no recall under incomplete knowledge, a decision tree should be paralleled by a probability model as a best choice model or online selection model algorithm. Another use of decision trees is as a descriptive means for calculating conditional probabilities.

Decision trees, influence diagrams, utility functions, and other decision analysis tools and methods are taught to undergraduate students in schools of business, health economics, and public health, and are examples of operations research or management science methods. These tools are also used to predict decisions of householders in normal and emergency scenarios.

### Decision-Tree Elements

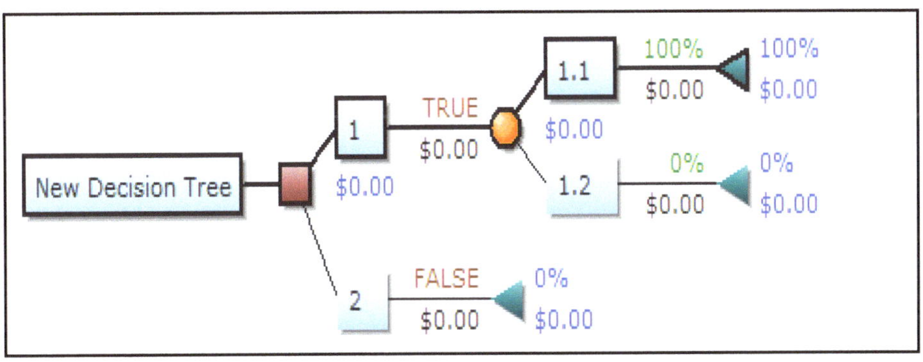


Drawn from left to right, a decision tree has only burst nodes (splitting paths) but no sink nodes (converging paths). So used manually they can grow very big and are then often hard to draw fully by hand. Traditionally, decision trees have been created manually – as the aside example shows – although increasingly, specialized software is employed.

### Decision Rules

The decision tree can be linearized into decision rules, where the outcome is the contents of the leaf node, and the conditions along the path form a conjunction in the if clause. In general, the rules have the form:

- if condition1 and condition2 and condition3 then outcome.

Decision rules can be generated by constructing association rules with the target variable on the right. They can also denote temporal or causal relations.

### Decision Tree Using Flowchart Symbols

Commonly a decision tree is drawn using flowchart symbols as it is easier for many to read and understand. Note there is a conceptual error in the "Proceed" calculation of the tree shown below; the error relates to the calculation of "costs" awarded in a legal action.

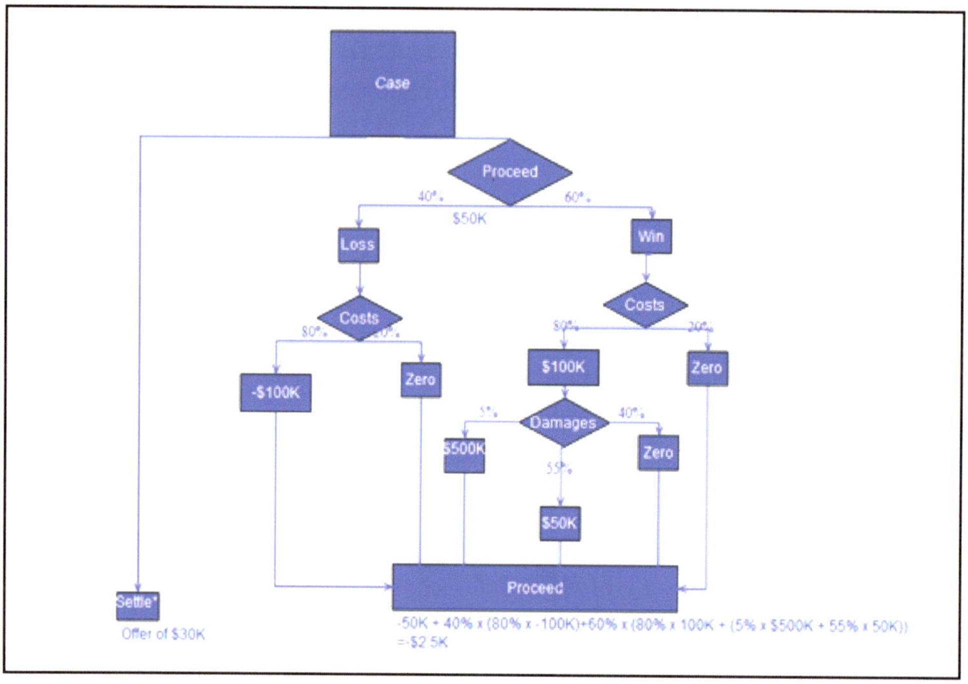


## Analysis Example

Analysis can take into account the decision maker's (e.g., the company's) preference or utility function, for example:

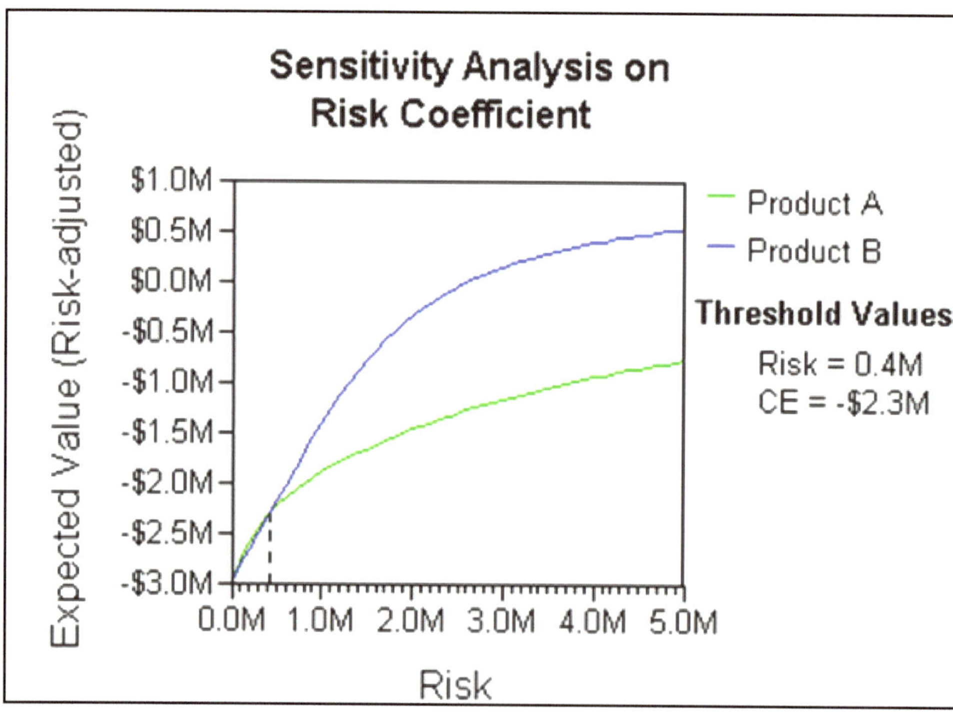

The basic interpretation in this situation is that the company prefers B's risk and payoffs under realistic risk preference coefficients (greater than \$400K—in that range of risk aversion, the company would need to model a third strategy, "Neither A nor B"). Another example, commonly used in operations research courses, is the distribution of lifeguards on beaches (a.k.a. the "Life's a Beach" example). The example describes two beaches with lifeguards to be distributed on each beach. There is maximum budget B that can be distributed among the two beaches (in total), and using a marginal returns table, analysts can decide how many lifeguards to allocate to each beach.

| Lifeguards on Each Beach | Drownings Prevented in Total, Beach #1 | Drownings Prevented in Total, Beach #2 |
|---|---|---|
| 1 | 3 | 1 |
| 2 | 0 | 4 |

In this example, a decision tree can be drawn to illustrate the principles of diminishing returns on beach #1.

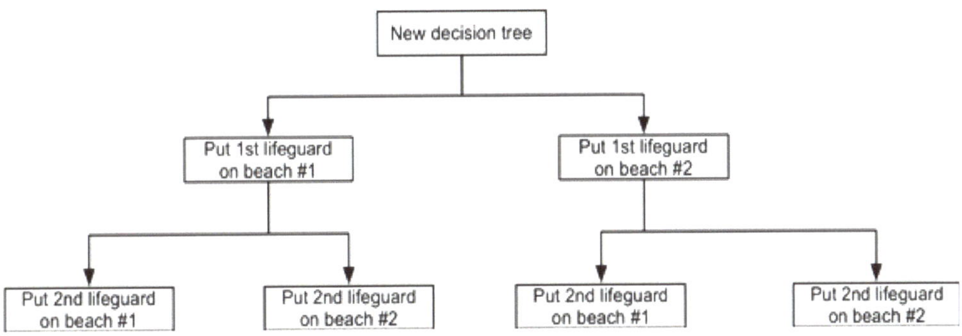


**Fig: Beach Decision Tree**

The decision tree illustrates that when sequentially distributing lifeguards, placing a first lifeguard on beach #1 would be optimal if there is only the budget for 1 lifeguard. But if there is a budget for two guards, then placing both on beach #2 would prevent more overall drownings.

### Influence Diagram

Much of the information in a decision tree can be represented more compactly as an influence diagram, focusing attention on the issues and relationships between events.

### Association Rule Induction

Decision trees can also be seen as generative models of induction rules from empirical data. An optimal decision tree is then defined as a tree that accounts for most of the data, while minimizing the number of levels (or "questions"). Several algorithms to generate such optimal trees have been devised, such as ID3/4/5, CLS, ASSISTANT, and CART.

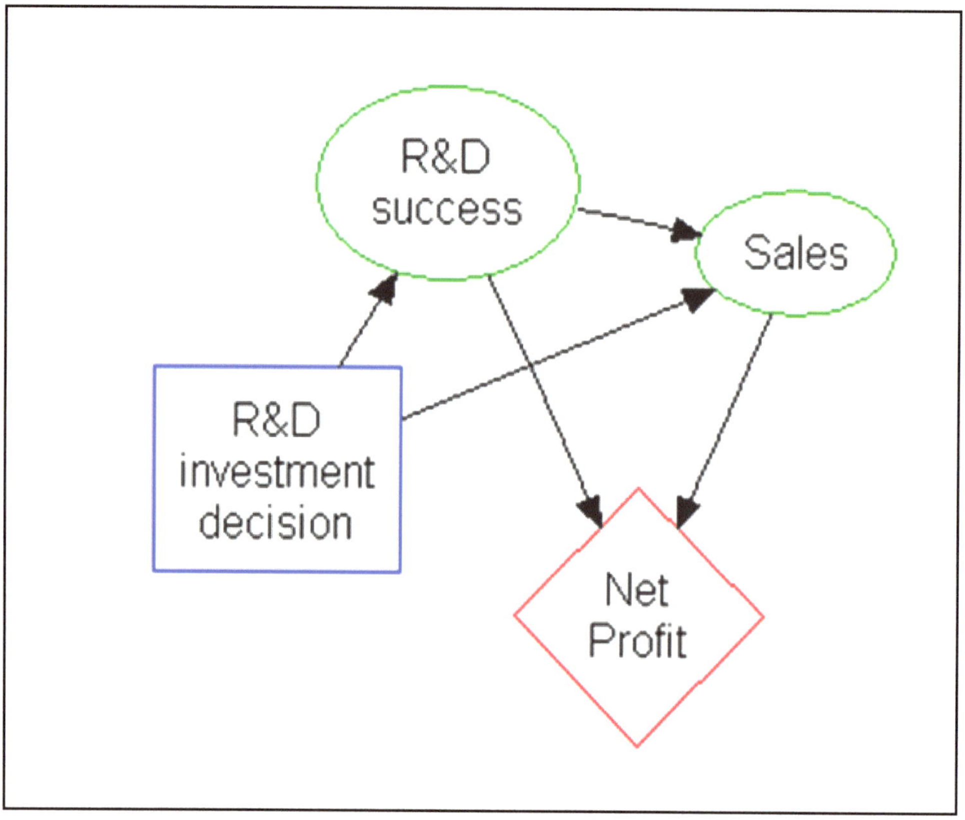


**Fig: The Rectangle on the Left Represents a Decision, the Ovals Represent Actions, and the Diamond Represents Results**

### Advantages and Disadvantages

Among decision support tools, decision trees (and influence diagrams) have several advantages. Decision trees:

- Are simple to understand and interpret. People are able to understand decision tree models after a brief explanation.
- Have value even with little hard data. Important insights can be generated based on experts describing a situation (its alternatives, probabilities, and costs) and their preferences for outcomes.
- Help determine worst, best, and expected values for different scenarios.
- Use a white box model. If a given result is provided by a model.
- Can be combined with other decision techniques.
- The action of more than one decision-maker can be considered.

Disadvantages of decision trees:

- They are unstable, meaning that a small change in the data can lead to a large change in the structure of the optimal decision tree.
- They are often relatively inaccurate. Many other predictors perform better with similar data. This can be remedied by replacing a single decision tree with a random forest of decision trees, but a random forest is not as easy to interpret as a single decision tree.
- For data including categorical variables with different numbers of levels, information gain in decision trees is biased in favor of those attributes with more levels.
- Calculations can get very complex, particularly if many values are uncertain and/or if many outcomes are linked.

### Optimizing a Decision Tree

A few things should be considered when improving the accuracy of the decision tree classifier. The following are some possible optimizations to consider when looking to make sure the decision tree model produced makes the correct decision or classification. Note that these things are not the only things to consider but only some.

### Increasing the Number of Levels of the Tree

The accuracy of the decision tree can change based on the depth of the decision tree. In many cases, the tree's leaves are pure nodes. When a node is pure, it means that all the data in that node belongs to a single class. For example, if the classes in the data set are Cancer and Non-Cancer a leaf node would be considered pure when all the sample data in a leaf node is part of only one class, either cancer or non-cancer. It is important to note that a deeper tree is not always better when optimizing the decision tree.

A deeper tree can influence the runtime in a negative way. If a certain classification algorithm is being used, then a deeper tree could mean the runtime of this classification algorithm is significantly slower. There is also the possibility that the actual algorithm building the decision tree will get significantly slower as the tree gets deeper. If the tree-building algorithm being used splits pure nodes, then a decrease in the overall accuracy of the tree classifier could be experienced. Occasionally, going deeper in the tree can cause an accuracy decrease in general, so it is very important to test modifying the depth of the decision tree and selecting the depth that produces the best results.

Possible advantages of increasing the number D:

- Accuracy of the decision-tree classification model increases.

Possible disadvantages of increasing D

- Runtime issues.
- Decrease in accuracy in general.
- Pure node splits while going deeper can cause issues.

The ability to test the differences in classification results when changing D is imperative. We must be able to easily change and test the variables that could affect the accuracy and reliability of the decision tree-model.

### The Choice of Node-Splitting Functions

The node splitting function used can have an impact on improving the accuracy of the decision tree. For example, using the information-gain function may yield better results than using the phi function. The phi function is known as a measure of "goodness" of a candidate split at a node in the decision tree. The information gain function is known as a measure of the "reduction in entropy". In the following, we will build two decision trees. One decision tree will be built using the phi function to split the nodes and one decision tree will be built using the information gain function to split the nodes.

The main advantages and disadvantages of information gain and phi function

- One major drawback of information gain is that the feature that is chosen as the next node in the tree tends to have more unique values.
- An advantage of information gain is that it tends to choose the most impactful features that are close to the root of the tree. It is a very good measure for deciding the relevance of some features.
- The phi function is also a good measure for deciding the relevance of some features based on "goodness".

This is the information gain function formula. The formula states the information gain is a function of the entropy of a node of the decision tree minus the entropy of a candidate split at node t of a decision tree.

$$I_{\text{gain}}(s) = H(t) - H(s,t)$$

This is the phi function formula. The phi function is maximized when the chosen feature splits the samples in a way that produces homogenous splits and have around the same number of samples in each split.

$$\Phi(s,t) = (2 * P_L * P_R) * Q(s \mid t)$$

We will set D, which is the depth of the decision tree we are building, to three (D = 3). We also have the following data set of cancer and non-cancer samples and the mutation features that the samples either have or do not have. If a sample has a feature mutation then the sample is positive for that mutation, and it will be represented by one. If a sample does not have a feature mutation then the sample is negative for that mutation, and it will be represented by zero.

To summarize, C stands for cancer and NC stands for non-cancer. The letter M stands for mutation, and if a sample has a particular mutation it will show up in the table as a one and otherwise zero.

**Table: The Sample Data**

| | M1 | M2 | M3 | M4 | M5 |
|---|---|---|---|---|---|
| C1 | 0 | 1 | 0 | 1 | 1 |
| NC1 | 0 | 0 | 0 | 0 | 0 |
| NC2 | 0 | 0 | 1 | 1 | 0 |
| NC3 | 0 | 0 | 0 | 0 | 0 |
| C2 | 1 | 1 | 1 | 1 | 1 |
| NC4 | 0 | 0 | 0 | 1 | 0 |

Now, we can use the formulas to calculate the phi function values and information gain values for each M in the dataset. Once all the values are calculated the tree can be produced. The first thing to be done is to select the root node. In information gain and the phi function we consider the optimal split to be the mutation that produces the highest value for information gain or the phi function. Now assume that M1 has the highest phi function value and M4 has the highest information gain value. The M1 mutation will be the root of our phi function tree and M4 will be the root of our information gain tree.

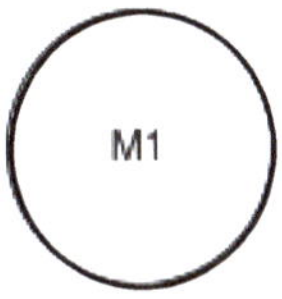


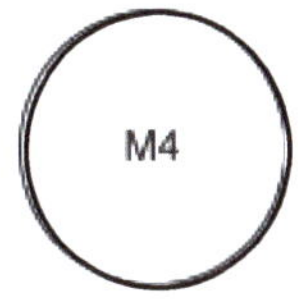


Now, once we have chosen the root node we can split the samples into two groups based on whether a sample is positive or negative for the root node mutation. The groups will be called group A and group B. For example, if we use M1 to split the samples in the root node we get NC2 and C2 samples in group A and the rest of the samples NC4, NC3, NC1, C1 in group B.

Disregarding the mutation chosen for the root node, proceed to place the next best features that have the highest values for information gain or the phi function in the left or right child nodes of the decision tree. Once we choose the root node and the two child nodes for the tree of depth = 3 we can just add the leaves. The leaves will represent the final classification decision the model has produced based on the mutations a sample either has or does not have. The left tree is the decision tree we obtain from using information gain to split the nodes and the right tree is what we obtain from using the phi function to split the nodes.

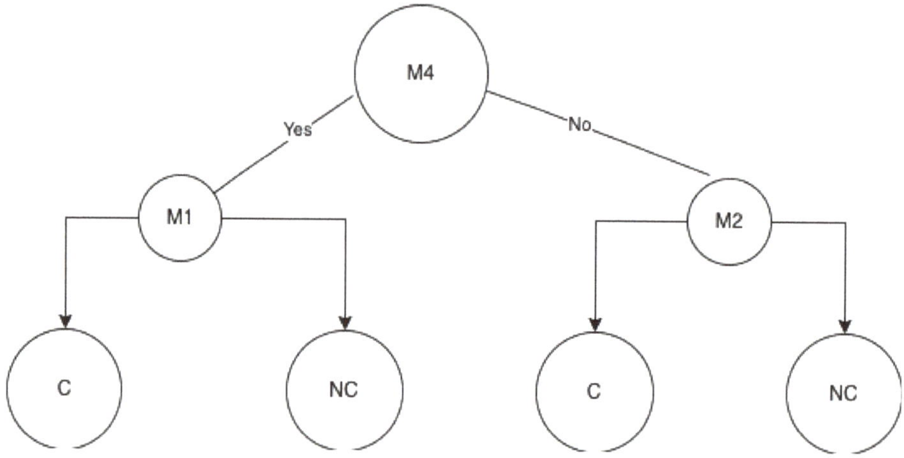


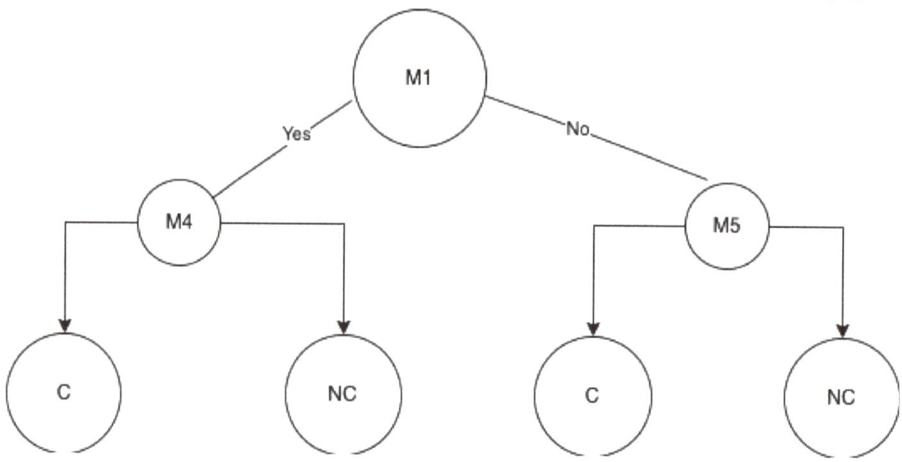


**Fig: Now Assume the Classification Results from Both Trees are Given Using a Confusion Matrix**

**Table: Information Gain Confusion Matrix**

| Predicted Actual | C | NC |
|---|---|---|
| C | 1 | 1 |
| NC | 0 | 4 |

**Table: Phi Function Confusion Matrix**

| Predicted Actual | C | NC |
|---|---|---|
| C | 2 | 0 |
| NC | 1 | 3 |

The tree using information gain has the same results when using the phi function when calculating the accuracy. When we classify the samples based on the model using information gain we get one true positive, one false positive, zero false negatives, and four true negatives. For the model using the phi function we get two true positives, zero false positives, one false negative, and three true negatives.

### Other Techniques

The information is not where it ends for building and optimizing a decision tree. There are many techniques for improving the decision tree classification models we build. One of the techniques is making our decision tree model from a bootstrapped dataset. The bootstrapped dataset helps remove the bias that occurs when building a decision tree model with the same data the model is tested with. The ability to leverage the power of random forests can also help significantly improve the overall accuracy of the model being built. This method generates many decisions from many decision trees and tallies up the votes from each decision tree to make the final classification. There are many techniques, but the main objective is to test building your decision tree model in different ways to make sure it reaches the highest performance level possible.

## Rule-Based Modeling

Rule-based modeling is a modeling approach that uses a set of rules that indirectly specifies a mathematical model. The rule-set can either be translated into a model such as Markov chains or differential equations, or be treated using tools that directly work on the rule-set in place of a translated model, as the latter is typically much bigger. Rule-based modeling is especially effective in cases where the rule-set is significantly simpler than the model it implies, meaning that the model is a repeated manifestation of a limited number of patterns. An important domain where this is often the case is biochemical models of living organisms. Groups of mutually corresponding substances are subject to mutually corresponding interactions.

BioNetGen is a suite of software tools used to generate mathematical models consisting of ordinary differential equations without generating the equations directly. For example below is an example rule in the BioNetGen format:

$$A(a,a)+B(b)->A(a!1).B(b!1)$$

### For Biochemical Systems

Early efforts to use rule-based modeling in simulation of biochemical systems include the stochastic simulation systems StochSim A widely used tool for rule-based modeling of biochemical networks is BioNetGen It is released under the GNU GPL, version 3. BioNetGen includes a language to describe chemical substances, including the states they can assume and the bindings they can undergo. These rules can be used to create a reaction network model or to perform computer simulations directly on the rule set. The biochemical modeling framework Virtual Cell includes a BioNetGen interpreter. A close alternative is the Kappa language. Another alternative is BioChemical Space language.

### Rule-Based Machine Learning

Rule-based machine learning (RBML) is a term in computer science intended to encompass any machine learning method that identifies, learns, or evolves 'rules' to store, manipulate or apply. The defining characteristic of a rule-based machine learner is the identification and utilization of a set of relational rules that collectively represent the knowledge captured by the system. Rule-based machine learning approaches include learning classifier systems, association rule learning, artificial immune systems, and any other method that relies on a set of rules, each covering contextual knowledge. While rule-based machine learning is conceptually a type of rule-based system, it is distinct from traditional rule-based systems, which are often hand-crafted, and other rule-based decision makers. This is because rule-based machine learning applies some form of learning algorithm to automatically identify useful rules, rather than a human needing to apply prior domain knowledge to manually construct rules and curate a rule set.

#### Rules

Rules typically take the form of an '{IF:THEN} expression', (e.g. {IF 'condition' THEN 'result'}, or as a more specific example, {IF 'red' AND 'octagon' THEN 'stop-sign}). An individual rule is not in itself a model, since the rule is only applicable when its condition is satisfied. Therefore rule-based machine learning methods typically comprise a set of rules, or knowledge base, that collectively make up the prediction model.

## 3.3.2 Linear Models and Generalized Linear Models

### Linear Model

In statistics, the term linear model refers to any model which assumes linearity in the system. The most common occurrence is in connection with regression models and the term is often taken as synonymous with linear regression model. However, the term is also used in time series analysis with a different meaning. In each case, the designation "linear" is used to identify a subclass of models for which substantial reduction in the complexity of the related statistical theory is possible.

#### Linear Regression Models

For the regression case, the statistical model is as follows. Given a (random) sample $(Y_i, X_{i1}, \ldots, X_{ip}), i = 1, \ldots, n$ the relation between the observations $Y_i$ and the independent variables $X_{ij}$ is formulated as

$$Y_i = \beta_0 + \beta_1\phi_1(X_{i1}) + \cdots + \beta_p\phi_p(X_{ip}) + \varepsilon_i \qquad i = 1, \ldots, n$$

where $\phi_1, \ldots, \phi_p$ may be nonlinear functions. The quantities $\varepsilon_i$ are random variables representing errors in the relationship. The "linear" part of the designation relates to the appearance of the regression coefficients, $\beta_j$ in a linear way in the above relationship. Alternatively, one may say that the predicted values corresponding to the above model, namely

$$\hat{Y}_i = \beta_0 + \beta_1\phi_1(X_{i1}) + \cdots + \beta_p\phi_p(X_{ip}) \qquad (i = 1, \ldots, n),$$

are linear functions of the $\beta_j$.

Given that estimation is undertaken on the basis of a least squares analysis, estimates of the unknown parameters $\beta_j$ are determined by minimising a sum of squares function

$$S = \sum_{i=1}^{n} \varepsilon_i^2 = \sum_{i=1}^{n} \left(Y_i - \beta_0 - \beta_1\phi_1(X_{i1}) - \cdots - \beta_p\phi_p(X_{ip})\right)^2.$$

From this, it can readily be seen that the "linear" aspect of the model means the following:

- the function to be minimised is a quadratic function of the $\beta_j$ for which minimisation is a relatively simple problem;
- the derivatives of the function are linear functions of the $\beta_j$ making it easy to find the minimising values;
- the minimising values $\beta_j$ are linear functions of the observations Y i $Y_i$;
- the minimising values $\beta_j$ are linear functions of the random errors $\varepsilon_i$ which makes it relatively easy to determine the statistical properties of the estimated values of $\beta_j$.

### Time Series Models

An example of a linear time series model is an autoregressive moving average model. Here the model for values $\{X_t\}$ in a time series can be written in the form

$$X_t = c + \varepsilon_t + \sum_{i=1}^{p} \phi_i X_{t-i} + \sum_{i=1}^{q} \theta_i \varepsilon_{t-i}.$$

where again the quantities $\varepsilon_i$ are random variables representing innovations which are new random effects that appear at a certain time but also affect values of X at later times. In this instance the use of the term "linear model" refers to the structure of the above relationship in representing $X_t$ as a linear function of past values of the same time series and of current and past values of the innovations. This particular aspect of the structure means that it is relatively simple to derive relations for the mean and covariance properties of the time series. Note that here the "linear" part of the term "linear model" is not referring to the coefficients

$\phi_i$ *and* $\theta_i$, as it would be in the case of a regression model, which looks structurally similar.

### Other Uses in Statistics

There are some other instances where "nonlinear model" is used to contrast with a linearly structured model, although the term "linear model" is not usually applied. One example of this is nonlinear dimensionality reduction.

## Generalized Linear Model

A generalized linear model (GLM) is a flexible generalization of ordinary linear regression. The GLM generalizes linear regression by allowing the linear model to be related to the response variable via a link function and by allowing the magnitude of the variance of each measurement to be a function of its predicted value.

Generalized linear models were formulated by John Nelder and Robert Wedderburn as a way of unifying various other statistical models, including linear regression, logistic regression and Poisson regression. They proposed an iteratively reweighted least squares method for maximum likelihood estimation (MLE) of the model parameters. MLE remains popular and is the default method on many statistical computing packages. Other approaches, including Bayesian regression and least squares fitting to variance stabilized responses, have been developed.

### Intuition

Ordinary linear regression predicts the expected value of a given unknown quantity (the response variable, a random variable) as a linear combination of a set of observed values (predictors). This implies that a constant change in a predictor leads to a constant change in the response variable (i.e. a linear-response model). This is appropriate when the response variable can vary, to a good approximation, indefinitely in either direction, or more generally for any quantity that only varies by a relatively small amount compared to the variation in the predictive variables, e.g., human heights.

However, these assumptions are inappropriate for some types of response variables. For example, in cases where the response variable is expected to be always positive and varying over a wide range, constant input changes lead to geometrically (i.e. exponentially) varying, rather than constantly varying, output changes. As an example, suppose a linear prediction model learns from some data (perhaps primarily drawn from large beaches) that a 10 degree temperature decrease would lead to 1,000 fewer people visiting the beach. This model is unlikely to generalize well over different sized beaches. More specifically, the problem is that if you use the model to predict the new attendance with a temperature drop of 10 for a beach that regularly receives 50 beachgoers, you would predict an impossible attendance value of -950. Logically, a more realistic model would instead predict a constant rate of increased beach attendance (e.g. an increase of 10 degrees leads to a doubling in beach attendance, and a drop of 10 degrees leads to a halving in attendance). Such a model is termed an exponential-response model (or log-linear model, since the logarithm of the response is predicted to vary linearly).

Similarly, a model that predicts a probability of making a yes/no choice (a Bernoulli variable) is even less suitable as a linear-response model, since probabilities are bounded on both ends (they must be between 0 and 1). Imagine, for example, a model that predicts the likelihood of a given person going to the beach as a function of temperature. A reasonable model might predict, for example, that a change in 10 degrees makes a person two times more or less likely to go to the beach. But what does "twice as likely" mean in terms of a probability? It cannot literally mean to double the probability value (e.g. 50% becomes 100%, 75% becomes 150%, etc.). Rather, it is the odds that are doubling: from 2:1 odds, to 4:1 odds, to 8:1 odds, etc. Such a model is a log-odds or logistic model.

Generalized linear models cover all these situations by allowing for response variables that have arbitrary distributions (rather than simply normal distributions), and for an arbitrary function of the response variable (the link function) to vary linearly with the predictors (rather than assuming that the response itself must vary linearly). For example, the case of predicted number of beach attendees would typically be modeled with a Poisson distribution and a log link, while the case of predicted probability of beach attendance would typically be modelled with a Bernoulli distribution (or binomial distribution, depending on exactly how the problem is phrased) and a log-odds (or logit) link function.

### Model Components

The GLM consists of three elements:

- A particular distribution for modeling Y from among those which are considered exponential families of probability distributions,
- A linear predictor $\eta = X\beta$, and
- A link function g q such that $\mathrm{E}(Y \mid X) = \mu = g^{-1}(\eta)$.

### Link Function

The link function provides the relationship between the linear predictor and the mean of the distribution function. There are many commonly used link functions, and their choice is informed by several considerations. There is always a well-defined canonical link function which is derived from the exponential of the response's density function. However, in some cases it makes sense to try to match the domain of the link function to the range of the distribution function's mean, or use a non-canonical link function for algorithmic purposes, for example Bayesian probit regression. count of occurrences of different types (1, ..., K) out of N total K-way occurrences

In the cases of the exponential and gamma distributions, the domain of the canonical link function is not the same as the permitted range of the mean. In particular, the linear predictor may be positive, which would give an impossible negative mean. When maximizing the likelihood, precautions must be taken to avoid this. An alternative is to use a noncanonical link function.

In the case of the Bernoulli, binomial, categorical and multinomial distributions, the support of the distributions is not the same type of data as the parameter being predicted. In all of these cases, the predicted parameter is one or more probabilities, i.e. real numbers in the range $[0,1]$. The resulting model is known as logistic regression (or multinomial logistic regression in the case that K-way rather than binary values are being predicted).

For the Bernoulli and binomial distributions, the parameter is a single probability, indicating the likelihood of occurrence of a single event. The Bernoulli still satisfies the basic condition of the generalized linear model in that, even though a single outcome will always be either 0 or 1, the expected value will nonetheless be a real-valued probability, i.e. the probability of occurrence of a "yes" (or 1) outcome. Similarly, in a binomial distribution, the expected value is Np, i.e. the expected proportion of "yes" outcomes will be the probability to be predicted.

For categorical and multinomial distributions, the parameter to be predicted is a K-vector of probabilities, with the further restriction that all probabilities must add up to 1. Each probability indicates the likelihood of occurrence of one of the K possible values. For the multinomial distribution, and for the vector form of the categorical distribution, the expected values of the elements of the vector can be related to the predicted probabilities similarly to the binomial and Bernoulli distributions.

### Examples

General Linear Models:

- A possible point of confusion has to do with the distinction between generalized linear models and general linear models, two broad statistical models. Co-originator John Nelder has expressed regret over this terminology.
- The general linear model may be viewed as a special case of the generalized linear model with identity link and responses normally distributed. As most exact results of interest are obtained only for the general linear model, the general linear model has undergone a

somewhat longer historical development. Results for the generalized linear model with non-identity link are asymptotic (tending to work well with large samples).

Linear Regression:

- A simple, very important example of a generalized linear model (also an example of a general linear model) is linear regression. In linear regression, the use of the least-squares estimator is justified by the Gauss–Markov theorem, which does not assume that the distribution is normal.
- From the perspective of generalized linear models, however, it is useful to suppose that the distribution function is the normal distribution with constant variance and the link function is the identity, which is the canonical link if the variance is known. Under these assumptions, the least-squares estimator is obtained as the maximum-likelihood parameter estimate.
- For the normal distribution, the generalized linear model has a closed form expression for the maximum-likelihood estimates, which is convenient. Most other GLMs lack closed form estimates.

Binary Data:

- When the response data, Y, are binary (taking on only values 0 and 1), the distribution function is generally chosen to be the Bernoulli distribution and the interpretation of $\mu_i$ is then the probability, p, of $Y_i$ taking on the value one.
- There are several popular link functions for binomial functions.
- **Identity Link:** The identity link g(p) = p is also sometimes used for binomial data to yield a linear probability model. However, the identity link can predict nonsense "probabilities" less than zero or greater than one. This can be avoided by using a transformation like cloglog, probit or logit (or any inverse cumulative distribution function). A primary merit of the identity link is that it can be estimated using linear math—and other standard link functions are approximately linear matching the identity link near p = 0.5.

Multinomial Regression:

- The binomial case may be easily extended to allow for a multinomial distribution as the response (also, a Generalized Linear Model for counts, with a constrained total). There are two ways in which this is usually done:

### Correlated or Clustered Data

The standard GLM assumes that the observations are uncorrelated. Extensions have been developed to allow for correlation between observations, as occurs for example in longitudinal studies and clustered designs:

- Generalized estimating equations (GEEs) allow for the correlation between observations without the use of an explicit probability model for the origin of the correlations, so there is no explicit likelihood. They are suitable when the random effects and their variances are not of inherent interest, as they allow for the correlation without explaining its origin. The focus is on estimating the average response over the population ("population-averaged" effects) rather than the regression parameters that would enable prediction of the effect of changing one or more components of X on a given individual. GEEs are usually used in conjunction with Huber–White standard errors.
- Generalized linear mixed models (GLMMs) are an extension to GLMs that includes random effects in the linear predictor, giving an explicit probability model that explains the origin of the correlations. The resulting "subject-specific" parameter estimates are suitable when the focus is on estimating the effect of changing one or more components of X on a given individual. GLMMs are also referred to as multilevel models and as mixed model. In general, fitting GLMMs is more computationally complex and intensive than fitting GEEs.

## 3.3.3 Attention Mechanisms in Neural Networks

In recent years, attention mechanisms have become a fundamental component of neural networks, particularly in natural language processing (NLP) and computer vision. The concept of attention mimics the way humans selectively focus on important parts of a scene or text while processing information. In deep learning, attention mechanisms allow models to dynamically allocate resources to relevant parts of the input, thereby improving efficiency and accuracy. Initially introduced to enhance machine translation models, attention mechanisms have since evolved and are now widely used in transformer architectures and other advanced AI models.

Attention mechanisms have revolutionized deep learning by enabling models to selectively focus on relevant information, improving accuracy and efficiency in various AI applications. From their initial use in sequence-to-sequence models to their widespread adoption in Transformers, attention mechanisms have reshaped the landscape of NLP and computer vision. While challenges such as computational complexity and interpretability remain, ongoing research continues to refine and extend attention-based techniques. As AI advances, attention mechanisms will play an increasingly critical role in creating intelligent systems capable of understanding and generating human-like responses across diverse domains. The future of attention-based models promises further innovation, making them a cornerstone of next-generation AI systems.

## The Evolution of Attention Mechanisms

The earliest neural networks operated on fixed-length input representations, leading to inefficiencies when handling long sequences. The introduction of recurrent neural networks (RNNs) and long short-term memory (LSTM) networks improved sequential data processing but still struggled with long-range dependencies. Attention mechanisms emerged as a solution, enabling models to selectively weigh input elements based on relevance. The first notable application was in sequence-to-sequence models for language translation, where attention allowed the decoder to focus on specific words in the input sequence while generating an output sentence.

## The Concept of Attention

Attention mechanisms operate by computing a weighted sum of input features, where the weights represent the relevance of each input element. These weights, or attention scores, determine how much influence each input component has on the output. The general formula for attention includes three key components:

- **Query (Q):** Represents the feature that is seeking relevant information.
- **Key (K):** Represents potential matches to the query.
- **Value (V):** Represents the actual information retrieved.

The model computes the similarity between the query and key, assigns a weight to each value, and produces an output based on the weighted sum. This process allows the model to prioritize important features while disregarding irrelevant ones.

## Types of Attention Mechanisms

### Additive Attention

Additive attention, introduced in early sequence-to-sequence models, computes attention scores by applying a feedforward neural network to the concatenation of query and key vectors. This method is computationally expensive but effective for smaller datasets. Additive attention remains widely used in applications where interpretability is critical.

### Dot-Product Attention

Dot-product attention, also known as multiplicative attention, computes attention scores using the dot product of query and key vectors. This approach is computationally efficient because it eliminates the need for additional neural network layers. A scaled version of dot-product attention is used in the Transformer model, ensuring stability when dealing with large vector representations.

### Self-Attention

Self-attention, a breakthrough in deep learning, enables models to focus on different parts of the same input sequence. Unlike traditional attention mechanisms that rely on separate input and output sequences, self-attention calculates dependencies within the same sequence. This mechanism is the foundation of modern transformer models, including BERT and GPT, which power state-of-the-art NLP applications.

## The Transformer Model and Attention

The Transformer model revolutionized deep learning by fully utilizing self-attention mechanisms. Unlike recurrent networks, which process sequences sequentially, Transformers operate on entire input sequences in parallel, significantly improving efficiency. The key innovation in Transformers is multi-head self-attention, where multiple attention mechanisms run in parallel to capture diverse linguistic or visual features.

Multi-head attention involves splitting the query, key, and value vectors into multiple smaller representations, allowing each head to focus on different aspects of the input. These individual attention outputs are then concatenated and transformed into a final representation. This approach enhances the model's ability to capture intricate relationships within the data.

## Attention in NLP Applications

Attention mechanisms have significantly improved NLP tasks such as machine translation, text summarization, and sentiment analysis. In machine translation, attention allows the model to align words in different languages, ensuring that each translated word corresponds to the correct source word. In text summarization, attention helps extract key information from lengthy documents while filtering out less relevant details.

Pretrained language models like BERT (Bidirectional Encoder Representations from Transformers) leverage self-attention to understand contextual relationships in text. By considering both left and right contexts, these models generate more accurate language representations. GPT (Generative Pre-trained Transformer) uses self-attention to generate coherent and contextually relevant text, making it ideal for conversational AI and content generation.

## Attention in Computer Vision

While attention was initially developed for NLP, it has also transformed computer vision tasks such as image recognition, object detection, and image captioning.

Traditional convolutional neural networks (CNNs) apply fixed-size filters to images, limiting their ability to capture long-range dependencies. Attention mechanisms enable CNNs to selectively focus on important regions of an image, improving performance in complex visual tasks.

Visual attention models guide networks to process high-importance image regions while ignoring less relevant areas. In object detection, attention mechanisms help models locate and classify objects within an image, improving accuracy and robustness. Vision Transformers (ViTs) extend the principles of self-attention to computer vision, enabling models to analyze entire images without the constraints of traditional convolutional filters.

## Challenges and Limitations of Attention Mechanisms

Despite their success, attention mechanisms present several challenges. One major issue is computational complexity. Since self-attention requires computing pairwise interactions between all elements in a sequence, processing long sequences can be resource-intensive. Researchers have developed efficient alternatives, such as sparse attention and memory-efficient Transformers, to mitigate this challenge.

Another limitation is interpretability. While attention scores provide insights into model focus, they do not always correlate with human intuition. Some studies have shown that attention mechanisms can be influenced by hidden biases, leading to unreliable explanations. Ongoing research aims to improve interpretability by integrating attention with causal reasoning and human-centric evaluation methods.

## Future Directions in Attention Research

Attention mechanisms continue to evolve, with ongoing research focusing on improving efficiency, interpretability, and generalization. One promising direction is hierarchical attention, which structures attention mechanisms to operate at multiple levels of granularity. This approach enhances model comprehension by capturing both global and local dependencies.

Efficient attention techniques, such as sparse attention and adaptive attention span, aim to reduce computational overhead without sacrificing accuracy. These methods selectively compute attention scores for a subset of relevant inputs, making them suitable for real-time applications.

Another emerging area is cross-modal attention, which enables AI models to process information from multiple modalities, such as text and images. This technique is essential for applications like video understanding and multimodal language processing, where integrating diverse data sources enhances performance.

CHAPTER 4

# Application Areas

## 4.1 HEALTHCARE AND MEDICAL DIAGNOSTICS

Artificial intelligence in healthcare is the application of artificial intelligence (AI) to analyze and understand complex medical and healthcare data. In some cases, it can exceed or augment human capabilities by providing better or faster ways to diagnose, treat, or prevent disease.

As the widespread use of AI in healthcare is still relatively new, research is ongoing into its applications across various medical subdisciplines and related industries. AI programs are being applied to practices such as diagnostics, treatment protocol development, drug development, personalized medicine, and patient monitoring and care. Since radiographs are the most commonly performed imaging tests in radiology, the potential for AI to assist with triage and interpretation of radiographs is particularly significant.

Using AI also presents unprecedented ethical concerns related to issues such as data privacy, automation of jobs, and amplifying already existing biases. Furthermore, new technologies such as AI are often resisted by healthcare leaders, leading to slow and erratic adoption. In contrast, there are also several cases where AI has been put to use in healthcare without proper testing. A systematic review and thematic analysis in 2023 showed that most stakeholders including health professionals, patients, and the general public doubted that care involving AI could be empathetic. Moreover, meta-studies have found that the scientific literature on AI in healthcare often suffers from a lack of reproducibility.

### 4.1.1 History

Research in the 1960s and 1970s produced the first problem-solving program, or expert system, known as Dendral. While it was designed for applications in organic chemistry, it provided the basis for a subsequent system MYCIN, considered one of the most significant early uses of artificial intelligence in medicine. MYCIN and other systems such as INTERNIST-1 and CASNET did not achieve routine use by practitioners, however.

The 1980s and 1990s brought the proliferation of the microcomputer and new levels of network connectivity. During this time, there was a recognition by researchers and developers that AI systems in healthcare must be designed to accommodate the absence of perfect data and build on the expertise of physicians. Approaches involving fuzzy set theory, Bayesian networks, and artificial neural networks, have been applied to intelligent computing systems in healthcare.

Medical and technological advancements occurring over this half-century period that have enabled the growth of healthcare-related applications of AI to include:

- Improvements in computing power resulting in faster data collection and data processing.
- Growth of genomic sequencing databases.
- Widespread implementation of electronic health record systems.
- Improvements in natural language processing and computer vision, enabling machines to replicate human perceptual processes.
- Enhanced the precision of robot-assisted surgery.
- Increased tree-based machine learning models that allow flexibility in establishing health predictors.
- Improvements in deep learning techniques and data logs for rare diseases.

### 4.1.2 Applications in Healthcare Systems

#### Disease Diagnosis

Accurate and early diagnosis of diseases is still a challenge in healthcare. Recognizing medical conditions and their symptoms is a complex problem. AI can assist clinicians with its data processing capabilities to save time and improve accuracy. Through the use of machine learning, artificial intelligence can be able to substantially aid doctors in patient diagnosis through the analysis of mass electronic health records (EHRs). AI can help early prediction, for example, of Alzheimer's disease and dementias, by looking through large numbers of similar cases and possible treatments. The recent and continued advancements in Al technology has shown immense potential in giving recommendations for disease treatment, and delivery diagnosis. Artificial Intelligence in healthcare, can help to reduce inefficiency in healthcare delivery and allow healthcare professionals provide safe and standardized care to their patients. The recent advances in Al has the potential to transform many areas of healthcare as providers are seeking transformative models of delivering treatments, and are open to leveraging Artificial Intelligence in their practice.

Doctors' decision making could also be supported by AI in urgent situations, for example in the emergency department. Here AI algorithms can help prioritize more serious cases and reduce waiting time. Decision support systems augmented with AI can offer real-time suggestions and faster data interpretation to aid the decisions made by healthcare professionals.

In 2023 a study reported higher satisfaction rates with ChatGPT-generated responses compared with those from physicians for medical questions posted on Reddit's r/AskDocs. Evaluators preferred ChatGPT's responses to physician responses in 78.6% of 585 evaluations, noting better quality and empathy. The authors noted that these were isolated questions taken from an online forum, not in the context of an established patient-physician relationship. Moreover, responses were not graded on the accuracy of medical information, and some have argued that the experiment was not properly blinded, with the evaluators being coauthors of the study.

Recent developments in statistical physics, machine learning, and inference algorithms are also being explored for their potential in improving medical diagnostic approaches.

## Electronic Health Records

Electronic health records (EHR) are crucial to the digitalization and information spread of the healthcare industry. Now that around 80% of medical practices use EHR, some anticipate the use of artificial intelligence to interpret the records and provide new information to physicians.

One application uses natural language processing (NLP) to make more succinct reports that limit the variation between medical terms by matching similar medical terms. For example, the term heart attack and myocardial infarction mean the same things, but physicians may use one over the other based on personal preferences. NLP algorithms consolidate these differences so that larger datasets can be analyzed. Another use of NLP identifies phrases that are redundant due to repetition in a physician's notes and keeps the relevant information to make it easier to read. Other applications use concept processing to analyze the information entered by the current patient's doctor to present similar cases and help the physician remember to include all relevant details.

Beyond making content edits to an EHR, there are AI algorithms that evaluate an individual patient's record and predict a risk for a disease based on their previous information and family history. One general algorithm is a rule-based system that makes decisions similarly to how humans use flow charts. This system takes in large amounts of data and creates a set of rules that connect specific observations to concluded diagnoses. Thus, the algorithm can take in a new patient's data and try to predict the likeliness that they will have a certain condition or disease. Since the algorithms can evaluate a patient's information based on collective data, they can find any outstanding issues to bring to a physician's attention and save time. One study conducted by the Centerstone research institute found that predictive modeling of EHR data has achieved 70–72% accuracy in predicting individualized treatment response. These methods are helpful due to the fact that the amount of online health records doubles every five years. Physicians do not have the bandwidth to process all this data manually, and AI can leverage this data to assist physicians in treating their patients.

### Drug Interactions

Improvements in natural language processing led to the development of algorithms to identify drug-drug interactions in medical literature. Drug-drug interactions pose a threat to those taking multiple medications simultaneously, and the danger increases with the number of medications being taken. To address the difficulty of tracking all known or suspected drug-drug interactions, machine learning algorithms have been created to extract information on interacting drugs and their possible effects from medical literature. Efforts were consolidated in 2013 in the DDIExtraction Challenge, in which a team of researchers at Carlos III University assembled a corpus of literature on drug-drug interactions to form a standardized test for such algorithms. Competitors were tested on their ability to accurately determine, from the text, which drugs were shown to interact and what the characteristics of their interactions were. Researchers continue to use this corpus to standardize the measurement of the effectiveness of their algorithms.

Other algorithms identify drug-drug interactions from patterns in user-generated content, especially electronic health records and/or adverse event reports. Organizations such as the FDA Adverse Event Reporting System (FAERS) and the World Health Organization's VigiBase allow doctors to submit reports of possible negative reactions to medications. Deep learning algorithms have been developed to parse these reports and detect patterns that imply drug-drug interactions.

### Telemedicine

The increase of telemedicine, the treatment of patients remotely, has shown the rise of possible AI applications. AI can assist in caring for patients remotely by monitoring their information through sensors. A wearable device may allow for constant monitoring of a patient and the ability to notice changes that may be less distinguishable by humans. The information can be compared to other data that has already been collected using artificial intelligence algorithms that alert physicians if there are any issues to be aware of. Another application of artificial intelligence is chat-bot therapy. Some researchers charge that the reliance on chatbots for mental healthcare does not offer the reciprocity and accountability of care that should exist in the relationship between the consumer of mental healthcare and the care provider (be it a chat-bot or psychologist), though.

**Fig: An Elderly Man Using a Pulse Oximeter to Measure his Blood Oxygen Levels**

Since the average age has risen due to a longer life expectancy, artificial intelligence could be useful in helping take care of older populations. Tools such as environment and personal sensors can identify a person's regular activities and alert a caretaker if a behavior or a measured vital is abnormal. Although the technology is useful, there are also discussions about limitations of monitoring in order to respect a person's privacy since there are technologies that are designed to map out home layouts and detect human interactions.

## Workload Management

AI has the potential to streamline care coordination and reduce the workload. AI algorithms can automate administrative tasks, prioritize patient needs and facilitate seamless communication in a healthcare team. This enables healthcare providers to focus more on direct patient care and ensures the efficient and coordinated delivery of healthcare services.

AI-powered medical transcription tools are capable of reducing clinician's burnout although they aren't saving the practices money or making care delivery more efficient. AI Scribes which can transcribe medical notes for healthcare providers have become increasingly popular as they can utilize AI to listen and transcribe patients appointment. In Mass General Brigham, a 40% reduction in burnout during a survey of an AI Scribe was found, while in MultiCare, a health system located in Washington, discovered a 63% reduction in burnout due to use of AI scribe. Though these results are impressive, Axios reports it is still quite early to determine if AI tools are truly efficient in the healthcare settings.

### 4.1.3 Clinical Applications

#### Cardiovascular

Artificial intelligence algorithms have shown promising results in accurately diagnosing and risk stratifying patients with concern for coronary artery disease, showing potential as an initial triage tool. Other algorithms have been used in predicting patient mortality, medication effects, and adverse events following treatment for acute coronary syndrome. Wearables, smartphones, and internet-based technologies have also shown the ability to monitor patients' cardiac data points, expanding the amount of data and the various settings AI models can use and potentially enabling earlier detection of cardiac events occurring outside of the hospital. A research in 2019 found that AI can be used to predict heart attack with up to 90% accuracy. Another growing area of research is the utility of AI in classifying heart sounds and diagnosing valvular disease. Challenges of AI in cardiovascular medicine have included the limited data available to train machine learning models, such as limited data on social determinants of health as they pertain to cardiovascular disease. A key limitation in early studies evaluating AI were omissions of data comparing algorithmic performance to humans. Examples of studies which assess AI performance relative to physicians includes how AI is non-inferior to humans in interpretation of cardiac echocardiograms and that AI can diagnose heart attack better than human physicians in the emergency setting, reducing both low-value testing and missed diagnoses. In cardiovascular tissue engineering and organoid studies, AI is increasingly used to analyze microscopy images, and integrate electrophysiological read outs.

#### Dermatology

Medical imaging (such as X-ray and photography) is a commonly used tool in dermatology and the development of deep learning has been strongly tied to image processing. Therefore, there is a natural fit between the dermatology and deep learning. Machine learning learning holds great potential to process these images for better diagnoses. Han et al. showed keratinocytic skin cancer detection from face photographs. Esteva et al. demonstrated dermatologist-level classification of skin cancer from lesion images. Noyan et al. demonstrated a convolutional neural network that achieved 94% accuracy at identifying skin cells from microscopic Tzanck smear images. A concern raised with this work is that it has not engaged with disparities related to skin color or differential treatment of patients with non-white skin tones.

According to some researchers, AI algorithms have been shown to be more effective than dermatologists at identifying cancer. However, a 2021 review article found that a majority of papers analyzing the performance of AI algorithms designed for skin cancer classification failed to use external test sets. Only four research studies were found in which the AI algorithms were tested on clinics, regions, or populations distinct from those it was trained on, and in each of those four studies, the performance of dermatologists was found to be on par with that of the algorithm. Moreover, only one study was set in the context of a full clinical examination; others were based on interaction through web-apps or online questionnaires, with most based entirely on context-free images of lesions. In this study, it was found that dermatologists significantly outperformed the algorithms.

It has also been suggested that AI could be used to automatically evaluate the outcome of maxillo-facial surgery or cleft palate therapy in regard to facial attractiveness or age appearance.

## Gastroenterology

AI can play a role in various facets of the field of gastroenterology. Endoscopic exams such as esophagogastroduodenoscopies (EGD) and colonoscopies rely on rapid detection of abnormal tissue. By enhancing these endoscopic procedures with AI, clinicians can more rapidly identify diseases, determine their severity, and visualize blind spots. Early trials in using AI detection systems of early stomach cancer have shown sensitivity close to expert endoscopists.

AI can assist doctors treating ulcerative colitis in detecting the microscopic activity of the disease in people and predicting when flare-ups will happen. For example, an AI-powered tool was developed to analyse digitised bowel samples (biopsies). The tool was able to distinguish with 80% accuracy between samples that show remission of colitis and those with active disease. It also predicted the risk of a flare-up happening with the same accuracy. These rates of successfully using microscopic disease activity to predict disease flare are similar to the accuracy of pathologists.

### Obstetrics and Gynaecology

Artificial intelligence utilises massive amounts of data to help with predicting illness, prevention, and diagnosis, as well as patient monitoring. In obstetrics, artificial intelligence is utilized in magnetic resonance imaging, ultrasound, and foetal cardiotocography. AI contributes in the resolution of a variety of obstetrical diagnostic issues.

### Infectious Diseases

AI has shown potential in both the laboratory and clinical spheres of infectious disease medicine. During the COVID-19 pandemic, AI has been used for early detection, tracking virus spread and analysing virus behaviour, among other things. However, there were only a few examples of AI being used directly in clinical practice during the pandemic itself.

Other applications of AI around infectious diseases include support-vector machines identifying antimicrobial resistance, machine learning analysis of blood smears to detect malaria, and improved point-of-care testing of Lyme disease based on antigen detection. Additionally, AI has been investigated for improving diagnosis of meningitis, sepsis, and tuberculosis, as well as predicting treatment complications in hepatitis B and hepatitis C patients.

### Musculoskeletal

AI has been used to identify causes of knee pain that doctors miss, that disproportionately affect Black patients. Underserved populations experience higher levels of pain. These disparities persist even after controlling for the objective severity of diseases like osteoarthritis, as graded by human physicians using medical images, raising the possibility that underserved patients' pain stems from factors external to the knee, such as stress. Researchers have conducted a study using a machine-learning algorithm to show that standard radiographic measures of severity overlook objective but undiagnosed features that disproportionately affect diagnosis and management of underserved populations with knee pain. They proposed that new algorithmic measure ALG-P could potentially enable expanded access to treatments for underserved patients.

### Neurology

The use of AI technologies has been explored for use in the diagnosis and prognosis of Alzheimer's disease (AD). For diagnostic purposes, machine learning models have been developed that rely on structural MRI inputs. The input datasets for these models are drawn from databases such as the Alzheimer's Disease Neuroimaging Initiative. Researchers have developed models that rely on convolutional neural networks with the aim of improving early diagnostic accuracy. Generative adversarial networks are a form of deep learning that have also performed well in diagnosing AD. There have also been efforts to develop machine learning models into forecasting tools that can predict the prognosis of patients with AD. Forecasting patient outcomes through generative models has been proposed by researchers as a means of synthesizing training and validation sets. They suggest that generated patient forecasts could be used to provide future models larger training datasets than current open access databases.

## Oncology

AI has been explored for use in cancer diagnosis, risk stratification, molecular characterization of tumors, and cancer drug discovery. A particular challenge in oncologic care that AI is being developed to address is the ability to accurately predict which treatment protocols will be best suited for each patient based on their individual genetic, molecular, and tumor-based characteristics. AI has been trialed in cancer diagnostics with the reading of imaging studies and pathology slides. In January 2020, Google DeepMind announced an algorithm capable of surpassing human experts in breast cancer detection in screening scans. A number of researchers, including Trevor Hastie, Joelle Pineau, and Robert Tibshirani among others, published a reply claiming that DeepMind's research publication in Nature lacked key details on methodology and code, "effectively undermin[ing] its scientific value" and making it impossible for the scientific community to confirm the work. In the MIT Technology Review, author Benjamin Haibe-Kains characterized DeepMind's work as "an advertisement" having little to do with science.

In July 2020, it was reported that an AI algorithm developed by the University of Pittsburgh achieves the highest accuracy to date in identifying prostate cancer, with 98% sensitivity and 97% specificity. In 2023 a study reported the use of AI for CT-based radiomics classification at grading the aggressiveness of retroperitoneal sarcoma with 82% accuracy compared with 44% for lab analysis of biopsies.

## Ophthalmology

Artificial intelligence-enhanced technology is being used as an aid in the screening of eye disease and prevention of blindness. In 2018, the U.S. Food and Drug Administration authorized the marketing of the first medical device to diagnose a specific type of eye disease, diabetic retinopathy using an artificial intelligence algorithm. Moreover, AI technology may be used to further improve "diagnosis rates" because of the potential to decrease detection time.

## Pathology

For many diseases, pathological analysis of cells and tissues is considered to be the gold standard of disease diagnosis. Methods of digital pathology allows microscopy slides to be scanned and digitally analyzed. AI-assisted pathology tools have been developed to assist with the diagnosis of a number of diseases, including breast cancer, hepatitis B, gastric cancer, and colorectal cancer.

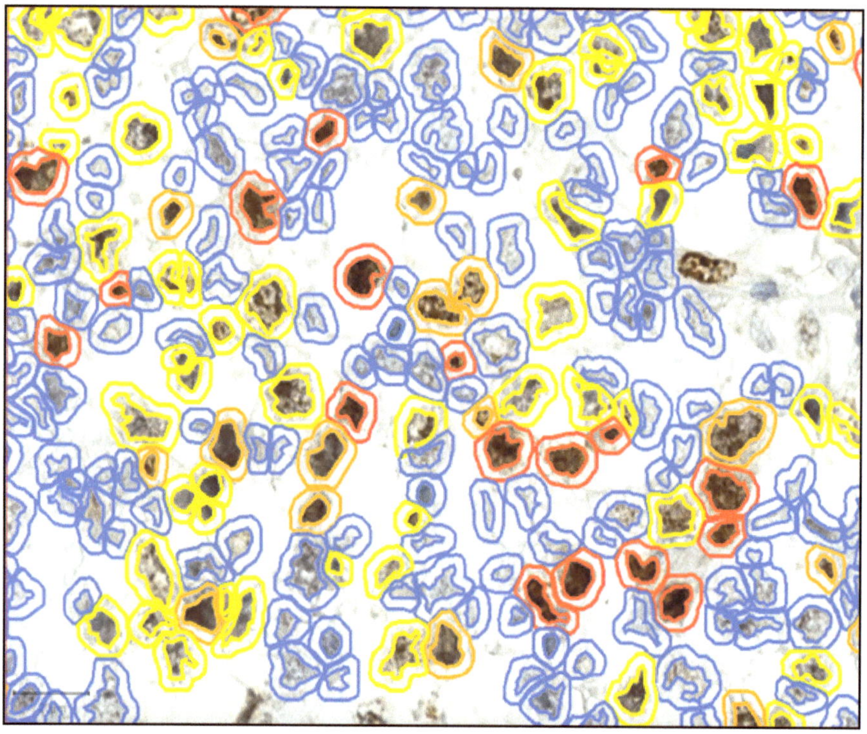

**Fig: Ki67 Stain Calculation by the Open-Source Software QuPath in a Pure Seminoma, which Gives a Measure of the Proliferation Rate of the Tumor. The Colors Represent the Intensity of Expression: Blue-No Expression, Yellow-Low, Orange-Moderate, and Red-High Expression**

AI has also been used to predict genetic mutations and prognosticate disease outcomes. AI is well-suited for use in low-complexity pathological analysis of large-scale screening samples, such as colorectal or breast cancer screening, thus lessening the burden on pathologists and allowing for faster turnaround of sample analysis. Several deep learning and artificial neural network models have shown accuracy similar to that of human pathologists, and a study of deep learning assistance in diagnosing metastatic breast cancer in lymph nodes showed that the accuracy of humans with the assistance of a deep learning program was higher than either the humans alone or the AI program alone. Additionally, implementation of digital pathology is predicted to save over $12 million for a university center over the course of five years, though savings attributed to AI specifically have not yet been widely researched. The use of augmented and virtual reality could prove to be a stepping stone to wider implementation of AI-assisted pathology, as they can highlight areas of concern on a pathology sample and present them in real-time to a pathologist for more efficient review. AI also has the potential to identify histological findings at levels beyond what the human eye can see, and has shown the ability to use genotypic and phenotypic data to more accurately detect the tumor of origin for metastatic cancer. One of the major current barriers to widespread implementation of AI-assisted pathology tools is the lack of prospective, randomized, multi-center controlled trials in determining the true clinical utility of AI for pathologists and patients, highlighting a current area of need in AI and healthcare research.

### Primary Care

Primary care has become one key development area for AI technologies. AI in primary care has been used for supporting decision making, predictive modeling, and business analytics. There are only a few examples of AI decision support systems that were prospectively assessed on clinical efficacy when used in practice by physicians. But there are cases where the use of these systems yielded a positive effect on treatment choice by physicians.

### Psychiatry

In psychiatry, AI applications are still in a phase of proof-of-concept. Areas where the evidence is widening quickly include predictive modelling of diagnosis and treatment outcomes, chatbots, conversational agents that imitate human behaviour and which have been studied for anxiety and depression.

Challenges include the fact that many applications in the field are developed and proposed by private corporations, such as the screening for suicidal ideation implemented by Facebook in 2017. Such applications outside the healthcare system raise various professional, ethical and regulatory questions. Another issue is often with the validity and interpretability of the models. Small training datasets contain bias that is inherited by the models, and compromises the generalizability and stability of these models. Such models may also have the potential to be discriminatory against minority groups that are underrepresented in samples.

In 2023, US-based National Eating Disorders Association replaced its human helpline staff with a chatbot but had to take it offline after users reported receiving harmful advice from it.

### Radiology

AI is being studied within the field of radiology to detect and diagnose diseases through computerized tomography (CT) and magnetic resonance (MR) imaging. It may be particularly useful in settings where demand for human expertise exceeds supply, or where data is too complex to be efficiently interpreted by human readers. Several deep learning models have shown the capability to be roughly as accurate as healthcare professionals in identifying diseases through medical imaging, though few of the studies reporting these findings have been externally validated. AI can also provide non-interpretive benefit to radiologists, such as reducing noise in images, creating high-quality images from lower doses of radiation, enhancing MR image quality, and automatically assessing image quality. Further research investigating the use of AI in nuclear medicine focuses on image reconstruction, anatomical landmarking, and the enablement of lower doses in imaging studies. The analysis of images for supervised AI applications in radiology encompasses two primary techniques at present: (1) convolutional neural network-based analysis; and (2) utilization of radiomics.

AI is also used in breast imaging for analyzing screening mammograms and can participate in improving breast cancer detection rate as well as reducing radiologist's reading workload.

### Pharmacy

Artificial intelligence in pharmacy is the application of artificial intelligence (AI) to the discovery, development, and the treatment of patients with medications. AI in pharmacy practices has the potential to revolutionize all aspects of pharmaceutical research as well as to improve the clinical application of pharmaceuticals to prevent, treat, or cure disease. AI, a technology that enables machines to simulate human intelligence, has found applications in pharmaceutical research, drug manufacturing, drug delivery systems, clinical trial optimization, treatment plans, and patient-centered services.

## 4.1.4 Industry

The trend of large health companies merging allows for greater health data accessibility. Greater health data lays the groundwork for the implementation of AI algorithms.

A large part of industry focus of implementation of AI in the healthcare sector is in the clinical decision support systems. As more data is collected, machine learning algorithms adapt and allow for more robust responses and solutions. Numerous companies are exploring the possibilities of the incorporation of big data in the healthcare industry. Many companies investigate the market opportunities through the realms of "data assessment, storage, management, and analysis technologies" which are all crucial parts of the healthcare industry.

The following are examples of large companies that have contributed to AI algorithms for use in healthcare:

- IBM's Watson Oncology is in development at Memorial Sloan Kettering Cancer Center and Cleveland Clinic. IBM is also working with CVS Health on AI applications in chronic disease treatment and with Johnson &

Johnson on analysis of scientific papers to find new connections for drug development. In May 2017, IBM and Rensselaer Polytechnic Institute began a joint project entitled Health Empowerment by Analytics, Learning and Semantics (HEALS), to explore using AI technology to enhance healthcare.

- Microsoft's Hanover project, in partnership with Oregon Health & Science University's Knight Cancer Institute, analyzes medical research to predict the most effective cancer drug treatment options for patients. Other projects include medical image analysis of tumor progression and the development of programmable cells.
- Google's DeepMind platform is being used by the UK National Health Service to detect certain health risks through data collected via a mobile app. A second project with the NHS involves the analysis of medical images collected from NHS patients to develop computer vision algorithms to detect cancerous tissues.
- Tencent is working on several medical systems and services. These include AI Medical Innovation System (AIMIS), an AI-powered diagnostic medical imaging service; WeChat Intelligent Healthcare; and Tencent Doctorwork
- Intel's venture capital arm Intel Capital invested in 2016 in the startup Lumiata, which uses AI to identify at-risk patients and develop care options.

Digital consultant apps use AI to give medical consultation based on personal medical history and common medical knowledge. Users report their symptoms into the app, which uses speech recognition to compare against a database of illnesses. Babylon then offers a recommended action, taking into account the user's medical history. Entrepreneurs in healthcare have been effectively using seven business model archetypes to take AI solution[buzzword] to the marketplace. These archetypes depend on the value generated for the target user (e.g. patient focus vs. healthcare provider and payer focus) and value capturing mechanisms (e.g. providing information or connecting stakeholders).

IFlytek launched a service robot "Xiao Man", which integrated artificial intelligence technology to identify the registered customer and provide personalized recommendations in medical areas. It also works in the field of medical imaging. Similar robots are also being made by companies such as UBTECH ("Cruzr") and Softbank Robotics ("Pepper"). The Indian startup Haptik recently developed a WhatsApp chatbot which answers questions associated with the deadly coronavirus in India. Similarly, a software platform ChatBot in partnership with medtech startup Infermedica launched COVID-19 Risk Assessment ChatBot.

Fig; Elon Musk Premiering the Surgical Robot that Implants the Neuralink Brain Chip

- Neuralink has come up with a next-generation neuroprosthetic which intricately interfaces with thousands of neural pathways in the brain. Their process allows a chip, roughly the size of a quarter, to be inserted in the place of a chunk of a skull by a precision surgical robot to avoid accidental injury .

With the market for AI expanding constantly, large tech companies such as Apple, Google, Amazon, and Baidu all have their own AI research divisions, as well as millions of dollars allocated for acquisition of smaller AI based companies. Many automobile manufacturers are beginning to use machine learning healthcare in their cars as well. Companies such as BMW, GE, Tesla, Toyota, and Volvo all have new research campaigns to find ways of learning a driver's vital statistics to ensure they are awake, paying attention to the road, and not under the influence of substances.

### 4.1.5 Expanding Care to Developing Nations

Artificial intelligence continues to expand in its abilities to diagnose more people accurately in nations where fewer doctors are accessible to the public. Many new technology companies such as SpaceX and the Raspberry Pi Foundation have enabled more developing countries to have access to computers and the internet than ever before. With the increasing capabilities of AI over the internet, advanced machine learning algorithms can allow patients to get accurately diagnosed when they would previously have no way of knowing if they had a life-threatening disease or not. Using AI in developing nations that do not have the resources will diminish the need for outsourcing and can improve patient care. AI can allow for not only diagnosis of patient in areas where healthcare is scarce, but also allow for a good patient experience by resourcing files to find the best treatment for a patient. The ability of AI to adjust course as it goes also allows the patient to have their treatment modified based on what works for them; a level of individualized care that is nearly non-existent in developing countries.

### 4.1.6 Regulation

While research on the use of AI in healthcare aims to validate its efficacy in improving patient outcomes before its broader adoption, its use may nonetheless introduce several new types of risk to patients and healthcare providers, such as algorithmic bias, Do not resuscitate implications, and other machine morality issues. AI may also compromise the protection of patients' rights, such as the right to informed consent and the right to medical data protection. These challenges of the clinical use of AI have brought about a potential need for regulations. AI studies need to be completely and transparently reported to have value to inform regulatory approval. Depending on the phase of study, international consensus-based reporting guidelines (TRIPOD+AI, DECIDE-AI, CONSORT-AI) have been developed to provide recommendations on the key details that need to be reported.

**Fig: A Man Speaking at the GDPR Compliance Workshop at the 2019 Entrepreneurship Summit**

Currently, there are regulations pertaining to the collection of patient data. This includes policies such as the Health Insurance Portability and Accountability Act (HIPAA) and the European General Data Protection Regulation (GDPR). The GDPR pertains to patients within the EU and details the consent requirements for patient data use when entities collect patient healthcare data. Similarly, HIPAA protects healthcare data from patient records in the United States. In May 2016, the White House announced its plan to host a series of workshops and formation of the National Science and Technology Council (NSTC) Subcommittee on Machine Learning and Artificial Intelligence. In October 2016, the group published The National Artificial Intelligence Research and Development Strategic Plan, outlining its proposed priorities for Federally-funded AI research and development (within government and academia). The report notes a strategic R&D plan for the subfield of health information technology is in development stages.

There is concern that large language models can overwhelm people with both accurate health information and also misinformation, leading to potential challenges in public health. This calls for the need for policy and user guidance related to health information through AI.

### United Nations (WHO/ITU)

The joint ITU-WHO Focus Group on Artificial Intelligence for Health (FG-AI4H) has built a platform - known as the ITU-WHO AI for Health Framework - for the testing and benchmarking of AI applications in health domain. As of November 2018, eight use cases are being benchmarked, including assessing breast cancer risk from histopathological imagery, guiding anti-venom selection from snake images, and diagnosing skin lesions.

### US FDA

In January 2021, the US FDA published a new Action Plan, entitled Artificial Intelligence (AI) /Machine Learning (ML)-Based Software as a Medical Device (SaMD) Action Plan. This plan lays out the FDA's future plans for regulation of medical devices that would include artificial intelligence in their software. There are five main actions the FDA plans to take to increase regulation: 1. Tailored Regulatory Framework for Ai/M:-based SaMD, 2. Good Machine Learning Practice (GMLP), 3. Patient-Centered Approach Incorporating Transparency to Users, 4. Regulatory Science Methods Related to Algorithm Bias & Robustness, and 5. Real-World Performance(RWP). This plan was in direct response to stakeholders' feedback on a 2019 discussion paper also published by the FDA.

According to the U.S. Department of Health and Human Services, the Office for Civil Rights (OCR) has issued guidance on the ethical use of AI in healthcare. The guidance outlines four core ethical principles that must be followed: respect for autonomy, beneficence, non-maleficence, and justice. Respect for autonomy requires that individuals have control over their own data and decisions. Beneficence requires that AI be used to do good, such as improving the quality of care and reducing health disparities.

Non-maleficence requires that AI be used to do no harm, such as avoiding discrimination in decisions. Finally, justice requires that AI be used fairly, such as using the same standards for decisions no matter a person's race, gender, or income level. Moreover, as of March 2021, the OCR hired a Chief Artificial Intelligence Officer (OCAIO) to pursue the "implementation of the HHS AI strategy". The OCR also has issued rules and regulations to protect the privacy of individuals' health information.

These regulations require healthcare providers to follow certain privacy rules when using AI. The OCR also requires healthcare providers to keep a record of how they use AI and to ensure that their AI systems are secure. Overall, the U.S. has taken steps to protect individuals' privacy and ethical issues related to AI in healthcare

The U.S. is not the only country to develop or initiate regulations of data privacy with AI. Other countries have implemented data protection regulations, more specifically with company privacy invasions. In Denmark, the Danish Expert Group on Data Ethics has adopted recommendations on 'Data for the Benefit of the People'. These recommendations are intended to encourage the responsible use of data in the business sector, with a focus on data processing. The recommendations include a focus on equality and non-discrimination with regard to bias in AI, as well as human dignity. The importance of human dignity is stressed, as it is said to outweigh profit and must be respected in all data processes

The European Union has implemented the General Data Protection Regulation (GDPR) to protect citizens' personal data, which applies to the use of AI in healthcare. In addition, the European Commission has established guidelines to ensure the ethical development of AI, including the use of algorithms to ensure fairness and transparency. With GDPR, the European Union was the first to regulate AI through data protection legislation.

The Union finds privacy as a fundamental human right, it wants to prevent unconsented and secondary uses of data by private or public health facilities. By streamlining access to personal data for health research and findings, they are able to instate the right and importance of patient privacy. In the United States, the Health Insurance Portability and Accountability Act (HIPAA) requires organizations to protect the privacy and security of patient information. The Centers for Medicare and Medicaid Services have also released guidelines for the development of AI-based medical applications.

### 4.1.7 Ethical Concerns

#### Data Collection

In order to effectively train Machine Learning and use AI in healthcare, massive amounts of data must be gathered. Acquiring this data, however, comes at the cost of patient privacy in most cases and is not well received publicly. For example, a survey conducted in the UK estimated that 63% of the population is uncomfortable with sharing their personal data in order to improve artificial intelligence technology. The scarcity of real, accessible patient data is a hindrance that deters the progress of developing and deploying more artificial intelligence in healthcare.

Furthermore, the lack of current regulations surrounding AI in the United States has generated concerns about mismanagement of patient data, such as with corporations utilizing patient data for financial gain. For example, Roche, a Swiss healthcare company, was found to have purchased healthcare data for approximately 2 million cancer patients at an estimated total cost of $1.9 billion. Naturally, this generates questions of ethical concern; Is there a monetary price that can be set for data, and should it depend on its perceived value or contributions to science? Is it fair to patients to sell their data? These concerns were addressed in a survey conducted by the Pew Research Center in 2022 that asked Americans for their opinions about the increased presence of AI in their daily lives, and the survey estimated that 37% of Americans were more concerned than excited about such increased presence, with 8% of participants specifically associating their concern with "people misusing AI". Ultimately, the current potential of artificial intelligence in healthcare is additionally hindered by concerns about mismanagement of data collected, especially in the United States.

#### Automation

A systematic review and thematic analysis in 2023 showed that most stakeholders including health professionals, patients, and the general public doubted that care involving AI could be empathetic.

According to a 2019 study, AI can replace up to 35% of jobs in the UK within the next 10 to 20 years. However, of these jobs, it was concluded that AI has not eliminated any healthcare jobs so far. Though if AI were to automate healthcare-related jobs, the jobs most susceptible to automation would be those dealing with digital information, radiology, and pathology, as opposed to those dealing with doctor-to-patient interaction.

Automation can provide benefits alongside doctors as well. Some believe that AI may avert healthcare worker burnout and cognitive overload, so that doctors who take advantage of AI in healthcare will provide greater quality healthcare than doctors and medical establishments who do not.

Recently, there have been many discussions between healthcare experts in terms of AI and elder care. In relation to elder care, AI bots have been helpful in guiding older residents living in assisted living with entertainment and company. These bots are allowing staff in the home to have more one-on-one time with each resident, but the bots are also programmed with more ability in what they are able to do; such as knowing different languages and different types of care depending on the patient's conditions. The bot is an AI machine, which means it goes through the same training as any other machine - using algorithms to parse the given data, learn from it and predict the outcome in relation to what situation is at hand

## Bias

Since AI makes decisions solely on the data it receives as input, it is important that this data represents accurate patient demographics. In a hospital setting, patients do not have full knowledge of how predictive algorithms are created or calibrated. Therefore, these medical establishments can unfairly code their algorithms to discriminate against minorities and prioritize profits rather than providing optimal care. A recent scoping review identified 18 equity challenges along with 15 strategies that can be implemented to help address them when AI applications are developed using many-to-many mapping.

There can also be unintended bias in these algorithms that can exacerbate social and healthcare inequities. Since AI's decisions are a direct reflection of its input data, the data it receives must have accurate representation of patient demographics. For instance, if populations are less represented in healthcare data it is likely to create bias in AI tools that lead to incorrect assumptions of a demographic and impact the ability to provide appropriate care. White males are overly represented in medical data sets. Therefore, having minimal patient data on minorities can lead to AI making more accurate predictions for majority populations, leading to unintended worse medical outcomes for minority populations. Collecting data from minority communities can also lead to medical discrimination. For instance, HIV is a prevalent virus among minority communities and HIV status can be used to discriminate against patients. In addition to biases that may arise from sample selection, different clinical systems used to collect data may also impact AI functionality. For example, radiographic systems and their outcomes (e.g., resolution) vary by provider. Moreover, clinician work practices, such as the positioning of the patient for radiography, can also greatly influence the data and make comparability difficult. However, these biases are able to be eliminated through careful implementation and a methodical collection of representative data.

A final source of algorithmic bias, which has been called "label choice bias", arises when proxy measures are used to train algorithms, that build in bias against certain groups. For example, a widely used algorithm predicted health care costs as a proxy for health care needs, and used predictions to allocate resources to help patients with complex health needs. This introduced bias because Black patients have lower costs, even when they are just as unhealthy as White patients. Solutions to the "label choice bias" aim to match the actual target (what the algorithm is predicting) more closely to the ideal target (what researchers want the algorithm to predict), so for the prior example, instead of predicting cost, researchers would focus on the variable of healthcare needs which is rather more significant. Adjusting the target led to almost double the number of Black patients being selected for the program.

## 4.2 FINANCE AND RISK ASSESSMENT

Artificial Intelligence has significantly transformed the financial sector by automating decision-making processes, optimizing risk assessments, and improving fraud detection. However, the adoption of AI in finance also brings challenges, primarily related to the opacity of complex machine learning models. Explainable AI (XAI) addresses these concerns by providing transparency and interpretability, ensuring financial professionals, regulators, and stakeholders understand how AI-driven decisions are made. The implementation of XAI in finance is crucial for trust, regulatory compliance, and mitigating financial risks.

Explainable AI is essential for the responsible use of AI in finance and risk assessment. By enhancing transparency, mitigating bias, and ensuring regulatory compliance, XAI fosters trust in AI-driven financial decisions. The integration of explainability techniques in financial AI models improves decision-making, enhances customer confidence, and strengthens risk management. As AI continues to shape the financial industry, the adoption of XAI will be crucial in ensuring ethical, transparent, and fair financial practices.

### 4.2.1 The Importance of Explainability in Financial AI Systems

AI-driven models in finance are frequently used for credit scoring, loan approvals, fraud detection, and risk assessment. Traditional AI models, especially deep learning networks, function as black boxes, making it difficult to explain why a particular decision was reached. Explainability is essential to ensure fairness, reduce bias, and provide customers with understandable reasons for financial decisions. By integrating XAI, financial institutions can ensure accountability, enhance customer trust, and comply with stringent regulatory requirements.

### 4.2.2 Applications of XAI in Finance and Risk Assessment

Explainable AI has various applications in financial decision-making. In credit scoring, XAI ensures that customers understand why they were approved or denied credit, helping institutions avoid discriminatory lending practices. For fraud detection, explainable models provide insights into suspicious transactions, enabling financial analysts to differentiate between legitimate and fraudulent activities. In investment management, XAI assists portfolio managers by explaining market predictions, thereby increasing confidence in AI-driven trading strategies. Moreover, regulatory compliance benefits from XAI as financial institutions must justify AI decisions to auditors and governing bodies.

### 4.2.3 Techniques for Achieving Explainability in Financial AI

Several techniques enhance the explainability of AI models in finance. Feature importance methods, such as SHAP (Shapley Additive Explanations) and LIME (Local Interpretable Model-agnostic Explanations), highlight the most significant factors influencing AI predictions. Decision trees and rule-based models offer inherently interpretable frameworks, making them useful for transparent financial modeling. Counterfactual explanations provide alternative scenarios, illustrating how minor changes in inputs can affect financial outcomes. Hybrid models that combine neural networks with interpretable components also contribute to improving AI transparency in financial applications.

### 4.2.4 Trust and Fairness in AI-Driven Financial Systems

Trust is a fundamental aspect of financial AI applications. Without explainability, financial decisions can be perceived as arbitrary, leading to customer dissatisfaction and potential regulatory penalties. XAI ensures fairness by identifying and mitigating biases within training data and algorithms.

For instance, AI models trained on biased historical data may discriminate against certain demographics in loan approvals. Explainability helps detect such biases, ensuring equitable financial decision-making. Additionally, transparent AI models allow customers to contest and understand financial decisions, enhancing trust in automated systems.

### 4.2.5 Regulatory and Legal Implications of XAI in Finance

Financial regulators emphasize the importance of transparency in AI-driven decision-making. Regulations such as the European Union's General Data Protection Regulation (GDPR) include provisions for the "right to explanation," requiring financial institutions to justify automated decisions affecting customers. Similarly, the U.S. Fair Lending Laws mandate that credit and lending decisions must be explainable and free from discriminatory biases.

Adopting XAI ensures compliance with these regulations while reducing legal risks associated with AI-driven financial decisions. Moreover, financial audits and risk assessments benefit from XAI, as transparent models enable easier verification and validation.

### 4.2.6 Challenges in Implementing XAI for Finance and Risk Management

Despite its advantages, implementing XAI in finance presents challenges. One major issue is the trade-off between model accuracy and interpretability. Highly accurate deep learning models often lack transparency, while simpler, more interpretable models may not perform as well.

Additionally, financial data is often complex and dynamic, making it difficult to create consistent and explainable models. Another challenge is the need for specialized training for financial professionals to understand and utilize AI explanations effectively. Furthermore, integrating XAI into existing financial infrastructures requires significant investment in technology and expertise.

### 4.2.7 Future Directions for XAI in Financial Risk Assessment

The future of XAI in finance lies in developing more sophisticated methods that balance accuracy and interpretability. Hybrid models that integrate deep learning with interpretable components will likely become more prevalent. AI research is also focusing on causality-based explanations, moving beyond correlation-based models to provide more meaningful financial insights.

The expansion of regulatory frameworks will drive further adoption of XAI, making transparency a standard requirement in financial AI applications. Additionally, advancements in human-AI collaboration will enable financial professionals to work alongside AI systems, refining and validating AI-generated insights.

## 4.3 AUTONOMOUS SYSTEMS

### 4.3.1 Autonomous System (Internet)

An autonomous system (AS) is a collection of connected Internet Protocol (IP) routing prefixes under the control of one or more network operators on behalf of a single administrative entity or domain, that presents a common and clearly defined routing policy to the Internet. Each AS is assigned an autonomous system number (ASN), for use in Border Gateway Protocol (BGP) routing.

Autonomous System Numbers are assigned to Local Internet Registries (LIRs) and end-user organizations by their respective Regional Internet Registries (RIRs), which in turn receive blocks of ASNs for reassignment from the Internet Assigned Numbers Authority (IANA). The IANA also maintains a registry of ASNs which are reserved for private use (and should therefore not be announced to the global Internet).

Originally, the definition required control by a single entity, typically an Internet service provider (ISP) or a very large organization with independent connections to multiple networks, that adhered to a single and clearly defined routing policy. In

March 1996, the newer definition came into use because multiple organizations can run BGP using private AS numbers to an ISP that connects all those organizations to the Internet. Even though there may be multiple autonomous systems supported by the ISP, the Internet only sees the routing policy of the ISP. That ISP must have an officially registered ASN.

Until 2007, AS numbers were defined as 16-bit integers, which allowed for a maximum of 65,536 assignments. Since then, the IANA has begun to also assign 32-bit AS numbers to regional Internet registries (RIRs). These numbers are written preferably as simple integers, in a notation referred to as "asplain", ranging from 0 to 4,294,967,295 (hexadecimal 0xFFFF FFFF). Or, alternatively, in the form called "asdot+" which looks like x.y, where x and y are 16-bit numbers. Numbers of the form 0.y are exactly the old 16-bit AS numbers.

The special 16-bit ASN 23456 ("AS_TRANS") was assigned by IANA as a placeholder for 32-bit ASN values for the case when 32-bit-ASN capable routers ("new BGP speakers") send BGP messages to routers with older BGP software ("old BGP speakers") which do not understand the new 32-bit ASNs.

The first and last ASNs of the original 16-bit integers (0 and 65,535) and the last ASN of the 32-bit numbers (4,294,967,295) are reserved and should not be used by operators; AS0 is used by all five RIRs to invalidate unallocated space. ASNs 64,496 to 64,511 of the original 16-bit range and 65,536 to 65,551 of the 32-bit range are reserved for use in documentation. ASNs 64,512 to 65,534 of the original 16-bit AS range, and 4,200,000,000 to 4,294,967,294 of the 32-bit range are reserved for Private Use.

The number of unique autonomous networks in the routing system of the Internet exceeded 5,000 in 1999, 30,000 in late 2008, 35,000 in mid-2010, 42,000 in late 2012, 54,000 in mid-2016 and 60,000 in early 2018. By December 2020, the number of allocated ASNs exceeded 100,000. As of 2025, there are roughly 120,000 allocated ASNs.

## Assignment

AS numbers are assigned in blocks by Internet Assigned Numbers Authority (IANA) to regional Internet registries (RIRs). The appropriate RIR then assigns ASNs to entities within its designated area from the block assigned by IANA.

Entities wishing to receive an ASN must complete the application process of their RIR, LIR or upstream service provider and be approved before being assigned an ASN. Current IANA ASN assignments to RIRs can be found on the IANA website. RIRs, as part of NRO, can revoke AS numbers as part of their Internet governance abilities.

## ASN Table

A complete table of available 16-bit and 32-bit ASN:

| Number | Bits | Description | Reference |
|---|---|---|---|
| 0 | 16 | Reserved for RPKI unallocated space invalidation | RFC 6483, RFC 7607 |
| 1–23455 | 16 | Public ASNs | |
| 23456 | 16 | Reserved for AS Pool Transition | RFC 6793 |
| 23457–64495 | 16 | Public ASNs | |
| 64496–64511 | 16 | Reserved for use in documentation and sample code | RFC 5398 |
| 64512–65534 | 16 | Reserved for private use | RFC 1930, RFC 6996 |
| 65535 | 16 | Reserved | RFC 7300 |
| 65536–65551 | 32 | Reserved for use in documentation and sample code | RFC 5398, RFC 6793 |
| 65552–131071 | 32 | Reserved | |
| 131072–4199999999 | 32 | Public 32-bit ASNs | |
| 4200000000–4294967294 | 32 | Reserved for private use | RFC 6996 |
| 4294967295 | 32 | Reserved | RFC 7300 |

## Types

Autonomous systems (AS) can be grouped into four categories, depending on their connectivity and operating policy.

- **Multihomed:** An AS that maintains connections to more than one other AS. This allows the AS to remain connected to the Internet in the event of a complete failure of one of their connections. However, unlike a transit AS, this type of AS would not allow traffic from one AS to pass through on its way to another AS.
- **Stub:** An AS that is connected to only one other AS. This may be an apparent waste of an AS number if the network's routing policy is the same as its upstream AS's. However, the stub AS may have peering with other autonomous systems that is not reflected in public route-view

servers. Specific examples include private interconnections in the financial and transportation sectors.

- **Transit:** An AS that acts as a router between two ASes is called a transit. Since not all ASes are directly connected with every other AS, a transit AS carries data traffic between one AS to another AS to which it has links.
- **Internet Exchange Point (IX or IXP):** A physical infrastructure through which ISPs or content delivery networks (CDNs) exchange Internet traffic between their networks (autonomous systems). These are often groups of local ISPs that band together to exchange data by splitting the costs of a local networking hub, avoiding the higher costs (and bandwidth charges) of a Transit AS. IXP ASNs are usually transparent. By having presence in an IXP, ASes shorten the transit path to other participating ASes, thereby reducing network latency and improving round-trip delay.

### AS-SET

Autonomous systems can be included in one or more AS-SETs, for example AS-SET of RIPE NCC "AS-12655" has AS1, AS2 and AS3 as its members, but AS1 is also included in other sets in ARIN (AS-INCAPSULA) and APNIC (AS-IMCL). Another AS-SET sources can be RADB, LEVEL3 (tier 1 network now called Lumen Technologies) and also ARIN has ARIN-NONAUTH source of AS-SETs. AS-SETs are created by network operators in an Internet Routing Registry (IRR), like other route objects, and can be included in other AS-SETs and even form cycles.

AS-SET names usually start with "AS-", but can also have a hierarchical name. For example, the administrator of AS 64500 may create an AS-SET called "AS64500:AS-UPSTREAMS", to avoid conflict with other similarly named AS-SETs.

AS-SETs are often used to simplify management of published routing policies. A routing policy is published in the IRR using "import" and "export" (or the newer "mp-import" and "mp-export") attributes, which each contain the source or destination AS number and the AS number imported or exported. Instead of single AS numbers, AS-SETs can be referenced in these attributes, which simplifies management of complex routing policies.

## 4.3.2 Autonomous Robot

An autonomous robot is a robot that acts without recourse to human control. Historic examples include space probes. Modern examples include self-driving vacuums and cars. Industrial robot arms that work on assembly lines inside factories may also be considered autonomous robots, though their autonomy is restricted due to a highly structured environment and their inability to locomote.

## Components and Criteria of Robotic Autonomy

### Self-Maintenance

The first requirement for complete physical autonomy is the ability for a robot to take care of itself. Many of the battery-powered robots on the market today can find and connect to a charging station, and some toys like Sony's Aibo are capable of self-docking to charge their batteries. Self-maintenance is based on "proprioception", or sensing one's own internal status. In the battery charging example, the robot can tell proprioceptively that its batteries are low, and it then seeks the charger. Another common proprioceptive sensor is for heat monitoring. Increased proprioception will be required for robots to work autonomously near people and in harsh environments. Common proprioceptive sensors include thermal, optical, and haptic sensing, as well as the Hall effect (electric).

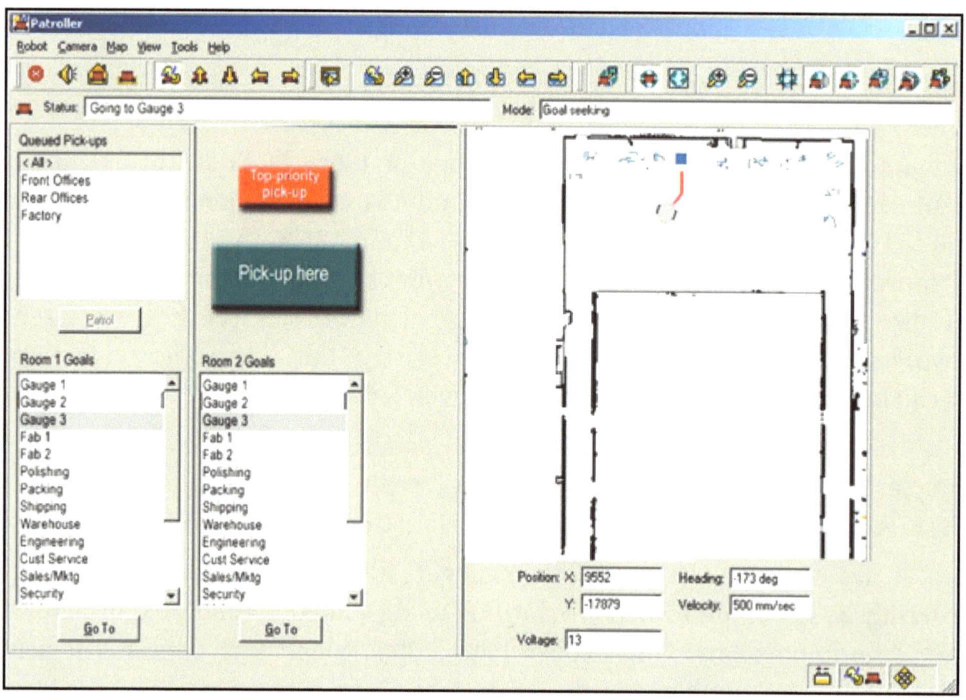


**Fig: Robot GUI Display Showing Battery Voltage and other Proprioceptive Data in Lower Right-Hand Corner. The Display is for User Information only. Autonomous Robots Monitor and Respond to Proprioceptive Sensors without Human Intervention to Keep Themselves Safe and Operating Properly**

### Sensing the Environment

Exteroception is sensing things about the environment. Autonomous robots must have a range of environmental sensors to perform their task and stay out of trouble. The autonomous robot can recognize sensor failures and minimize the impact on the performance caused by failures.

- Common exteroceptive sensors include the electromagnetic spectrum, sound, touch, chemical (smell, odor), temperature, range to various objects, and altitude.

Some robotic lawn mowers will adapt their programming by detecting the speed in which grass grows as needed to maintain a perfectly cut lawn, and some vacuum cleaning robots have dirt detectors that sense how much dirt is being picked up and use this information to tell them to stay in one area longer.

### Task Performance

The next step in autonomous behavior is to actually perform a physical task. A new area showing commercial promise is domestic robots, with a flood of small vacuuming robots beginning with iRobot and Electrolux in 2002. While the level of intelligence is not high in these systems, they navigate over wide areas and pilot in tight situations around homes using contact and non-contact sensors. Both of these robots use proprietary algorithms to increase coverage over simple random bounce.

The next level of autonomous task performance requires a robot to perform conditional tasks. For instance, security robots can be programmed to detect intruders and respond in a particular way depending upon where the intruder is. For example, Amazon launched its Astro for home monitoring, security and eldercare in September 2021.

### Indoor navigation: Autonomous Navigation

For a robot to associate behaviors with a place (localization) requires it to know where it is and to be able to navigate point-to-point. Such navigation began with wire-guidance in the 1970s and progressed in the early 2000s to beacon-based triangulation. Current commercial robots autonomously navigate based on sensing natural features. The first commercial robots to achieve this were Pyxus' HelpMate hospital robot and the CyberMotion guard robot, both designed by robotics pioneers in the 1980s. These robots originally used manually created CAD floor plans, sonar sensing and wall-following variations to navigate buildings. The next generation, such as MobileRobots' PatrolBot and autonomous wheelchair, both introduced in 2004, have the ability to create their own laser-based maps of a building and to navigate open areas as well as corridors. Their control system changes its path on the fly if something blocks the way.

At first, autonomous navigation was based on planar sensors, such as laser range-finders, that can only sense at one level. The most advanced systems now fuse information from various sensors for both localization (position) and navigation. Systems such as Motivity can rely on different sensors in different areas, depending upon which provides the most reliable data at the time, and can re-map a building autonomously.

Rather than climb stairs, which requires highly specialized hardware, most indoor robots navigate handicapped-accessible areas, controlling elevators, and electronic doors. With such electronic access-control interfaces, robots can now freely navigate indoors. Autonomously climbing stairs and opening doors manually are topics of research at the current time.

As these indoor techniques continue to develop, vacuuming robots will gain the ability to clean a specific user-specified room or a whole floor. Security robots will be able to cooperatively surround intruders and cut off exits. These advances also bring concomitant protections: robots' internal maps typically permit "forbidden areas" to be defined to prevent robots from autonomously entering certain regions.

### Outdoor Navigation: Autonomous Navigation

Outdoor autonomy is most easily achieved in the air, since obstacles are rare. Cruise missiles are rather dangerous highly autonomous robots. Pilotless drone aircraft are increasingly used for reconnaissance.

Some of these unmanned aerial vehicles (UAVs) are capable of flying their entire mission without any human interaction at all except possibly for the landing where a person intervenes using radio remote control. Some drones are capable of safe, automatic landings, however. SpaceX operates a number of autonomous spaceport drone ships, used to safely land and recover Falcon 9 rockets at sea.

Outdoor autonomy is the most difficult for ground vehicles, due to:

- Three-dimensional terrain.
- Great disparities in surface density.
- Weather exigencies.
- Instability of the sensed environment.

### Open Problems in Autonomous Robotics Autonomous Navigation

There are several open problems in autonomous robotics which are special to the field rather than being a part of the general pursuit of AI. According to George A. Bekey's Autonomous Robots: From Biological Inspiration to Implementation and Control, problems include things such as making sure the robot is able to function correctly and not run into obstacles autonomously.

Reinforcement learning has been used to control and plan the navigation of autonomous robots, specifically when a group of them operate in collaboration with each other.

Energy autonomy and foraging:

- Researchers concerned with creating true artificial life are concerned not only with intelligent control, but further with the capacity of the robot to find its own resources through foraging (looking for food, which includes both energy and spare parts).

- This is related to autonomous foraging, a concern within the sciences of behavioral ecology, social anthropology, and human behavioral ecology; as well as robotics, artificial intelligence, and artificial life.

## Societal Impact and Issues

As autonomous robots have grown in ability and technical levels, there has been increasing societal awareness and news coverage of the latest advances, and also some of the philosophical issues, economic effects, and societal impacts that arise from the roles and activities of autonomous robots.

Elon Musk, a prominent business executive and billionaire has warned for years of the possible hazards and pitfalls of autonomous robots; however, his own company is one of the most prominent companies that is trying to devise new advanced technologies in this area.

In 2021, a United Nations group of government experts, known as the Convention on Certain Conventional Weapons – Group of Governmental Experts on Lethal Autonomous Weapons Systems, held a conference to highlight the ethical concerns which arise from the increasingly advanced technology for autonomous robots to wield weapons and to play a military role.

## Technical Development

### Early Robots

The first autonomous robots were known as Elmer and Elsie, constructed in the late 1940s by W. Grey Walter. They were the first robots programmed to "think" the way biological brains do and were meant to have free will. Elmer and Elsie were often labeled as tortoises because of how they were shaped and the manner in which they moved. They were capable of phototaxis, the movement that occurs in response to light stimulus.

### Space Probes

The Mars rovers MER-A and MER-B (now known as Spirit rover and Opportunity rover) found the position of the Sun and navigated their own routes to destinations, on the fly, by:

- Mapping the surface with 3D vision.
- Computing safe and unsafe areas on the surface within that field of vision.
- Computing optimal paths across the safe area towards the desired destination.

- Driving along the calculated route.
- Repeating this cycle until either the destination is reached, or there is no known path to the destination.

The planned ESA Rover, Rosalind Franklin rover, is capable of vision based relative localisation and absolute localisation to autonomously navigate safe and efficient trajectories to targets by:

- Reconstructing 3D models of the terrain surrounding the Rover using a pair of stereo cameras.
- Determining safe and unsafe areas of the terrain and the general "difficulty" for the Rover to navigate the terrain.
- Computing efficient paths across the safe area towards the desired destination.
- Driving the Rover along the planned path.
- Building up a navigation map of all previous navigation data.

During the final NASA Sample Return Robot Centennial Challenge in 2016, a rover, named Cataglyphis, successfully demonstrated fully autonomous navigation, decision-making, and sample detection, retrieval, and return capabilities. The rover relied on a fusion of measurements from inertial sensors, wheel encoders, Lidar, and camera for navigation and mapping, instead of using GPS or magnetometers. During the 2-hour challenge, Cataglyphis traversed over 2.6 km and returned five different samples to its starting position.

### General-Use Autonomous Robots

**Fig: The Seekur and MDARS Robots Demonstrate their Autonomous Navigation and Security Capabilities at an Airbase**

**Fig: Sophia, a Robot Known for Human-Like Appearance and Interactions**

**Fig: AMR Transfer Cart for In-Factory Transfer Needs**

The Seekur robot was the first commercially available robot to demonstrate MDARS-like capabilities for general use by airports, utility plants, corrections facilities and Homeland Security.

The DARPA Grand Challenge and DARPA Urban Challenge have encouraged development of even more autonomous capabilities for ground vehicles, while this has been the demonstrated goal for aerial robots since 1990 as part of the AUVSI International Aerial Robotics Competition. AMR transfer carts developed by Seyiton are used to transfer loads of up to 1500 kilograms inside factories.

Between 2013 and 2017, TotalEnergies has held the ARGOS Challenge to develop the first autonomous robot for oil and gas production sites. The robots had to face adverse outdoor conditions such as rain, wind and extreme temperatures.

Some significant current robots include:

- Sophia is an autonomous robot that is known for its human-like appearance and behavior compared to previous robotic variants. As of 2018, Sophia's architecture includes scripting software, a chat system, and OpenCog, an AI system designed for general reasoning. Sophia imitates human gestures and facial expressions and is able to answer certain questions and to make simple conversations on predefined topics (e.g. on the weather). The AI program analyses conversations and extracts data that allows it to improve responses in the future.
- Nine other robot humanoid "siblings" who were also created by Hanson Robotics. Fellow Hanson robots are Alice, Albert Einstein Hubo, BINA48, Han, Jules, Professor Einstein, Philip K. Dick Android, Zeno, and Joey Chaos. Around 2019–20, Hanson released "Little Sophia" as a companion that could teach children how to code, including support for Python, Blockly, and Raspberry Pi.

### Military Autonomous Robots

Lethal autonomous weapons (LAWs) are a type of autonomous robot military system that can independently search for and engage targets based on programmed constraints and descriptions. LAWs are also known as lethal autonomous weapon systems (LAWS), autonomous weapon systems (AWS), robotic weapons, killer robots or slaughterbots. LAWs may operate in the air, on land, on water, under water, or in space. The autonomy of current systems as of 2018 was restricted in the sense that a human gives the final command to attack – though there are exceptions with certain "defensive" systems.

- UGV Interoperability Profile (UGV IOP), Robotics and Autonomous Systems – Ground IOP (RAS-G IOP), was originally a research program started by the United States Department of Defense (DoD) to organize and maintain open architecture interoperability standards for Unmanned Ground Vehicles (UGV). The IOP was initially created by U.S. Army Robotic Systems Joint Project Office (RS JPO):
- In October 2019, Textron and Howe & Howe unveiled their Ripsaw M5 vehicle, and on 9 January 2020, the U.S. Army awarded them a contract

for the Robotic Combat Vehicle-Medium (RCV-M) program. Four Ripsaw M5 prototypes are to be delivered and used in a company-level to determine the feasibility of integrating unmanned vehicles into ground combat operations in late 2021. It can reach speeds of more than 40 mph (64 km/h), has a combat weight of 10.5 tons and a payload capacity of 8,000 lb (3,600 kg). The RCV-M is armed with a 30 mm autocannon and a pair of anti-tank missiles. The standard armor package can withstand 12.7×108mm rounds, with optional add-on armor increasing weight to up to 20 tons. If disabled, it will retain the ability to shoot, with its sensors and radio uplink prioritized to continue transmitting as its primary function.

- Crusher is a 13,200-pound (6,000 kg) autonomous off-road Unmanned Ground Combat Vehicle developed by researchers at the Carnegie Mellon University's National Robotics Engineering Center for DARPA. It is a follow-up on the previous Spinner vehicle. DARPA's technical name for the Crusher is Unmanned Ground Combat Vehicle and Perceptor Integration System, and the whole project is known by the acronym UPI, which stands for Unmanned Ground Combat Vehicle PerceptOR Integration.
- CATS Warrior will be an autonomous wingman drone capable of take-off & landing from land & in sea from an aircraft carrier, it will team up with the existing fighter platforms of the IAF like Tejas, Su-30 MKI and Jaguar which will act like its mothership.
- The Warrior is primarily envisioned for the Indian Air Force use and a similar, smaller version will be designed for the Indian Navy. It would be controlled by the mothership and accomplish tasks such as scouting, absorbing enemy fire, attacking the targets if necessary with its internal & external pylons weapons or sacrifice itself by crashing into the target.
- The SGR-A1 is a type of autonomous sentry gun that was jointly developed by Samsung Techwin (now Hanwha Aerospace) and Korea University to assist South Korean troops in the Korean Demilitarized Zone. It is widely considered as the first unit of its kind to have an integrated system that includes surveillance, tracking, firing, and voice recognition. While units of the SGR-A1 have been reportedly deployed, their number is unknown due to the project being "highly classified".

## Types of Robots

### Humanoid

Tesla Robot and NVIDIA GROOT are humanoid robots. Humanoids are machines that are designed to mimic the human form in appearance and behavior. These robots typically have a head, torso, arms, and legs, making them look like humans.

### Delivery Robot

**Fig: A Food Delivery Robot**

### Charging Robot

An automatic charging robot, unveiled on July 27, 2022, is an arm-shaped robot to charge an electric vehicle. It has been running a pilot operation at Hyundai Motor Group's headquarters since 2021. VISION AI System based on deep learning technology has been applied. When an electric vehicle is parked in front of the charger, the robot arm recognizes the charger of the electric vehicle and derives coordinates. And automatically insert a connector into the electric car and operate fast charging. The robot arm is configured in a vertical multi-joint structure so that it can be applied to chargers at different locations for each vehicle. In addition, waterproof and dustproof functions are applied.

### Construction Robots

Construction robots are used directly on job sites and perform work such as building, material handling, earthmoving, and surveillance.

### Research and Education Mobile Robots

Research and education mobile robots are mainly used during a prototyping phase in the process of building full scale robots. They are a scaled down version of bigger robots with the same types of sensors, kinematics and software stack (e.g. ROS). They are often extendable and provide comfortable programming interface and development tools. Next to full scale robot prototyping they are also used for education, especially at university level, where more and more labs about programming autonomous vehicles are being introduced.

## Legislation

In March 2016, a bill was introduced in Washington, D.C., allowing pilot ground robotic deliveries. The program was to take place from September 15 through the end of December 2017. The robots were limited to a weight of 50 pounds unloaded and a maximum speed of 10 miles per hour. In case the robot stopped moving because of malfunction the company was required to remove it from the streets within 24 hours. There were allowed only 5 robots to be tested per company at a time. A 2017 version of the Personal Delivery Device Act bill was under review as of March 2017.

In February 2017, a bill was passed in the US state of Virginia via the House bill, HB2016, and the Senate bill, SB1207, that will allow autonomous delivery robots to travel on sidewalks and use crosswalks statewide beginning on July 1, 2017. The robots will be limited to a maximum speed of 10 mph and a maximum weight of 50 pounds. In the states of Idaho and Florida there are also talks about passing the similar legislature.

It has been discussed that robots with similar characteristics to invalid carriages (e.g. 10 mph maximum, limited battery life) might be a workaround for certain classes of applications. If the robot was sufficiently intelligent and able to recharge itself using the existing electric vehicle (EV) charging infrastructure it would only need minimal supervision and a single arm with low dexterity might be enough to enable this function if its visual systems had enough resolution.

In November 2017, the San Francisco Board of Supervisors announced that companies would need to get a city permit in order to test these robots. In addition, the Board banned sidewalk delivery robots from making non-research deliveries.

## 4.3.3 Autonomous Underwater Vehicle

An autonomous underwater vehicle (AUV) is a robot that travels underwater without requiring continuous input from an operator. AUVs constitute part of a larger group of undersea systems known as unmanned underwater vehicles, a classification that includes non-autonomous remotely operated underwater vehicles (ROVs) – controlled and powered from the surface by an operator/pilot via an umbilical or using remote control. In military applications an AUV is more often referred to as an unmanned undersea vehicle (UUV). Underwater gliders are a subclass of AUVs. Homing torpedoes can also be considered as a subclass of AUVs.

## History

The first AUV was developed at the Applied Physics Laboratory at the University of Washington as early as 1957 by Stan Murphy, Bob Francois and later on, Terry Ewart. The "Self-Propelled Underwater Research Vehicle", or SPURV, was used to study diffusion, acoustic transmission, and submarine wakes. Other early AUVs were developed at the Massachusetts Institute of Technology in the 1970s. One of these is on display in the Hart Nautical Gallery in MIT. At the same time, AUVs were also developed in the Soviet Union (although this was not commonly known until much later).

## Applications

This type of underwater vehicles has recently become an attractive alternative for underwater search and exploration since they are cheaper than manned vehicles. Over the past years, there have been abundant attempts to develop underwater vehicles to meet the challenge of exploration and extraction programs in the oceans. Recently, researchers have focused on the development of AUVs for long-term data collection in oceanography and coastal management.

### Commercial

The oil and gas industry uses AUVs to make detailed maps of the seafloor before they start building subsea infrastructure; pipelines and sub sea completions can be installed in the most cost effective manner with minimum disruption to the environment. The AUV allows survey companies to conduct precise surveys of areas where traditional bathymetric surveys would be less effective or too costly. Also, post-lay pipe surveys are now possible, which includes pipeline inspection. The use of AUVs for pipeline inspection and inspection of underwater man-made structures is becoming more common. There also is development of AUVs for potential seabed mining and/or harvesting of polymetallic nodule rocks.

### Research

Scientists use AUVs to study lakes, the ocean, and the ocean floor. A variety of sensors can be affixed to AUVs to measure the concentration of various elements or compounds, the absorption or reflection of light, and the presence of microscopic life. Examples include conductivity-temperature-depth sensors (CTDs), fluorometers, and pH sensors. Additionally, AUVs can be configured as tow-vehicles to deliver customized sensor packages to specific locations.

**Fig: A University of South Florida researcher deploys Tavros02, a solar-powered "tweeting" AUV (SAUV)**

The Applied Physics Lab at the University of Washington has been creating iterations of its Seaglider AUV platform since the 1950s. Though the Seaglider was originally designed for oceanographic research, in recent years it has seen much interest from organizations such as the U.S. Navy or the oil and gas industry. The fact that these autonomous gliders are relatively inexpensive to manufacture and operate is indicative of most AUV platforms that will see success in myriad applications.

An example of an AUV interacting directly with its environment is the Crown-Of-Thorns Starfish Robot (COTSBot) created by the Queensland University of Technology (QUT). The COTSBot finds and eradicates crown-of-thorns starfish (Acanthaster planci), a species that damages the Great Barrier Reef. It uses a neural network to identify the starfish and injects bile salts to kill it.

The Queensland University of Technology has also developed the RangerBot AUV as a predecessor to the COTSBot to help monitor the Great Barrier Reef and reefs around the world. The RangerBot was developed for single person deployment and offers real-time on-board vision for navigation, obstacle detection, and management tasks.

## Hobby

Many roboticists construct AUVs as a hobby. Several competitions exist which allow these homemade AUVs to compete against each other while accomplishing objectives. Like their commercial brethren, these AUVs can be fitted with cameras, lights, or sonar. As a consequence of limited resources and inexperience, hobbyist AUVs can rarely compete with commercial models on operational depth, durability, or sophistication. Finally, these hobby AUVs are usually not oceangoing, being operated most of the time in pools or lake beds. A simple AUV can be constructed from a microcontroller, PVC pressure housing, automatic door lock actuator, syringes, and a DPDT relay. Some participants in competitions create designs that rely on open-source software.

## Illegal Drug Traffic

Submarines that travel autonomously to a destination by means of GPS navigation have been made by illegal drug traffickers.

## Air Crash Investigations

Autonomous underwater vehicles, for example AUV ABYSS, have been used to find wreckage of missing airplanes, e.g. Air France Flight 447, and the Bluefin-21 AUV was used in the search for Malaysia Airlines Flight 370.

## Military Applications

Fig: MK 18 MOD 1 Swordfish UUV

Fig: Mk 18 Mod 2 Kingfish UUV

Fig: Kingfish UUV Launch

The U.S. Navy Unmanned Undersea Vehicle (UUV) Master Plan identified the following UUV missions in 2004:

- Intelligence, surveillance, and reconnaissance.
- Mine countermeasures.
- Anti-submarine warfare.
- Inspection/identification.
- Oceanography.
- Communication/navigation network nodes.
- Payload delivery.
- Information operations.
- Time-critical strikes.

By 2014, the Navy Master Plan divided all UUVs into four classes:

- Man-portable vehicle class: 25–100 lb displacement; 10–20 hours endurance; launched from small water craft manually (i.e., REMUS; Mk 18 Mod 1 Swordfish UUV).
- Lightweight vehicle class: up to 500 lb displacement, 20–40 hours endurance; launched from RHIB using launch-retriever system or by cranes from surface ships (i.e., Mk 18 Mod 2 Kingfish UUV).
- Heavyweight vehicle class: up to 3,000 lb displacement, 40–80 hours endurance, launched from submarines.
- Large vehicle class: up to 10 long tons displacement; launched from surface ships and submarines.

In 2019, the Navy ordered five Orca UUVs, its first acquisition of unmanned submarines with combat capability.

In 2022–23, during the Russian invasion of Ukraine, Ukrainian armed forces made a number of advancements in uncrewed surface vessel (USV) technology using autonomous control architecture, sometimes with mid-mission telerobotic updates. Employed in a multi-USV attack on Russian naval vessels at the Sevastopol Naval Base in October 2022 and the Russian naval facilities at Novorossiysk in November 2022, and in August 2023 there were additional attacks on Novorossiysk. The Russian navy adapted both defences and fleet strategy as a result of these attacks, such that, by January 2024, the Ukrainian navy was developing AUVs to increase offensive capability against improved Russian USV defenses.

## Vehicle Designs

Hundreds of different AUVs have been designed over the past 50 or so years, but only a few companies sell vehicles in any significant numbers. There are around 10 companies that sell AUVs on the international market, including Kongsberg

Maritime, HII (formerly Hydroid, and previously owned by Kongsberg Maritime)), Bluefin Robotics, Teledyne Gavia (previously known as Hafmynd), International Submarine Engineering (ISE) Ltd, Atlas Elektronik, RTsys, MSubs and OceanScan.

Vehicles range in size from man portable lightweight AUVs to large diameter vehicles of over 10 metres length. Large vehicles have advantages in terms of endurance and sensor payload capacity; smaller vehicles benefit significantly from lower logistics (for example: support vessel footprint; launch and recovery systems).

Some manufacturers have benefited from domestic government sponsorship including Bluefin and Kongsberg. The market is effectively split into three areas: scientific (including universities and research agencies), commercial offshore (offshore energy, marine minerals etc.) and defence related applications (mine countermeasures, battle space preparation). The majority of these roles utilize a similar design and operate in a cruise (torpedo-type) mode. They collect data while following a preplanned route at speeds between 1 and 4 knots.

Commercially available AUVs include various designs, such as the small REMUS 100 AUV originally developed by Woods Hole Oceanographic Institution in the US and now produced commercially by HII; the HUGIN Family of AUVs comprising HUGIN, HUGIN Edge, HUGIN Superior and HUGIN Endurance developed by Kongsberg Maritime and Norwegian Defence Research Establishment; the Bluefin Robotics 12-and-21-inch-diameter (300 and 530 mm) vehicles; the ISE Ltd. Explorer; Cellula Robotics' Solus LR; the RT Sys Comet and NemoSens AUVs; Teledyne's Gavia, Osprey and SeaRaptor; and the L3 Harris Ocean Server Iver range of AUVs.

Most AUVs fall into the survey class or cruising AUVs, in a cylindrical or torpedo shape with a powered propeller. This is seen as the best compromise between size, usable volume, hydrodynamic efficiency and ease of handling. There are some vehicles that make use of a modular design, enabling components to be changed easily by the operators. Some recent developments move away from the traditional cylindrical shape in favour of other arrangements such as Saab's Sabretooth hybrid R/AUV or the recently launched HUGIN Edge. These either optimise the shape according to the operational requirements (Sabretooth) or to benefit from low drag hydrodynamic performance (HUGIN Edge).

The market has matured since 2010 with greater emphasis on data than on vehicle characteristics. Operators are more technically aware and the utilisation of AUVs has increased commensurately. More operators use their systems autonomously, rather than supervising the vehicles using an acoustic link. Consequently, on-board processing and in-mission autonomy have become more important features for AUVs. Most AUVs have what is considered navigational or event-based autonomy. They will follow a geographic mission plan with distinct events to operate sensors, change course or return to the surface. Some AUVs have adaptive autonomy, for example the ability to adjust course to avoid obstacles along the planned route. The current state of the art is a vehicle that collects, processes and acts on the data it has acquired without operator input.

As of 2008, a new class of AUVs is being developed, which mimics designs found in nature. Although most are currently in their experimental stages, these biomimetic (or bionic) vehicles are able to achieve higher degrees of efficiency in propulsion and maneuverability by copying successful designs in nature. Two such vehicles are Festo's AquaJelly (AUV) and the EvoLogics BOSS Manta Ray.

### Sensors

AUVs carry sensors to navigate autonomously and map features of the ocean. Typical sensors include compasses, depth sensors, sidescan and other sonars, magnetometers, thermistors and conductivity probes. Some AUVs are outfitted with biological sensors including fluorometers (also known as chlorophyll sensors), turbidity sensors, and sensors to measure pH, and amounts of dissolved oxygen. A demonstration at Monterey Bay, in California, in September 2006, showed that a 21-inch-diameter (530 mm) AUV can tow a 400-foot-long (120 m) hydrophone array while maintaining a 6-knot (11 km/h) cruising speed.

### Navigation

Radio waves cannot penetrate water very far, so as soon as an AUV dives it loses its GPS signal. Therefore, a standard way for AUVs to navigate underwater is through dead reckoning. Navigation can, however, be improved by using an underwater acoustic positioning system. When operating within a net of sea floor-deployed baseline transponders, this is known as LBL navigation. When a surface reference such as a support ship is available, ultra-short baseline (USBL) or short-baseline (SBL) positioning is used to calculate where the sub-sea vehicle is relative to the known (GPS) position of the surface craft by means of acoustic range and bearing measurements.

To improve estimation of its position, and reduce errors in dead reckoning (which grow over time), the AUV can also surface and take its own GPS fix. Between position fixes and for precise maneuvering, an Inertial Navigation System on board the AUV calculates through dead reckoning the AUV position, acceleration, and velocity. Estimates can be made using data from an Inertial Measurement Unit, and can be improved by adding a Doppler Velocity Log (DVL), which measures the rate of travel over the sea/lake floor. Typically, a pressure sensor measures the vertical position (vehicle depth), although depth and altitude can also be obtained from DVL measurements. These observations are filtered to determine a final navigation solution.

### Propulsion

There are a couple of propulsion techniques for AUVs. Some of them use a brushed or brush-less electric motor, gearbox, Lip seal, and a propeller which may be surrounded by a nozzle or not. All of these parts embedded in the AUV construction are involved in propulsion. Other vehicles use a thruster unit to maintain the modularity. Depending on the need, the thruster may be equipped with a nozzle for propeller collision protection or to reduce noise submission, or it may be equipped with a direct drive thruster to keep the efficiency at the highest level and the noises at the lowest level. Advanced AUV thrusters have a redundant shaft sealing system to guarantee a proper seal of the robot even if one of the seals fails during the mission.

Underwater gliders do not directly propel themselves. By changing their buoyancy and trim, they repeatedly sink and ascend; airfoil "wings" convert this up-and-down motion to forward motion. The change of buoyancy is typically done through the use of a pump that can take in or push out water. The vehicle's pitch can be controlled by moving the center of mass of the vehicle. For Slocum gliders this is done internally by moving the batteries, which are mounted on a screw. Because of their low speed and low-power electronics, the energy required to cycle trim states is far less than for regular AUVs, and gliders can have endurances of months and transoceanic ranges.

### Communications

Since radio waves do not propagate well under water, many AUV's incorporate acoustic modems to enable remote command and control. These modems typically utilize proprietary communications techniques and modulation schemes. In 2017 NATO ratified the ANEP-87 JANUS standard for subsea communications. This standard allows for 80 BPS communications links with flexible and extensible message formatting. Alternative communication techniques are being explored, including optical, inductive and RF based techniques, which may be combined in a multi-modal solutions. Evaluations are also being conducted on novel communication techniques which are able to utilize the infrastructure as a communication path to provide alternative communication paths and opportunities from the vehicles.

### Power

Most AUVs in use today are powered by rechargeable batteries (lithium ion, lithium polymer, nickel metal hydride etc.), and are implemented with some form of battery management system. Some vehicles use primary batteries which provide perhaps twice the endurance—at a substantial extra cost per mission. Previously some systems used aluminum based semi-fuel cells, but these require substantial maintenance, require expensive refills and produce waste product that must be handled safely. An emerging trend is to combine different battery and power systems with supercapacitors.

## 4.4 CRIMINAL JUSTICE AND LAW ENFORCEMENT

The integration of Artificial Intelligence (AI) in criminal justice and law enforcement has significantly enhanced investigative processes, crime prevention strategies, and judicial decision-making. However, as AI-driven systems become more complex, concerns regarding their transparency and accountability have arisen. Explainable AI (XAI) seeks to address these challenges by ensuring that AI decisions are interpretable, unbiased, and justifiable. In the context of law enforcement and the legal system, the ability to understand and trust AI-driven decisions is crucial for ethical considerations, fairness, and public confidence. Explainable AI is critical for the responsible deployment of AI in criminal justice and law enforcement. By enhancing transparency, mitigating bias, and ensuring regulatory compliance, XAI fosters trust in AI-driven decision-making. The integration of explainability techniques in predictive policing, facial recognition, risk assessment, and forensic analysis strengthens the ethical and legal foundation of AI applications in law enforcement. As AI continues to shape the future of criminal justice, adopting XAI will be essential in upholding fairness, accountability, and the protection of civil rights.

### 4.4.1 The Role of AI in Criminal Justice and Law Enforcement

AI is widely used in criminal justice and law enforcement for various applications, including predictive policing, facial recognition, criminal risk assessment, and forensic analysis. Law enforcement agencies leverage AI to analyze crime patterns and allocate resources more efficiently. In the judicial system, AI models assist in determining sentencing recommendations, assessing parole eligibility, and evaluating potential biases in legal decisions. AI also plays a crucial role in cybersecurity, detecting fraud, and preventing financial crimes. However, the opaque nature of many AI models raises concerns about their fairness, potential biases, and the legality of their recommendations.

### 4.4.2 The Importance of Explainability in AI for Law Enforcement

Explainability in AI ensures that law enforcement agencies and judicial systems can justify AI-driven decisions. Unlike traditional rule-based systems, modern AI models often rely on deep learning techniques, which can be difficult to interpret. Without explainability, there is a risk of AI perpetuating biases, making arbitrary decisions, or violating civil rights. Transparent AI models allow for better oversight, helping officers, judges, and policymakers assess the reasoning behind AI-generated predictions. Explainable AI also strengthens public trust by demonstrating that law enforcement decisions are based on fair and understandable criteria.

### 4.4.3 Applications of XAI in Criminal Justice and Legal Systems

XAI is applied across multiple areas of criminal justice and law enforcement. In predictive policing, explainable models provide insights into why certain areas are flagged for higher crime risk, ensuring that AI recommendations do not lead to over-policing specific communities. In facial recognition, XAI helps identify the features AI algorithms rely on, reducing the risk of wrongful arrests due to misidentification. AI-driven risk assessment tools used in parole and sentencing benefit from explainability by making sure that factors influencing decisions are transparent and justifiable. Additionally, forensic AI tools used to analyze evidence, such as DNA matching and fingerprint recognition, gain credibility when their decision-making processes are interpretable.

### 4.4.4 Techniques for Achieving Explainability in Criminal Justice AI

Several methods enhance the interpretability of AI models used in criminal justice. Feature importance techniques such as SHAP (Shapley Additive Explanations) and LIME (Local Interpretable Model-agnostic Explanations) highlight the most influential factors in AI decision-making. Decision trees and rule-based models provide inherently interpretable structures, making them preferable for legal applications. Counterfactual explanations demonstrate how altering certain variables would change AI recommendations, helping legal professionals understand the reasoning behind specific decisions. Hybrid models that combine deep learning with transparent architectures also contribute to improving AI interpretability in law enforcement.

### 4.4.5 Ethical and Legal Considerations in AI-Driven Law Enforcement

Ethical concerns in AI-driven law enforcement primarily revolve around fairness, bias, and accountability. AI models trained on biased historical data may reinforce existing racial, gender, or socioeconomic disparities in policing and sentencing. Explainable AI plays a crucial role in identifying and mitigating these biases, ensuring that AI-driven decisions do not disproportionately impact specific communities. Legal frameworks such as the European Union's General Data Protection Regulation (GDPR) and the U.S. Constitution emphasize the importance of due process and accountability in automated decision-making. By incorporating XAI, law enforcement agencies can ensure compliance with legal standards and uphold the principles of justice and fairness.

### 4.4.6 Challenges in Implementing XAI in Criminal Justice

Despite its benefits, implementing XAI in criminal justice presents several challenges. One significant issue is the trade-off between model complexity and interpretability. Deep learning models often achieve high accuracy but lack transparency, whereas simpler models may be more explainable but less effective in crime detection. Additionally, ensuring data privacy while making AI systems interpretable is a difficult task, as law enforcement agencies handle sensitive information. Another challenge is resistance from traditional law enforcement structures that may be hesitant to adopt AI-driven solutions due to concerns about reliability and operational integration. Furthermore, standardizing explainability methods across different AI applications in criminal justice remains an ongoing research challenge.

### 4.4.7 Future Directions for XAI in Law Enforcement and Criminal Justice

The future of XAI in criminal justice lies in the development of more interpretable deep learning models that balance accuracy and transparency. Research into causality-based AI explanations will help move beyond correlation-based models, providing more meaningful insights into crime patterns and risk assessments. The introduction of human-in-the-loop AI systems, where law enforcement officers and legal professionals interact with AI tools to validate and refine decisions, will further improve trust and usability. Additionally, policymakers and AI developers must collaborate to create standardized guidelines for explainability in law enforcement applications, ensuring fairness, accountability, and compliance with legal frameworks.

## 4.5 EDUCATION AND LEARNING ANALYTICS

Artificial Intelligence (AI) is playing an increasingly significant role in education and learning analytics by personalizing learning experiences, predicting student performance, and assisting educators in decision-making. AI-driven systems analyze vast amounts of educational data to optimize learning paths, provide recommendations, and identify students at risk of falling behind.

However, many AI models in education operate as "black boxes," making it difficult for educators, students, and policymakers to understand the rationale behind their recommendations. Explainable AI (XAI) seeks to address this issue by making AI models more transparent, interpretable, and accountable.

Explainable AI is essential for the responsible use of AI in education and learning analytics. By enhancing transparency, mitigating biases, and ensuring regulatory compliance, XAI fosters trust in AI-driven educational tools. The integration of explainability techniques in personalized learning, student performance prediction, and automated assessment improves decision-making and promotes fairness in education. As AI continues to shape the future of learning, adopting XAI will be crucial in creating an equitable and effective educational landscape.

### 4.5.1 The Need for Explainability in AI-Powered Education

Explainability in AI is crucial in educational settings for multiple reasons. First, it builds trust among educators, students, and administrators who rely on AI-driven insights for decision-making. Second, explainable models help ensure fairness and reduce biases in AI-based assessments and grading systems. Third, regulatory and ethical considerations require that educational AI models provide explanations for their predictions, particularly when student performance and opportunities are at stake. By enhancing explainability, XAI empowers stakeholders to make informed decisions and promotes responsible AI usage in education.

### 4.5.2 Applications of XAI in Learning Analytics

Explainable AI has a wide range of applications in learning analytics. One primary use is in personalized learning, where AI systems recommend tailored content to students based on their learning styles, progress, and past performance. By making these recommendations transparent, educators and students can understand why certain resources are suggested. AI also plays a role in early warning systems, predicting students at risk of academic failure. XAI allows educators to see the factors contributing to these predictions and intervene effectively. Furthermore, automated grading and assessment tools benefit from explainability, ensuring that AI-generated scores are justified and unbiased. XAI also aids in curriculum development by analyzing the effectiveness of teaching methodologies and suggesting improvements.

### 4.5.3 Techniques for Explainability in Educational AI Systems

Several methods enhance explainability in AI models used in education. Feature importance techniques such as SHAP (Shapley Additive Explanations) and LIME (Local Interpretable Model-agnostic Explanations) help educators understand which factors contribute most to AI predictions. Decision trees and rule-based models offer interpretable structures that are easy for non-technical users to comprehend. Counterfactual explanations, which show how changes in student performance metrics might alter AI recommendations, are particularly useful for educators. Additionally, hybrid models that combine deep learning with transparent decision-making elements can improve AI interpretability in education.

### 4.5.4 Trust and Fairness in AI-Based Learning Analytics

Building trust in AI-powered learning analytics requires ensuring that models are fair, unbiased, and accountable. AI models trained on historical data may inherit biases related to socioeconomic status, gender, or ethnicity, leading to unfair treatment of certain student groups. Explainable AI helps identify and mitigate these biases by providing insights into how models arrive at their decisions.

Moreover, transparency in AI recommendations allows educators and students to question, validate, and refine AI-driven insights, fostering a culture of trust and collaboration in education.

### 4.5.5 Ethical and Regulatory Considerations in XAI for Education

Ethical and regulatory concerns in AI-driven education systems center around transparency, accountability, and student privacy. Regulations such as the General Data Protection Regulation (GDPR) mandate that automated decisions affecting individuals must be explainable. Educational institutions must ensure that AI-powered assessments and recommendations do not disadvantage students unfairly. Additionally, data privacy is a critical concern, as AI systems rely on student data for training. XAI techniques should be designed to safeguard sensitive information while maintaining transparency. Educators and policymakers must work together to establish guidelines that balance AI innovation with ethical considerations in education.

### 4.5.6 Challenges in Implementing XAI in Education

Despite its benefits, implementing XAI in education poses challenges. One major issue is the trade-off between AI model complexity and interpretability. Deep learning models can provide highly accurate predictions, but their decision-making processes are often difficult to understand. Conversely, simpler models offer greater transparency but may lack predictive accuracy. Additionally, integrating XAI into existing educational technologies requires technical expertise and resource investment. Resistance from educators who may not fully understand or trust AI-driven insights can also hinder adoption. Moreover, standardizing explainability methods across diverse educational settings remains an ongoing challenge.

### 4.5.7 Future Directions for XAI in Learning Analytics

The future of XAI in education lies in developing more sophisticated and interpretable AI models. Researchers are exploring new techniques, such as causality-based explanations, which go beyond correlation-based predictions to provide deeper insights into student learning patterns. The integration of human-in-the-loop AI systems, where educators actively interact with AI-generated recommendations, will enhance explainability and usability. Additionally, AI-driven chatbots and virtual tutors with built-in explainability features will provide students with more transparent guidance. Policymakers and educational institutions must collaborate to create standardized frameworks for explainability in AI-powered learning analytics.

CHAPTER 5

# Challenges in Explainable AI

## 5.1 EXPLAINING COMPLEX MODELS (E.G., DEEP LEARNING, ENSEMBLES)

### 5.1.1 Deep Learning

Deep learning is a subset of machine learning that focuses on utilizing neural networks to perform tasks such as classification, regression, and representation learning. The field takes inspiration from biological neuroscience and is centered around stacking artificial neurons into layers and "training" them to process data. The adjective "deep" refers to the use of multiple layers (ranging from three to several hundred or thousands) in the network. Methods used can be either supervised, semi-supervised or unsupervised.

Some common deep learning network architectures include fully connected networks, deep belief networks, recurrent neural networks, convolutional neural networks, generative adversarial networks, transformers, and neural radiance fields. These architectures have been applied to fields including computer vision, speech recognition, natural language processing, machine translation, bioinformatics, drug design, medical image analysis, climate science, material inspection and board game programs, where they have produced results comparable to and in some cases surpassing human expert performance.

Early forms of neural networks were inspired by information processing and distributed communication nodes in biological systems, particularly the human brain. However, current neural networks do not intend to model the brain function of organisms, and are generally seen as low-quality models for that purpose.

Most modern deep learning models are based on multi-layered neural networks such as convolutional neural networks and transformers, although they can also include propositional formulas or latent variables organized layer-wise in deep generative models such as the nodes in deep belief networks and deep Boltzmann machines.

Fundamentally, deep learning refers to a class of machine learning algorithms in which a hierarchy of layers is used to transform input data into a progressively more abstract and composite representation. For example, in an image recognition model, the raw input may be an image (represented as a tensor of pixels). The first representational layer may attempt to identify basic shapes such as lines and circles, the second layer may compose and encode arrangements of edges, the third layer may encode a nose and eyes, and the fourth layer may recognize that the image contains a face.

Importantly, a deep learning process can learn which features to optimally place at which level on its own. Prior to deep learning, machine learning techniques often involved hand-crafted feature engineering to transform the data into a more suitable representation for a classification algorithm to operate on. In the deep learning approach, features are not hand-crafted and the model discovers useful feature representations from the data automatically. This does not eliminate the need for hand-tuning; for example, varying numbers of layers and layer sizes can provide different degrees of abstraction.

Deep learning architectures can be constructed with a greedy layer-by-layer method. Deep learning helps to disentangle these abstractions and pick out which features improve performance.

Deep learning algorithms can be applied to unsupervised learning tasks. This is an important benefit because unlabeled data are more abundant than the labeled data. Examples of deep structures that can be trained in an unsupervised manner are deep belief networks.

The term Deep Learning was introduced to the machine learning community by Rina Dechter in 1986, and to artificial neural networks by Igor Aizenberg and colleagues in 2000, in the context of Boolean threshold neurons. Although the history of its appearance is apparently more complicated.

## Interpretations

Deep neural networks are generally interpreted in terms of the universal approximation theorem or probabilistic inference.

The classic universal approximation theorem concerns the capacity of feedforward neural networks with a single hidden layer of finite size to approximate continuous functions. In 1989, the first proof was published by George Cybenko for sigmoid activation functions and was generalised to feed-forward multi-layer architectures in 1991 by Kurt Hornik. Recent work also showed that universal approximation also holds for non-bounded activation functions such as Kunihiko Fukushima's rectified linear unit.

The universal approximation theorem for deep neural networks concerns the capacity of networks with bounded width but the depth is allowed to grow. Lu et al. proved that if the width of a deep neural network with ReLU activation is strictly larger than the input dimension, then the network can approximate any Lebesgue integrable function; if the width is smaller or equal to the input dimension, then a deep neural network is not a universal approximator.

The probabilistic interpretation derives from the field of machine learning. It features inference, as well as the optimization concepts of training and testing, related to fitting and generalization, respectively. More specifically, the probabilistic interpretation considers the activation nonlinearity as a cumulative distribution function. The probabilistic interpretation led to the introduction of dropout as regularizer in neural networks. The probabilistic interpretation was introduced by researchers including Hopfield, Widrow and Narendra and popularized in surveys such as the one by Bishop.

## History

### Before 1980

There are two types of artificial neural network (ANN): feedforward neural network (FNN) or multilayer perceptron (MLP) and recurrent neural networks (RNN). RNNs have cycles in their connectivity structure, FNNs don't. In the 1920s, Wilhelm Lenz and Ernst Ising created the Ising model which is essentially a non-learning RNN architecture consisting of neuron-like threshold elements. In 1972, Shun'ichi Amari made this architecture adaptive. His learning RNN was republished by John Hopfield in 1982. Other early recurrent neural networks were published by Kaoru Nakano in 1971. Already in 1948, Alan Turing produced work on "Intelligent Machinery" that was not published in his lifetime, containing "ideas related to artificial evolution and learning RNNs".

Frank Rosenblatt (1958) proposed the perceptron, an MLP with 3 layers: an input layer, a hidden layer with randomized weights that did not learn, and an output layer. He later published a 1962 book that also introduced variants and computer experiments, including a version with four-layer perceptrons "with adaptive preterminal networks" where the last two layers have learned weights (here he credits H. D. Block and B. W. Knight). The book cites an earlier network by R. D. Joseph (1960) "functionally equivalent to a variation of" this four-layer system (the book mentions Joseph over 30 times). Should Joseph therefore be considered the originator of proper adaptive multilayer perceptrons with learning hidden units? Unfortunately, the learning algorithm was not a functional one, and fell into oblivion.

The first working deep learning algorithm was the Group method of data handling, a method to train arbitrarily deep neural networks, published by Alexey Ivakhnenko and Lapa in 1965. They regarded it as a form of polynomial regression, or a generalization of Rosenblatt's perceptron. A 1971 paper described a deep network with eight layers trained by this method, which is based on layer by layer training through regression analysis. Superfluous hidden units are pruned using a separate validation set. Since the activation functions of the nodes are Kolmogorov-Gabor polynomials, these were also the first deep networks with multiplicative units or "gates".

The first deep learning multilayer perceptron trained by stochastic gradient descent was published in 1967 by Shun'ichi Amari. In computer experiments conducted by Amari's student Saito, a five layer MLP with two modifiable layers learned internal representations to classify non-linearily separable pattern classes. Subsequent developments in hardware and hyperparameter tunings have made end-to-end stochastic gradient descent the currently dominant training technique.

In 1969, Kunihiko Fukushima introduced the ReLU (rectified linear unit) activation function. The rectifier has become the most popular activation function for deep learning. Deep learning architectures for convolutional neural networks (CNNs) with convolutional layers and downsampling layers began with the Neocognitron introduced by Kunihiko Fukushima in 1979, though not trained by backpropagation.

Backpropagation is an efficient application of the chain rule derived by Gottfried Wilhelm Leibniz in 1673 to networks of differentiable nodes. The terminology "back-propagating errors" was actually introduced in 1962 by Rosenblatt, but he did not know how to implement this, although Henry J. Kelley had a continuous precursor of backpropagation in 1960 in the context of control theory. The modern form of backpropagation was first published in Seppo Linnainmaa's master thesis (1970). G.M. Ostrovski et al. republished it in 1971. Paul Werbos applied backpropagation to neural networks in 1982 (his 1974 PhD thesis, reprinted in a 1994 book, did not yet describe the algorithm). In 1986, David E. Rumelhart et al. popularised backpropagation but did not cite the original work.

### 1980s-2000s

The time delay neural network (TDNN) was introduced in 1987 by Alex Waibel to apply CNN to phoneme recognition. It used convolutions, weight sharing, and backpropagation. In 1988, Wei Zhang applied a backpropagation-trained CNN to alphabet recognition. In 1989, Yann LeCun et al. created a CNN called LeNet for recognizing handwritten ZIP codes on mail. Training required 3 days. In 1990, Wei Zhang implemented a CNN on optical computing hardware. In 1991, a CNN was applied to medical image object segmentation and breast cancer detection in mammograms. LeNet-5 (1998), a 7-level CNN by Yann LeCun et al., that classifies digits, was applied by several banks to recognize hand-written numbers on checks digitized in 32x32 pixel images.

Recurrent neural networks (RNN) were further developed in the 1980s. Recurrence is used for sequence processing, and when a recurrent network is unrolled, it mathematically resembles a deep feedforward layer. Consequently, they have similar properties and issues, and their developments had mutual influences. In RNN, two early influential works were the Jordan network (1986) and the Elman network (1990), which applied RNN to study problems in cognitive psychology.

In the 1980s, backpropagation did not work well for deep learning with long credit assignment paths. To overcome this problem, in 1991, Jürgen Schmidhuber proposed a hierarchy of RNNs pre-trained one level at a time by self-supervised learning where each RNN tries to predict its own next input, which is the next unexpected input of the RNN below. This "neural history compressor" uses predictive coding to learn internal representations at multiple self-organizing time scales. This can substantially facilitate downstream deep learning. The RNN hierarchy can be collapsed into a single RNN, by distilling a higher level chunker network into a lower level automatizer network. In 1993, a neural history compressor solved a "Very Deep Learning" task that required more than 1000 subsequent layers in an RNN unfolded in time. The "P" in ChatGPT refers to such pre-training.

Sepp Hochreiter's diploma thesis (1991) implemented the neural history compressor, and identified and analyzed the vanishing gradient problem. Hochreiter proposed recurrent residual connections to solve the vanishing gradient problem. This led to the long short-term memory (LSTM), published in 1995. LSTM can learn "very deep learning" tasks with long credit assignment paths that require memories of events that happened thousands of discrete time steps before. That LSTM was not yet the modern architecture, which required a "forget gate", introduced in 1999, which became the standard RNN architecture.

In 1991, Jürgen Schmidhuber also published adversarial neural networks that contest with each other in the form of a zero-sum game, where one network's gain is the other network's loss. The first network is a generative model that models a probability distribution over output patterns. The second network learns by gradient descent to predict the reactions of the environment to these patterns. This was called "artificial curiosity". In 2014, this principle was used in generative adversarial networks (GANs).

During 1985–1995, inspired by statistical mechanics, several architectures and methods were developed by Terry Sejnowski, Peter Dayan, Geoffrey Hinton, etc., including the Boltzmann machine, restricted Boltzmann machine, Helmholtz machine, and the wake-sleep algorithm. These were designed for unsupervised learning of deep generative models. However, those were more computationally expensive compared to backpropagation. Boltzmann machine learning algorithm, published in 1985, was briefly popular before being eclipsed by the backpropagation algorithm in 1986. (p. 112 ). A 1988 network became state of the art in protein structure prediction, an early application of deep learning to bioinformatics.

Both shallow and deep learning (e.g., recurrent nets) of ANNs for speech recognition have been explored for many years. These methods never outperformed non-uniform internal-handcrafting Gaussian mixture model/Hidden Markov model (GMM-HMM) technology based on generative models of speech trained discriminatively. Key difficulties have been analyzed, including gradient diminishing and weak temporal correlation structure in neural predictive models. Additional difficulties were the lack of training data and limited computing power.

Most speech recognition researchers moved away from neural nets to pursue generative modeling. An exception was at SRI International in the late 1990s. Funded by the US government's NSA and DARPA, SRI researched in speech and speaker recognition. The speaker recognition team led by Larry Heck reported significant success with deep neural networks in speech processing in the 1998 NIST Speaker Recognition benchmark. It was deployed in the Nuance Verifier, representing the first major industrial application of deep learning.

The principle of elevating "raw" features over hand-crafted optimization was first explored successfully in the architecture of deep autoencoder on the "raw" spectrogram or linear filter-bank features in the late 1990s, showing its superiority over the Mel-Cepstral features that contain stages of fixed transformation from spectrograms. The raw features of speech, waveforms, later produced excellent larger-scale results.

### 2000s

Neural networks entered a lull, and simpler models that use task-specific handcrafted features such as Gabor filters and support vector machines (SVMs) became the preferred choices in the 1990s and 2000s, because of artificial neural networks' computational cost and a lack of understanding of how the brain wires its biological networks.

In 2003, LSTM became competitive with traditional speech recognizers on certain tasks. In 2006, Alex Graves, Santiago Fernández, Faustino Gomez, and Schmidhuber combined it with connectionist temporal classification (CTC) in stacks of LSTMs. In 2009, it became the first RNN to win a pattern recognition contest, in connected handwriting recognition.

In 2006, publications by Geoff Hinton, Ruslan Salakhutdinov, Osindero and Teh deep belief networks were developed for generative modeling. They are trained by training one restricted Boltzmann machine, then freezing it and training another one on top of the first one, and so on, then optionally fine-tuned using supervised backpropagation. They could model high-dimensional probability distributions, such as the distribution of MNIST images, but convergence was slow. The impact of deep learning in industry began in the early 2000s, when CNNs already processed an estimated 10% to 20% of all the checks written in the US, according to Yann LeCun. Industrial applications of deep learning to large-scale speech recognition started around 2010.

The 2009 NIPS Workshop on Deep Learning for Speech Recognition was motivated by the limitations of deep generative models of speech, and the possibility that given more capable hardware and large-scale data sets that deep neural nets might become practical. It was believed that pre-training DNNs using generative models of deep belief nets (DBN) would overcome the main difficulties of neural nets. However, it was discovered that replacing pre-training with large amounts of training data for straightforward backpropagation when using DNNs with large, context-dependent output layers produced error rates dramatically lower than then-state-of-the-art Gaussian mixture model (GMM)/Hidden Markov Model (HMM) and also than more-advanced generative model-based systems. The nature of the recognition errors produced by the two types of systems was characteristically different, offering technical insights into how to integrate deep learning into the existing highly efficient, run-time speech decoding system deployed by all major speech recognition systems. Analysis around 2009–2010, contrasting the GMM (and other generative speech models) vs. DNN models, stimulated early industrial investment in deep learning for speech recognition. That analysis was done with comparable performance (less than 1.5% in error rate) between discriminative DNNs and generative models. In 2010, researchers extended deep learning from TIMIT to large vocabulary speech recognition, by adopting large output layers of the DNN based on context-dependent HMM states constructed by decision trees.

### Deep Learning Revolution

The deep learning revolution started around CNN- and GPU-based computer vision. Although CNNs trained by backpropagation had been around for decades and GPU implementations of NNs for years, including CNNs, faster implementations of CNNs on GPUs were needed to progress on computer vision. Later, as deep learning becomes widespread, specialized hardware and algorithm optimizations were developed specifically for deep learning.

A key advance for the deep learning revolution was hardware advances, especially GPU. Some early work dated back to 2004. In 2009, Raina, Madhavan, and Andrew Ng reported a 100M deep belief network trained on 30 Nvidia GeForce GTX 280 GPUs, an early demonstration of GPU-based deep learning. They reported up to 70 times faster training.

In 2011, a CNN named DanNet by Dan Ciresan, Ueli Meier, Jonathan Masci, Luca Maria Gambardella, and Jürgen Schmidhuber achieved for the first time superhuman performance in a visual pattern recognition contest, outperforming traditional methods by a factor of 3. It then won more contests. They also showed how max-pooling CNNs on GPU improved performance significantly.

In 2012, Andrew Ng and Jeff Dean created an FNN that learned to recognize higher-level concepts, such as cats, only from watching unlabeled images taken from YouTube videos.

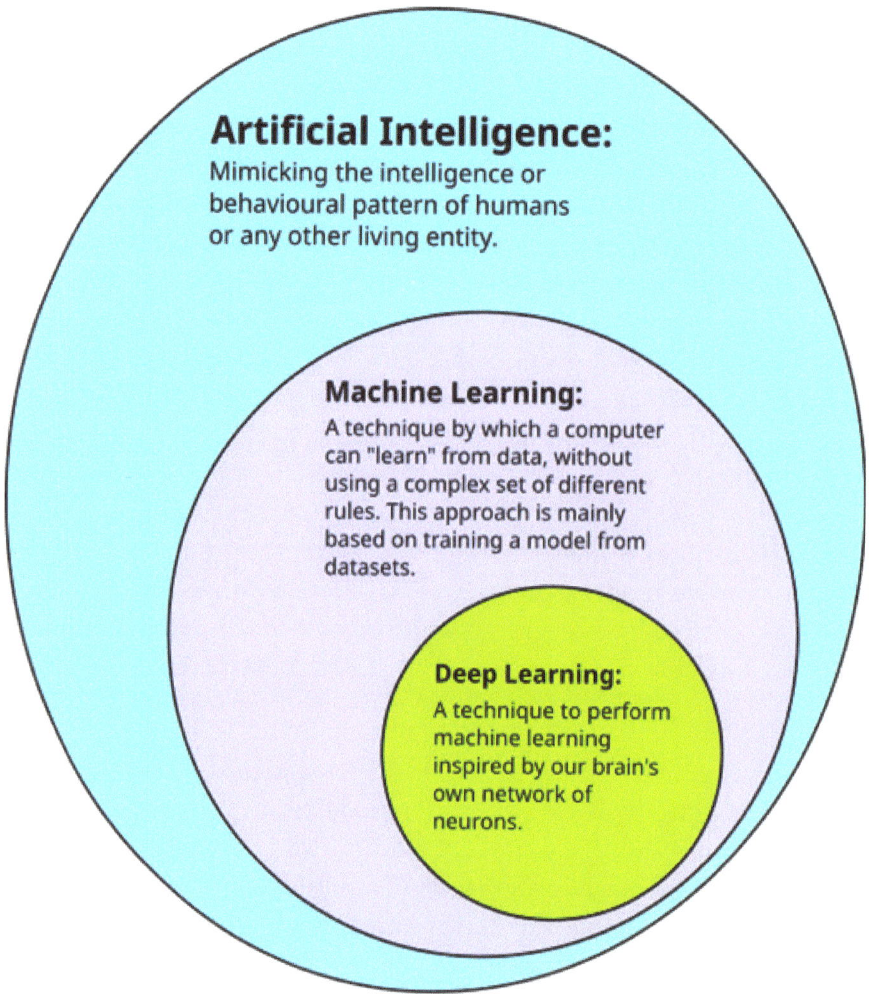


**Fig: How Deep Learning is a Subset of Machine Learning and how Machine Learning is a Subset of Artificial Intelligence (AI)**

In October 2012, AlexNet by Alex Krizhevsky, Ilya Sutskever, and Geoffrey Hinton won the large-scale ImageNet competition by a significant margin over shallow machine learning methods. Further incremental improvements included the VGG-16 network by Karen Simonyan and Andrew Zisserman and Google's Inceptionv3.

The success in image classification was then extended to the more challenging task of generating descriptions (captions) for images, often as a combination of CNNs and LSTMs. In 2014, the state of the art was training "very deep neural network" with 20 to 30 layers. Stacking too many layers led to a steep reduction in training accuracy, known as the "degradation" problem. In 2015, two techniques were developed to train very deep networks: the Highway Network was published in May 2015, and the residual neural network (ResNet) in Dec 2015. ResNet behaves like an open-gated Highway Net.

Around the same time, deep learning started impacting the field of art. Early examples included Google DeepDream (2015), and neural style transfer (2015), both of which were based on pretrained image classification neural networks, such as VGG-19.

Generative adversarial network (GAN) by (Ian Goodfellow et al., 2014) (based on Jürgen Schmidhuber's principle of artificial curiosity) became state of the art in generative modeling during 2014-2018 period. Excellent image quality is achieved by Nvidia's StyleGAN (2018) based on the Progressive GAN by Tero Karras et al. Here the GAN generator is grown from small to large scale in a pyramidal fashion. Image generation by GAN reached popular success, and provoked discussions concerning deepfakes. Diffusion models (2015) eclipsed GANs in generative modeling since then, with systems such as DALL·E 2 (2022) and Stable Diffusion (2022).

In 2015, Google's speech recognition improved by 49% by an LSTM-based model, which they made available through Google Voice Search on smartphone.

Deep learning is part of state-of-the-art systems in various disciplines, particularly computer vision and automatic speech recognition (ASR). Results on commonly used evaluation sets such as TIMIT (ASR) and MNIST (image classification), as well as a range of large-vocabulary speech recognition tasks have steadily improved. Convolutional neural networks were superseded for ASR by LSTM. but are more successful in computer vision.

Yoshua Bengio, Geoffrey Hinton and Yann LeCun were awarded the 2018 Turing Award for "conceptual and engineering breakthroughs that have made deep neural networks a critical component of computing".

## Neural Networks

Artificial neural networks (ANNs) or connectionist systems are computing systems inspired by the biological neural networks that constitute animal brains. Such systems learn (progressively improve their ability) to do tasks by considering examples, generally without task-specific programming. For example, in image recognition, they might learn to identify images that contain cats by analyzing example images that have been manually labeled as "cat" or "no cat" and using the analytic results to identify cats in other images. They have found most use in applications difficult to express with a traditional computer algorithm using rule-based programming.

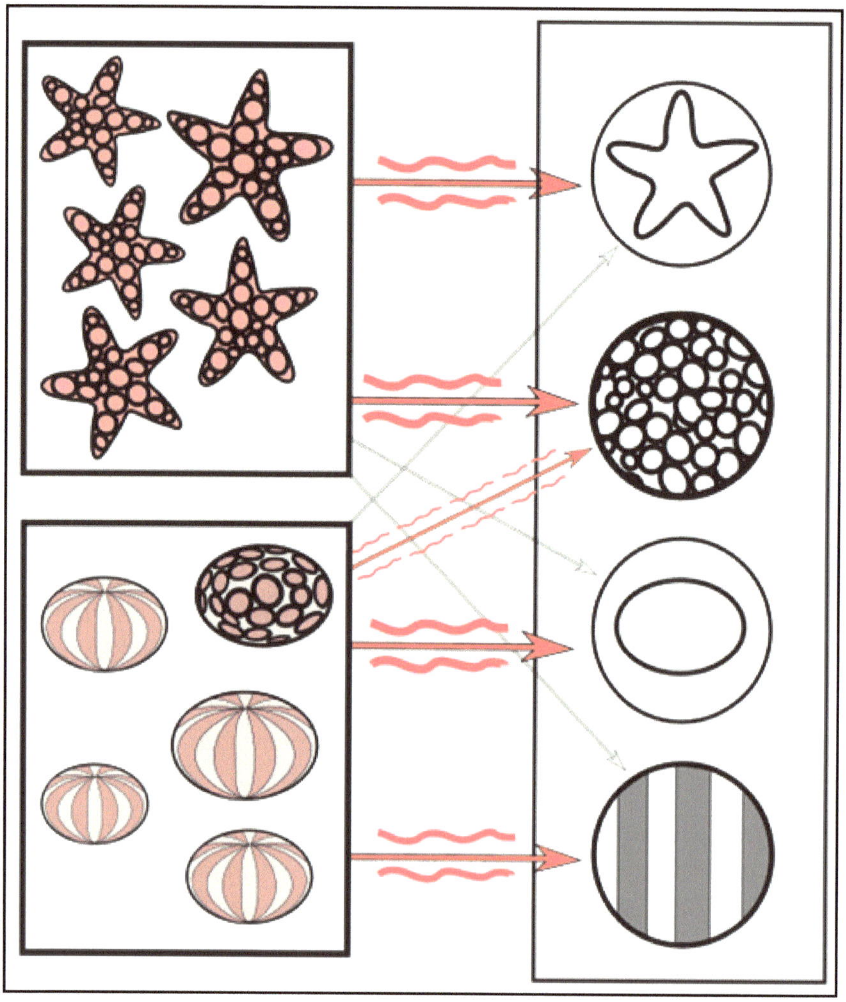

**Fig: Simplified Example of Training a Neural Network in Object Detection: The Network is Trained by Multiple Images that are Known to Depict Starfish and Sea Urchins, which are Correlated with "Nodes" that Represent Visual Features. The Starfish Match with a Ringed Texture and a Star Outline, whereas Most Sea Urchins Match with a Striped Texture and Oval Shape. However, the Instance of a Ring Textured Sea Urchin Creates a Weakly Weighted Association between them**

An ANN is based on a collection of connected units called artificial neurons, (analogous to biological neurons in a biological brain). Each connection (synapse) between neurons can transmit a signal to another neuron. The receiving (postsynaptic) neuron can process the signal(s) and then signal downstream neurons connected to it. Neurons may have state, generally represented by real numbers, typically between 0 and 1. Neurons and synapses may also have a weight that varies as learning proceeds, which can increase or decrease the strength of the signal that it sends downstream.

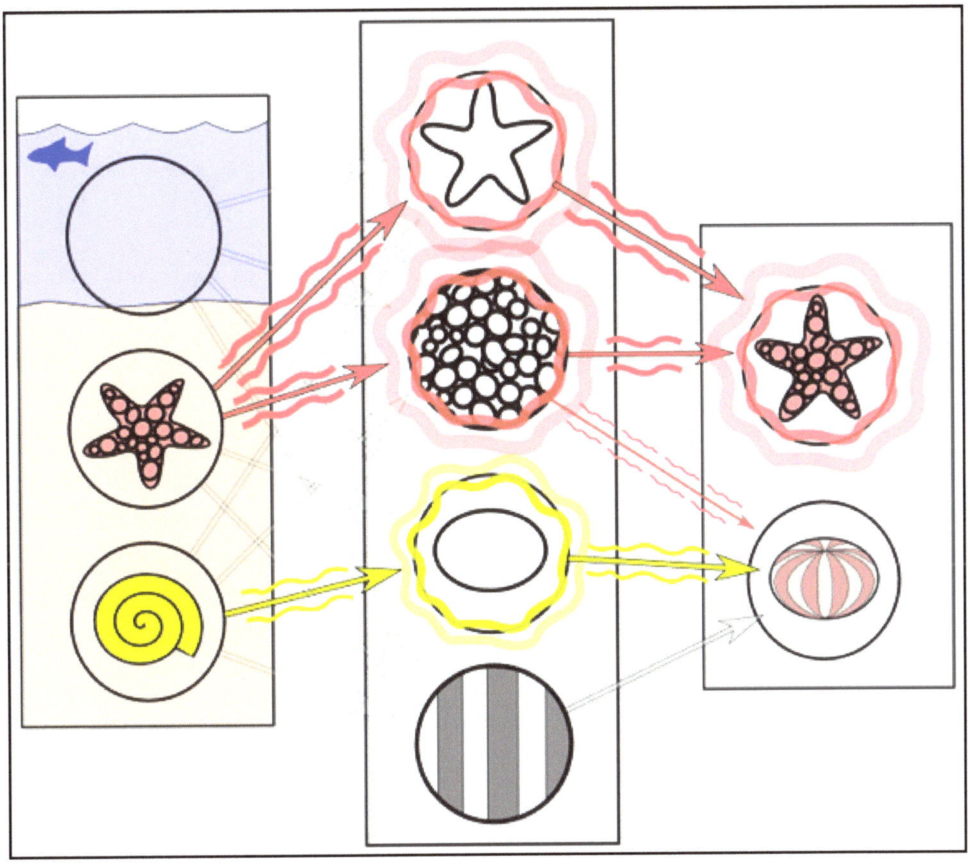

Fig: Subsequent Run of the Network on an Input Image (Left): The Network Correctly Detects the Starfish. However, the Weakly Weighted Association between Ringed Texture and Sea Urchin also Confers a Weak Signal to the Latter from One of Two Intermediate Nodes. In Addition, a Shell that was not Included in the Training Gives a Weak Signal for the Oval Shape, also Resulting in a Weak Signal for the Sea Urchin Output. These Weak Signals may Result in a False Positive Result for Sea Urchin. In Reality, Textures and Outlines would not be Represented by Single Nodes, but Rather by Associated Weight Patterns of Multiple Nodes

Typically, neurons are organized in layers. Different layers may perform different kinds of transformations on their inputs. Signals travel from the first (input), to the last (output) layer, possibly after traversing the layers multiple times.

The original goal of the neural network approach was to solve problems in the same way that a human brain would. Over time, attention focused on matching specific mental abilities, leading to deviations from biology such as backpropagation, or passing information in the reverse direction and adjusting the network to reflect that information. Neural networks have been used on a variety of tasks, including computer vision, speech recognition, machine translation, social network filtering, playing board and video games and medical diagnosis.

As of 2017, neural networks typically have a few thousand to a few million units and millions of connections. Despite this number being several order of magnitude less than the number of neurons on a human brain, these networks can perform many tasks at a level beyond that of humans (e.g., recognizing faces, or playing "Go").

### Deep Neural Networks

A deep neural network (DNN) is an artificial neural network with multiple layers between the input and output layers. There are different types of neural networks but they always consist of the same components: neurons, synapses, weights, biases, and functions. These components as a whole function in a way that mimics functions of the human brain, and can be trained like any other ML algorithm.

For example, a DNN that is trained to recognize dog breeds will go over the given image and calculate the probability that the dog in the image is a certain breed. The user can review the results and select which probabilities the network should display (above a certain threshold, etc.) and return the proposed label. Each mathematical manipulation as such is considered a layer, and complex DNN have many layers, hence the name "deep" networks.

DNNs can model complex non-linear relationships. DNN architectures generate compositional models where the object is expressed as a layered composition of primitives. The extra layers enable composition of features from lower layers, potentially modeling complex data with fewer units than a similarly performing shallow network. For instance, it was proved that sparse multivariate polynomials are exponentially easier to approximate with DNNs than with shallow networks.

Deep architectures include many variants of a few basic approaches. Each architecture has found success in specific domains. It is not always possible to compare the performance of multiple architectures, unless they have been evaluated on the same data sets.

DNNs are typically feedforward networks in which data flows from the input layer to the output layer without looping back. At first, the DNN creates a map of virtual neurons and assigns random numerical values, or "weights", to connections between them. The weights and inputs are multiplied and return an output between 0 and 1. If the network did not accurately recognize a particular pattern, an algorithm would adjust the weights. That way the algorithm can make certain parameters more influential, until it determines the correct mathematical manipulation to fully process the data.

Recurrent neural networks, in which data can flow in any direction, are used for applications such as language modeling. Long short-term memory is particularly effective for this use.

Convolutional neural networks (CNNs) are used in computer vision. CNNs also have been applied to acoustic modeling for automatic speech recognition (ASR).

Challenges:

- As with ANNs, many issues can arise with naively trained DNNs. Two common issues are overfitting and computation time.
- DNNs are prone to overfitting because of the added layers of abstraction, which allow them to model rare dependencies in the training data. Regularization methods such as Ivakhnenko's unit pruning or weight decay or sparsity can be applied during training to combat overfitting. Alternatively dropout regularization randomly omits units from the hidden layers during training. This helps to exclude rare dependencies. Another interesting recent development is research into models of just enough complexity through an estimation of the intrinsic complexity of the task being modelled. This approach has been successfully applied for multivariate time series prediction tasks such as traffic prediction. Finally, data can be augmented via methods such as cropping and rotating such that smaller training sets can be increased in size to reduce the chances of overfitting.
- DNNs must consider many training parameters, such as the size (number of layers and number of units per layer), the learning rate, and initial weights. Sweeping through the parameter space for optimal parameters may not be feasible due to the cost in time and computational resources. Various tricks, such as batching (computing the gradient on several training examples at once rather than individual examples) speed up computation. Large processing capabilities of many-core architectures (such as GPUs or the Intel Xeon Phi) have produced significant speedups in training, because of the suitability of such processing architectures for the matrix and vector computations.
- Alternatively, engineers may look for other types of neural networks with more straightforward and convergent training algorithms. CMAC (cerebellar model articulation controller) is one such kind of neural network. It doesn't require learning rates or randomized initial weights. The training process can be guaranteed to converge in one step with a new batch of data, and the computational complexity of the training algorithm is linear with respect to the number of neurons involved.

### Hardware

Since the 2010s, advances in both machine learning algorithms and computer hardware have led to more efficient methods for training deep neural networks that contain many layers of non-linear hidden units and a very large output layer. By 2019, graphics processing units (GPUs), often with AI-specific enhancements, had displaced CPUs as the dominant method for training large-scale commercial cloud AI . OpenAI estimated the hardware computation used in the largest deep learning projects from AlexNet (2012) to AlphaZero (2017) and found a 300,000-fold increase in the amount of computation required, with a doubling-time trendline of 3.4 months.

Special electronic circuits called deep learning processors were designed to speed up deep learning algorithms. Deep learning processors include neural processing units (NPUs) in Huawei cellphones and cloud computing servers such as tensor processing units (TPU) in the Google Cloud Platform. Cerebras Systems has also built a dedicated system to handle large deep learning models, the CS-2, based on the largest processor in the industry, the second-generation Wafer Scale Engine (WSE-2).

Atomically thin semiconductors are considered promising for energy-efficient deep learning hardware where the same basic device structure is used for both logic operations and data storage. In 2020, Marega et al. published experiments with a large-area active channel material for developing logic-in-memory devices and circuits based on floating-gate field-effect transistors (FGFETs).

In 2021, J. Feldmann et al. proposed an integrated photonic hardware accelerator for parallel convolutional processing. The authors identify two key advantages of integrated photonics over its electronic counterparts: (1) massively parallel data transfer through wavelength division multiplexing in conjunction with frequency combs, and (2) extremely high data modulation speeds. Their system can execute trillions of multiply-accumulate operations per second, indicating the potential of integrated photonics in data-heavy AI applications.

## Applications

### Automatic Speech Recognition

Large-scale automatic speech recognition is the first and most convincing successful case of deep learning. LSTM RNNs can learn "Very Deep Learning" tasks that involve multi-second intervals containing speech events separated by thousands of discrete time steps, where one time step corresponds to about 10 ms. LSTM with forget gates is competitive with traditional speech recognizers on certain tasks.

The initial success in speech recognition was based on small-scale recognition tasks based on TIMIT. The data set contains 630 speakers from eight major dialects of American English, where each speaker reads 10 sentences. Its small size lets many configurations be tried. More importantly, the TIMIT task concerns phone-sequence recognition, which, unlike word-sequence recognition, allows weak phone bigram language models. This lets the strength of the acoustic modeling aspects of speech recognition be more easily analyzed. The error rates listed below, including these early results and measured as percent phone error rates (PER), have been summarized since 1991.

| Method | Percent Phone Error Rate (PER) (%) |
|---|---|
| Randomly Initialized RNN | 26.1 |
| Bayesian Triphone GMM-HMM | 25.6 |
| Hidden Trajectory (Generative) Model | 24.8 |
| Monophone Randomly Initialized DNN | 23.4 |
| Monophone DBN-DNN | 22.4 |
| Triphone GMM-HMM with BMMI Training | 21.7 |
| Monophone DBN-DNN on fbank | 20.7 |
| Convolutional DNN | 20.0 |
| Convolutional DNN w. Heterogeneous Pooling | 18.7 |
| Ensemble DNN/CNN/RNN | 18.3 |
| Bidirectional LSTM | 17.8 |
| Hierarchical Convolutional Deep Maxout Network | 16.5 |

The debut of DNNs for speaker recognition in the late 1990s and speech recognition around 2009-2011 and of LSTM around 2003–2007, accelerated progress in eight major areas:

- Scale-up/out and accelerated DNN training and decoding.
- Sequence discriminative training.
- Feature processing by deep models with solid understanding of the underlying mechanisms.
- Adaptation of DNNs and related deep models.
- Multi-task and transfer learning by DNNs and related deep models.
- CNNs and how to design them to best exploit domain knowledge of speech.
- RNN and its rich LSTM variants.
- Other types of deep models including tensor-based models and integrated deep generative/discriminative models.

All major commercial speech recognition systems (e.g., Microsoft Cortana, Xbox, Skype Translator, Amazon Alexa, Google Now, Apple Siri, Baidu and iFlyTek voice search, and a range of Nuance speech products, etc.) are based on deep learning.

### Image Recognition

A common evaluation set for image classification is the MNIST database data set. MNIST is composed of handwritten digits and includes 60,000 training examples and 10,000 test examples. As with TIMIT, its small size lets users test multiple configurations. A comprehensive list of results on this set is available.

Deep learning-based image recognition has become "superhuman", producing more accurate results than human contestants. This first occurred in 2011 in recognition of traffic signs, and in 2014, with recognition of human faces.

Deep learning-trained vehicles now interpret 360° camera views. Another example is Facial Dysmorphology Novel Analysis (FDNA) used to analyze cases of human malformation connected to a large database of genetic syndromes.

### Visual Art Processing

Closely related to the progress that has been made in image recognition is the increasing application of deep learning techniques to various visual art tasks. DNNs have proven themselves capable, for example, of

- identifying the style period of a given painting.
- Neural Style Transfer – capturing the style of a given artwork and applying it in a visually pleasing manner to an arbitrary photograph or video.
- Generating striking imagery based on random visual input fields.

### Natural Language Processing

Neural networks have been used for implementing language models since the early 2000s. LSTM helped to improve machine translation and language modeling.

Other key techniques in this field are negative sampling and word embedding. Word embedding, such as word2vec, can be thought of as a representational layer in a deep learning architecture that transforms an atomic word into a positional representation of the word relative to other words in the dataset; the position is represented as a point in a vector space. Using word embedding as an RNN input layer allows the network to parse sentences and phrases using an effective compositional vector grammar.

A compositional vector grammar can be thought of as probabilistic context free grammar (PCFG) implemented by an RNN. Recursive auto-encoders built atop word embeddings can assess sentence similarity and detect paraphrasing. Deep neural architectures provide the best results for constituency parsing, sentiment analysis, information retrieval, spoken language understanding, machine translation, contextual entity linking, writing style recognition, named-entity recognition (token classification), text classification, and others.

Recent developments generalize word embedding to sentence embedding. Google Translate (GT) uses a large end-to-end long short-term memory (LSTM) network. Google Neural Machine Translation (GNMT) uses an example-based machine translation method in which the system "learns from millions of examples". It translates "whole sentences at a time, rather than pieces". Google Translate supports over one hundred languages. The network encodes the "semantics of the sentence rather than simply memorizing phrase-to-phrase translations". GT uses English as an intermediate between most language pairs.

### Drug Discovery and Toxicology

A large percentage of candidate drugs fail to win regulatory approval. These failures are caused by insufficient efficacy (on-target effect), undesired interactions (off-target effects), or unanticipated toxic effects. Research has explored use of deep learning to predict the biomolecular targets, off-targets, and toxic effects of environmental chemicals in nutrients, household products and drugs.

AtomNet is a deep learning system for structure-based rational drug design. AtomNet was used to predict novel candidate biomolecules for disease targets such as the Ebola virus and multiple sclerosis.

In 2017 graph neural networks were used for the first time to predict various properties of molecules in a large toxicology data set. In 2019, generative neural networks were used to produce molecules that were validated experimentally all the way into mice.

### Customer Relationship Management

Deep reinforcement learning has been used to approximate the value of possible direct marketing actions, defined in terms of RFM variables. The estimated value function was shown to have a natural interpretation as customer lifetime value.

### Recommendation Systems

Recommendation systems have used deep learning to extract meaningful features for a latent factor model for content-based music and journal recommendations. Multi-view deep learning has been applied for learning user preferences from multiple domains. The model uses a hybrid collaborative and content-based approach and enhances recommendations in multiple tasks.

### Bioinformatics

- An autoencoder ANN was used in bioinformatics, to predict gene ontology annotations and gene-function relationships.
- In medical informatics, deep learning was used to predict sleep quality based on data from wearables and predictions of health complications from electronic health record data.

- Deep neural networks have shown unparalleled performance in predicting protein structure, according to the sequence of the amino acids that make it up. In 2020, AlphaFold, a deep-learning based system, achieved a level of accuracy significantly higher than all previous computational methods.

### Deep Neural Network Estimations

Deep neural networks can be used to estimate the entropy of a stochastic process and called Neural Joint Entropy Estimator (NJEE). Such an estimation provides insights on the effects of input random variables on an independent random variable. Practically, the DNN is trained as a classifier that maps an input vector or matrix X to an output probability distribution over the possible classes of random variable Y, given input X. For example, in image classification tasks, the NJEE maps a vector of pixels' color values to probabilities over possible image classes. In practice, the probability distribution of Y is obtained by a Softmax layer with number of nodes that is equal to the alphabet size of Y. NJEE uses continuously differentiable activation functions, such that the conditions for the universal approximation theorem holds. It is shown that this method provides a strongly consistent estimator and outperforms other methods in case of large alphabet sizes.

### Medical Image Analysis

Deep learning has been shown to produce competitive results in medical application such as cancer cell classification, lesion detection, organ segmentation and image enhancement. Modern deep learning tools demonstrate the high accuracy of detecting various diseases and the helpfulness of their use by specialists to improve the diagnosis efficiency.

### Mobile Advertising

Finding the appropriate mobile audience for mobile advertising is always challenging, since many data points must be considered and analyzed before a target segment can be created and used in ad serving by any ad server. Deep learning has been used to interpret large, many-dimensioned advertising datasets. Many data points are collected during the request/serve/click internet advertising cycle. This information can form the basis of machine learning to improve ad selection.

### Image Restoration

Deep learning has been successfully applied to inverse problems such as denoising, super-resolution, inpainting, and film colorization. These applications include learning methods such as "Shrinkage Fields for Effective Image Restoration" which trains on an image dataset, and Deep Image Prior, which trains on the image that needs restoration.

### Financial Fraud Detection

Deep learning is being successfully applied to financial fraud detection, tax evasion detection, and anti-money laundering.

### Materials Science

In November 2023, researchers at Google DeepMind and Lawrence Berkeley National Laboratory announced that they had developed an AI system known as GNoME. This system has contributed to materials science by discovering over 2 million new materials within a relatively short timeframe. GNoME employs deep learning techniques to efficiently explore potential material structures, achieving a significant increase in the identification of stable inorganic crystal structures. The system's predictions were validated through autonomous robotic experiments, demonstrating a noteworthy success rate of 71%. The data of newly discovered materials is publicly available through the Materials Project database, offering researchers the opportunity to identify materials with desired properties for various applications. This development has implications for the future of scientific discovery and the integration of AI in material science research, potentially expediting material innovation and reducing costs in product development. The use of AI and deep learning suggests the possibility of minimizing or eliminating manual lab experiments and allowing scientists to focus more on the design and analysis of unique compounds.

### Military

The United States Department of Defense applied deep learning to train robots in new tasks through observation.

### Partial Differential Equations

Physics informed neural networks have been used to solve partial differential equations in both forward and inverse problems in a data driven manner. One example is the reconstructing fluid flow governed by the Navier-Stokes equations. Using physics informed neural networks does not require the often expensive mesh generation that conventional CFD methods rely on.

### Deep Backward Stochastic Differential Equation Method

Deep backward stochastic differential equation method is a numerical method that combines deep learning with Backward stochastic differential equation (BSDE). This method is particularly useful for solving high-dimensional problems in financial mathematics. By leveraging the powerful function approximation capabilities of deep neural networks, deep BSDE addresses the computational challenges faced by traditional numerical methods in high-dimensional settings. Specifically, traditional methods like finite difference methods or Monte Carlo simulations often struggle with the curse of dimensionality, where computational cost increases exponentially with the number of dimensions. Deep BSDE methods, however, employ deep neural networks to approximate solutions of high-dimensional partial differential equations (PDEs), effectively reducing the computational burden.

In addition, the integration of Physics-informed neural networks (PINNs) into the deep BSDE framework enhances its capability by embedding the underlying physical laws directly into the neural network architecture. This ensures that the solutions not only fit the data but also adhere to the governing stochastic differential equations. PINNs leverage the power of deep learning while respecting the constraints imposed by the physical models, resulting in more accurate and reliable solutions for financial mathematics problems.

### Image Reconstruction

Image reconstruction is the reconstruction of the underlying images from the image-related measurements. Several works showed the better and superior performance of the deep learning methods compared to analytical methods for various applications, e.g., spectral imaging and ultrasound imaging.

### Weather Prediction

Traditional weather prediction systems solve a very complex system of partial differential equations. GraphCast is a deep learning based model, trained on a long history of weather data to predict how weather patterns change over time. It is able to predict weather conditions for up to 10 days globally, at a very detailed level, and in under a minute, with precision similar to state of the art systems.

### Epigenetic Clock

An epigenetic clock is a biochemical test that can be used to measure age. Galkin et al. used deep neural networks to train an epigenetic aging clock of unprecedented accuracy using >6,000 blood samples. The clock uses information from 1000 CpG sites and predicts people with certain conditions older than healthy controls: IBD, frontotemporal dementia, ovarian cancer, obesity. The aging clock was planned to be released for public use in 2021 by an Insilico Medicine spinoff company Deep Longevity.

## Relation to Human Cognitive and Brain Development

Deep learning is closely related to a class of theories of brain development (specifically, neocortical development) proposed by cognitive neuroscientists in the early 1990s. These developmental theories were instantiated in computational models, making them predecessors of deep learning systems. These developmental models share the property that various proposed learning dynamics in the brain (e.g., a wave of nerve growth factor) support the self-organization somewhat analogous to the neural networks utilized in deep learning models. Like the neocortex, neural networks employ a hierarchy of layered filters in which each layer considers information from a prior layer (or the operating environment), and then passes its output (and possibly the original input), to other layers. This process yields a self-organizing stack of transducers, well-tuned to their operating environment. A 1995 description stated, "...the infant's brain seems to organize itself under the influence of waves of so-called trophic-factors ... different regions of the brain become connected sequentially, with one layer of tissue maturing before another and so on until the whole brain is mature".

A variety of approaches have been used to investigate the plausibility of deep learning models from a neurobiological perspective. On the one hand, several variants of the backpropagation algorithm have been proposed in order to increase its processing realism. Other researchers have argued that unsupervised forms of deep learning, such as those based on hierarchical generative models and deep belief networks, may be closer to biological reality. In this respect, generative neural network models have been related to neurobiological evidence about sampling-based processing in the cerebral cortex.

Although a systematic comparison between the human brain organization and the neuronal encoding in deep networks has not yet been established, several analogies have been reported. For example, the computations performed by deep learning units could be similar to those of actual neurons and neural populations. Similarly, the representations developed by deep learning models are similar to those measured in the primate visual system both at the single-unit and at the population levels.

## Commercial Activity

Facebook's AI lab performs tasks such as automatically tagging uploaded pictures with the names of the people in them.

Google's DeepMind Technologies developed a system capable of learning how to play Atari video games using only pixels as data input. In 2015 they demonstrated their AlphaGo system, which learned the game of Go well enough to beat a professional Go player. Google Translate uses a neural network to translate between more than 100 languages.

In 2017, Covariant.ai was launched, which focuses on integrating deep learning into factories. As of 2008, researchers at The University of Texas at Austin (UT) developed a machine learning framework called Training an Agent Manually via Evaluative Reinforcement, or TAMER, which proposed new methods for robots or computer programs to learn how to perform tasks by interacting with a human instructor. First developed as TAMER, a new algorithm called Deep TAMER was later introduced in 2018 during a collaboration between U.S. Army Research Laboratory (ARL) and UT researchers. Deep TAMER used deep learning to provide a robot with the ability to learn new tasks through observation. Using Deep TAMER, a robot learned a task with a human trainer, watching video streams or observing a human perform a task in-person. The robot later practiced the task with the help of some coaching from the trainer, who provided feedback such as "good job" and "bad job".

## Criticism and Comment

Deep learning has attracted both criticism and comment, in some cases from outside the field of computer science.

### Theory

A main criticism concerns the lack of theory surrounding some methods. Learning in the most common deep architectures is implemented using well-understood gradient descent. However, the theory surrounding other algorithms, such as contrastive divergence is less clear. (e.g., Does it converge? If so, how fast? What is it approximating?) Deep learning methods are often looked at as a black box, with most confirmations done empirically, rather than theoretically.

### Errors

Some deep learning architectures display problematic behaviors, such as confidently classifying unrecognizable images as belonging to a familiar category of ordinary images (2014) and misclassifying minuscule perturbations of correctly classified images (2013). Goertzel hypothesized that these behaviors are due to limitations in their internal representations and that these limitations would inhibit integration into heterogeneous multi-component artificial general intelligence (AGI) architectures. These issues may possibly be addressed by deep learning architectures that internally form states homologous to image-grammar decompositions of observed entities and events. Learning a grammar (visual or linguistic) from training data would be equivalent to restricting the system to commonsense reasoning that operates on concepts in terms of grammatical production rules and is a basic goal of both human language acquisition and artificial intelligence (AI).

### Cyber Threat

As deep learning moves from the lab into the world, research and experience show that artificial neural networks are vulnerable to hacks and deception. By identifying patterns that these systems use to function, attackers can modify inputs to ANNs in such a way that the ANN finds a match that human observers would not recognize. For example, an attacker can make subtle changes to an image such that the ANN finds a match even though the image looks to a human nothing like the search target. Such manipulation is termed an "adversarial attack".

In 2016 researchers used one ANN to doctor images in trial and error fashion, identify another's focal points, and thereby generate images that deceived it. The modified images looked no different to human eyes. Another group showed that printouts of doctored images then photographed successfully tricked an image classification system. One defense is reverse image search, in which a possible fake image is submitted to a site such as TinEye that can then find other instances of it. A refinement is to search using only parts of the image, to identify images from which that piece may have been taken.

Another group showed that certain psychedelic spectacles could fool a facial recognition system into thinking ordinary people were celebrities, potentially allowing one person to impersonate another. In 2017 researchers added stickers to stop signs and caused an ANN to misclassify them.

ANNs can however be further trained to detect attempts at deception, potentially leading attackers and defenders into an arms race similar to the kind that already defines the malware defense industry. ANNs have been trained to defeat ANN-based anti-malware software by repeatedly attacking a defense with malware that was continually altered by a genetic algorithm until it tricked the anti-malware while retaining its ability to damage the target.

In 2016, another group demonstrated that certain sounds could make the Google Now voice command system open a particular web address, and hypothesized that this could "serve as a stepping stone for further attacks (e.g., opening a web page hosting drive-by malware)".

In "data poisoning", false data is continually smuggled into a machine learning system's training set to prevent it from achieving mastery.

### Data Collection Ethics

The deep learning systems that are trained using supervised learning often rely on data that is created and/or annotated by humans. It has been argued that not only low-paid clickwork (such as on Amazon Mechanical Turk) is regularly deployed for this purpose, but also implicit forms of human microwork that are often not recognized as such. The philosopher Rainer Mühlhoff distinguishes five types of "machinic capture" of human microwork to generate training data: (1) gamification (the embedding of annotation or computation tasks in the flow of a game), (2) "trapping and tracking" (e.g. CAPTCHAs for image recognition or click-tracking on Google search results pages), (3) exploitation of social motivations (e.g. tagging faces on Facebook to obtain labeled facial images), (4) information mining (e.g. by leveraging quantified-self devices such as activity trackers) and (5) clickwork.

### 5.1.2 Ensembles

In statistics and machine learning, ensemble methods use multiple learning algorithms to obtain better predictive performance than could be obtained from any of the constituent learning algorithms alone. Unlike a statistical ensemble in statistical mechanics, which is usually infinite, a machine learning ensemble consists of only a concrete finite set of alternative models, but typically allows for much more flexible structure to exist among those alternatives.

Supervised learning algorithms search through a hypothesis space to find a suitable hypothesis that will make good predictions with a particular problem. Even if this space contains hypotheses that are very well-suited for a particular problem, it may be very difficult to find a good one. Ensembles combine multiple hypotheses to form one which should be theoretically better.

Ensemble learning trains two or more machine learning algorithms on a specific classification or regression task. The algorithms within the ensemble model are generally referred as "base models", "base learners", or "weak learners" in literature. These base models can be constructed using a single modelling algorithm, or several different algorithms.

The idea is to train a diverse set of weak models on the same modelling task, such that the outputs of each weak learner have poor predictive ability (i.e., high bias), and among all weak learners, the outcome and error values exhibit high variance. Fundamentally, an ensemble learning model trains at least two high-bias (weak) and high-variance (diverse) models to be combined into a better-performing model. The set of weak models — which would not produce satisfactory predictive results individually — are combined or averaged to produce a single, high performing, accurate, and low-variance model to fit the task as required.

Ensemble learning typically refers to bagging (bootstrap aggregating), boosting or stacking/blending techniques to induce high variance among the base models. Bagging creates diversity by generating random samples from the training observations and fitting the same model to each different sample — also known as homogeneous parallel ensembles.

Boosting follows an iterative process by sequentially training each base model on the up-weighted errors of the previous base model, producing an additive model to reduce the final model errors — also known as sequential ensemble learning. Stacking or blending consists of different base models, each trained independently (i.e. diverse/high variance) to be combined into the ensemble model — producing a heterogeneous parallel ensemble.

Common applications of ensemble learning include random forests (an extension of bagging), Boosted Tree models, and Gradient Boosted Tree Models. Models in applications of stacking are generally more task-specific — such as combining clustering techniques with other parametric and/or non-parametric techniques.

The broader term of multiple classifier systems also covers hybridization of hypotheses that are not induced by the same base learner.

Evaluating the prediction of an ensemble typically requires more computation than evaluating the prediction of a single model. In one sense, ensemble learning may be thought of as a way to compensate for poor learning algorithms by performing a lot of extra computation. On the other hand, the alternative is to do a lot more learning with one non-ensemble model.

An ensemble may be more efficient at improving overall accuracy for the same increase in compute, storage, or communication resources by using that increase on two or more methods, than would have been improved by increasing resource use for a single method. Fast algorithms such as decision trees are commonly used in ensemble methods (e.g., random forests), although slower algorithms can benefit from ensemble techniques as well.

By analogy, ensemble techniques have been used also in unsupervised learning scenarios, for example in consensus clustering or in anomaly detection.

## Ensemble Theory

Empirically, ensembles tend to yield better results when there is a significant diversity among the models. Many ensemble methods, therefore, seek to promote diversity among the models they combine. Although perhaps non-intuitive, more random algorithms (like random decision trees) can be used to produce a stronger ensemble than very deliberate algorithms (like entropy-reducing decision trees).

Using a variety of strong learning algorithms, however, has been shown to be more effective than using techniques that attempt to dumb-down the models in order to promote diversity. It is possible to increase diversity in the training stage of the model using correlation for regression tasks or using information measures such as cross entropy for classification tasks.

Theoretically, one can justify the diversity concept because the lower bound of the error rate of an ensemble system can be decomposed into accuracy, diversity, and the other term.

### The Geometric Framework

Ensemble learning, including both regression and classification tasks, can be explained using a geometric framework. Within this framework, the output of each individual classifier or regressor for the entire dataset can be viewed as a point in a multi-dimensional space. Additionally, the target result is also represented as a point in this space, referred to as the "ideal point."

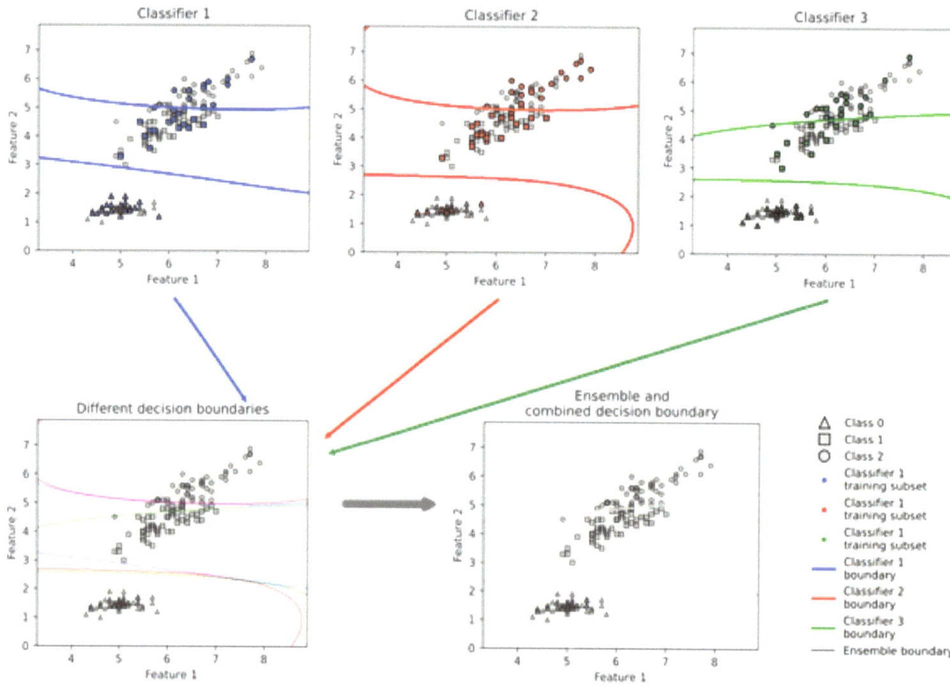


**Fig: An Ensemble of Classifiers Usually has Smaller Classification Error than Base Models**

The Euclidean distance is used as the metric to measure both the performance of a single classifier or regressor (the distance between its point and the ideal point) and the dissimilarity between two classifiers or regressors (the distance between their respective points). This perspective transforms ensemble learning into a deterministic problem.

For example, within this geometric framework, it can be proved that the averaging of the outputs (scores) of all base classifiers or regressors can lead to equal or better results than the average of all the individual models. It can also be proved that if the optimal weighting scheme is used, then a weighted averaging approach can outperform any of the individual classifiers or regressors that make up the ensemble or as good as the best performer at least.

## Ensemble Size

While the number of component classifiers of an ensemble has a great impact on the accuracy of prediction, there is a limited number of studies addressing this problem. A priori determining of ensemble size and the volume and velocity of big data streams make this even more crucial for online ensemble classifiers. Mostly statistical tests were used for determining the proper number of components.

More recently, a theoretical framework suggested that there is an ideal number of component classifiers for an ensemble such that having more or less than this number of classifiers would deteriorate the accuracy. It is called "the law of diminishing returns in ensemble construction." Their theoretical framework shows that using the same number of independent component classifiers as class labels gives the highest accuracy.

## Common Types of Ensembles

### Bayes Optimal Classifier

The Bayes optimal classifier is a classification technique. It is an ensemble of all the hypotheses in the hypothesis space. On average, no other ensemble can outperform it. The Naive Bayes classifier is a version of this that assumes that the data is conditionally independent on the class and makes the computation more feasible. Each hypothesis is given a vote proportional to the likelihood that the training dataset would be sampled from a system if that hypothesis were true. To facilitate training data of finite size, the vote of each hypothesis is also multiplied by the prior probability of that hypothesis. The Bayes optimal classifier can be expressed with the following equation:

$$y = \underset{c_j \in C}{\operatorname{argmax}} \sum_{h_i \in H} P(c_j \mid h_i) P(T \mid h_i) P(h_i)$$

This formula can be restated using Bayes' theorem, which says that the posterior is proportional to the likelihood times the prior:

$$P(h_i \mid T) \propto P(T \mid h_i) P(h_i)$$

Hence

$$y = \underset{c_j \in C}{\operatorname{argmax}} \sum_{h_i \in H} P(c_j \mid h_i) P(h_i \mid T)$$

### Bootstrap Aggregating (Bagging)

Bootstrap aggregation (bagging) involves training an ensemble on bootstrapped data sets. A bootstrapped set is created by selecting from original training data set with replacement. Thus, a bootstrap set may contain a given example zero, one, or multiple times. Ensemble members can also have limits on the features (e.g., nodes of a decision tree), to encourage exploring of diverse features. The variance of local information in the bootstrap sets and feature considerations promote diversity in the ensemble, and can strengthen the ensemble. To reduce overfitting, a member can be validated using the out-of-bag set (the examples that are not in its bootstrap set).

Inference is done by voting of predictions of ensemble members, called aggregation. It is illustrated below with an ensemble of four decision trees. The query example is classified by each tree. Because three of the four predict the positive class, the ensemble's overall classification is positive. Random forests like the one shown are a common application of bagging.

Fig: Three Datasets Bootstrapped from an Original Set. Example A Occurs Twice in Set 1 because these are Chosen with Replacement

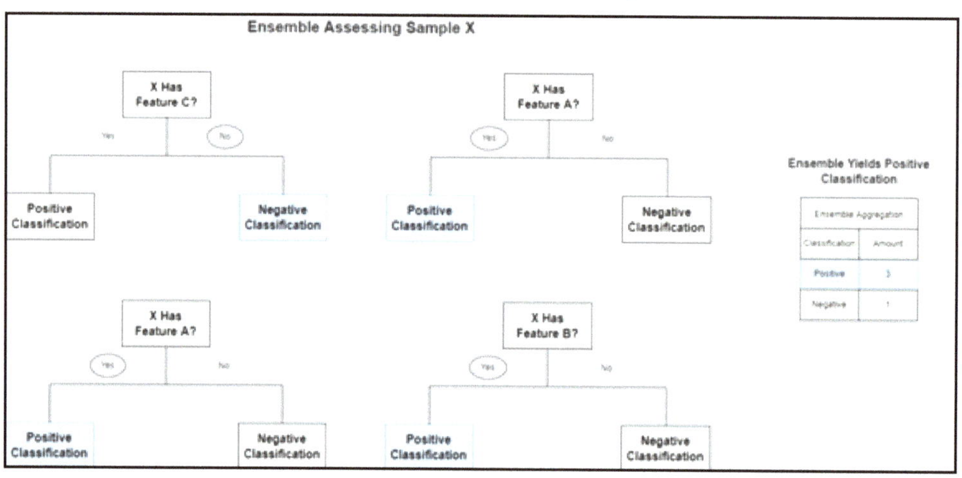


## Boosting

Boosting involves training successive models by emphasizing training data mis-classified by previously learned models. Initially, all data (D1) has equal weight and is used to learn a base model M1. The examples mis-classified by M1 are assigned a weight greater than correctly classified examples. This boosted data (D2) is used to train a second base model M2, and so on. Inference is done by voting.

In some cases, boosting has yielded better accuracy than bagging, but tends to over-fit more. The most common implementation of boosting is Adaboost, but some newer algorithms are reported to achieve better results.

### Bayesian Model Averaging

Bayesian model averaging (BMA) makes predictions by averaging the predictions of models weighted by their posterior probabilities given the data. BMA is known to generally give better answers than a single model, obtained, e.g., via stepwise regression, especially where very different models have nearly identical performance in the training set but may otherwise perform quite differently.

The question with any use of Bayes' theorem is the prior, i.e., the probability (perhaps subjective) that each model is the best to use for a given purpose. Conceptually, BMA can be used with any prior. R packages ensembleBMA and BMA use the prior implied by the Bayesian information criterion, (BIC), following Raftery (1995). R package BAS supports the use of the priors implied by Akaike information criterion (AIC) and other criteria over the alternative models as well as priors over the coefficients.

The difference between BIC and AIC is the strength of preference for parsimony. BIC's penalty for model complexity. Large-sample asymptotic theory establishes that if there is a best model, then with increasing sample sizes, BIC is strongly consistent, i.e., will almost certainly find it, while AIC may not, because AIC may continue to place excessive posterior probability on models that are more complicated than they need to be. On the other hand, AIC and AICc are asymptotically "efficient" (i.e., minimum mean square prediction error), while BIC is not .

Haussler et al. (1994) showed that when BMA is used for classification, its expected error is at most twice the expected error of the Bayes optimal classifier. Burnham and Anderson (1998, 2002) contributed greatly to introducing a wider audience to the basic ideas of Bayesian model averaging and popularizing the methodology.

### Bayesian Model Combination

Bayesian model combination (BMC) is an algorithmic correction to Bayesian model averaging (BMA). Instead of sampling each model in the ensemble individually, it samples from the space of possible ensembles (with model weights drawn randomly from a Dirichlet distribution having uniform parameters). This modification overcomes the tendency of BMA to converge toward giving all the weight to a single model. Although BMC is somewhat more computationally expensive than BMA, it tends to yield dramatically better results. BMC has been shown to be better on average (with statistical significance) than BMA and bagging.

Use of Bayes' law to compute model weights requires computing the probability of the data given each model. Typically, none of the models in the ensemble are exactly the distribution from which the training data were generated, so all of them correctly receive a value close to zero for this term. This would work well if the ensemble were big enough to sample the entire model-space, but this is rarely possible. Consequently, each pattern in the training data will cause the ensemble weight to shift toward the model in the ensemble that is closest to the distribution of the training data. It essentially reduces to an unnecessarily complex method for doing model selection.

The possible weightings for an ensemble can be visualized as lying on a simplex. At each vertex of the simplex, all of the weight is given to a single model in the ensemble. BMA converges toward the vertex that is closest to the distribution of the training data. By contrast, BMC converges toward the point where this distribution projects onto the simplex. In other words, instead of selecting the one model that is closest to the generating distribution, it seeks the combination of models that is closest to the generating distribution.

The results from BMA can often be approximated by using cross-validation to select the best model from a bucket of models. Likewise, the results from BMC may be approximated by using cross-validation to select the best ensemble combination from a random sampling of possible weightings.

### Bucket of Models

A "bucket of models" is an ensemble technique in which a model selection algorithm is used to choose the best model for each problem. When tested with only one problem, a bucket of models can produce no better results than the best model in the set, but when evaluated across many problems, it will typically produce much better results, on average, than any model in the set.

The most common approach used for model-selection is cross-validation selection (sometimes called a "bake-off contest"). It is described with the following pseudo-code:

```
For each model m in the bucket:
  Do c times: (where 'c' is some constant)
    Randomly divide the training dataset into two sets: A and B
    Train m with A
    Test m with B
Select the model that obtains the highest average score
```

Cross-Validation Selection can be summed up as: "try them all with the training set, and pick the one that works best". Gating is a generalization of Cross-Validation Selection. It involves training another learning model to decide which of the models in the bucket is best-suited to solve the problem. Often, a perceptron is used for the gating model. It can be used to pick the "best" model, or it can be used to give a linear weight to the predictions from each model in the bucket.

When a bucket of models is used with a large set of problems, it may be desirable to avoid training some of the models that take a long time to train. Landmark learning is a meta-learning approach that seeks to solve this problem. It involves training only the fast (but imprecise) algorithms in the bucket, and then using the performance of these algorithms to help determine which slow (but accurate) algorithm is most likely to do best.

### Amended Cross-Entropy Cost: An Approach for Encouraging Diversity in Classification Ensemble

The most common approach for training classifier is using Cross-entropy cost function. However, one would like to train an ensemble of models that have diversity so when we combine them it would provide best results. Assuming we use a simple ensemble of averaging K K classifiers. Then the Amended Cross-Entropy Cost is

$$e^k = H(p,q^k) - \frac{\lambda}{K}\sum_{j\neq k} H(q^j,q^k)$$

### Stacking

Stacking (sometimes called stacked generalization) involves training a model to combine the predictions of several other learning algorithms. First, all of the other algorithms are trained using the available data, then a combiner algorithm (final estimator) is trained to make a final prediction using all the predictions of the other algorithms (base estimators) as additional inputs or using cross-validated predictions from the base estimators which can prevent overfitting.

Stacking typically yields performance better than any single one of the trained models. It has been successfully used on both supervised learning tasks (regression, classification and distance learning ) and unsupervised learning (density estimation). It has also been used to estimate bagging's error rate. It has been reported to out-perform Bayesian model-averaging. The two top-performers in the Netflix competition utilized blending, which may be considered a form of stacking.

### Implementations in Statistics Packages

- **R:** At least three packages offer Bayesian model averaging tools, including the BMS (an acronym for Bayesian Model Selection) package, the BAS (an acronym for Bayesian Adaptive Sampling) package, and the BMA package.
- **Python:** Scikit-learn, a package for machine learning in Python offers packages for ensemble learning including packages for bagging, voting and averaging methods.

- **MATLAB:** Classification ensembles are implemented in Statistics and Machine Learning Toolbox.

## Ensemble Learning Applications

In recent years, due to growing computational power, which allows for training in large ensemble learning in a reasonable time frame, the number of ensemble learning applications has grown increasingly. Some of the applications of ensemble classifiers include:

### Remote Sensing

- **Land Cover Mapping:** Land cover mapping is one of the major applications of Earth observation satellite sensors, using remote sensing and geospatial data, to identify the materials and objects which are located on the surface of target areas. Generally, the classes of target materials include roads, buildings, rivers, lakes, and vegetation. Some different ensemble learning approaches based on artificial neural networks, kernel principal component analysis (KPCA), decision trees with boosting, random forest and automatic design of multiple classifier systems, are proposed to efficiently identify land cover objects.
- **Change Detection:** Change detection is an image analysis problem, consisting of the identification of places where the land cover has changed over time. Change detection is widely used in fields such as urban growth, forest and vegetation dynamics, land use and disaster monitoring. The earliest applications of ensemble classifiers in change detection are designed with the majority voting, Bayesian model averaging, and the maximum posterior probability. Given the growth of satellite data over time, the past decade sees more use of time series methods for continuous change detection from image stacks. One example is a Bayesian ensemble changepoint detection method called BEAST, with the software available as a package Rbeast in R, Python, and Matlab.

### Computer Security

- **Distributed Denial of Service:** Distributed denial of service is one of the most threatening cyber-attacks that may happen to an internet service provider. By combining the output of single classifiers, ensemble classifiers reduce the total error of detecting and discriminating such attacks from legitimate flash crowds.
- **Malware Detection:** Classification of malware codes such as computer viruses, computer worms, trojans, ransomware and spywares with the

usage of machine learning techniques, is inspired by the document categorization problem. Ensemble learning systems have shown a proper efficacy in this area.

- **Intrusion Detection:** An intrusion detection system monitors computer network or computer systems to identify intruder codes like an anomaly detection process. Ensemble learning successfully aids such monitoring systems to reduce their total error.

### Face Recognition

Face recognition, which recently has become one of the most popular research areas of pattern recognition, copes with identification or verification of a person by their digital images. Hierarchical ensembles based on Gabor Fisher classifier and independent component analysis preprocessing techniques are some of the earliest ensembles employed in this field.

### Emotion Recognition

While speech recognition is mainly based on deep learning because most of the industry players in this field like Google, Microsoft and IBM reveal that the core technology of their speech recognition is based on this approach, speech-based emotion recognition can also have a satisfactory performance with ensemble learning. It is also being successfully used in facial emotion recognition.

### Fraud Detection

Fraud detection deals with the identification of bank fraud, such as money laundering, credit card fraud and telecommunication fraud, which have vast domains of research and applications of machine learning. Because ensemble learning improves the robustness of the normal behavior modelling, it has been proposed as an efficient technique to detect such fraudulent cases and activities in banking and credit card systems.

### Financial Decision-Making

The accuracy of prediction of business failure is a very crucial issue in financial decision-making. Therefore, different ensemble classifiers are proposed to predict financial crises and financial distress. Also, in the trade-based manipulation problem, where traders attempt to manipulate stock prices by buying and selling activities, ensemble classifiers are required to analyze the changes in the stock market data and detect suspicious symptom of stock price manipulation.

### Medicine

Ensemble classifiers have been successfully applied in neuroscience, proteomics and medical diagnosis like in neuro-cognitive disorder (i.e. Alzheimer or myotonic dystrophy) detection based on MRI datasets, cervical cytology classification. Besides, ensembles have been successfully applied in medical segmentation tasks, for example brain tumor and hyperintensities segmentation.

## 5.2 USER-CENTRIC CHALLENGES

User-centered design (UCD) or user-driven development (UDD) is a framework of processes in which usability goals, user characteristics, environment, tasks and workflow of a product, service or brand are given extensive attention at each stage of the design process. This attention includes testing which is conducted during each stage of design and development from the envisioned requirements, through pre-production models to post production.

Testing is beneficial as it is often difficult for the designers of a product to understand the experiences of first-time users and each user's learning curve. UCD is based on the understanding of a user, their demands, priorities and experiences, and can lead to increased product usefulness and usability. UCD applies cognitive science principles to create intuitive, efficient products by understanding users' mental processes, behaviors, and needs. UCD differs from other product design philosophies in that it tries to optimize the product around how users engage with the product, in order that users are not forced to change their behavior and expectations to accommodate the product. The users are at the focus, followed by the product's context, objectives and operating environment, and then the granular details of task development, organization, and flow.

### 5.2.1 History

The term user-centered design (UCD) was coined by Rob Kling in 1977 and later adopted in Donald A. Norman's research laboratory at the University of California, San Diego. The concept became popular as a result of Norman's 1986 book User-Centered System Design: New Perspectives on Human-Computer Interaction and the concept gained further attention and acceptance in Norman's 1988 book The Design of Everyday Things, in which Norman describes the psychology behind what he deems 'good' and 'bad' design through examples. He exalts the importance of design in our everyday lives and the consequences of errors caused by bad designs.

Norman describes principles for building well-designed products. His recommendations are based on the user's needs, leaving aside what he considers secondary issues like aesthetics. The main highlights of these are:

- Simplifying the structure of the tasks such that the possible actions at any moment are intuitive.
- Making things visible, including the conceptual model of the system, actions, results of actions and feedback.

- Achieving correct mappings between intended results and required actions.
- Embracing and exploiting the constraints of systems.

In a later book, Emotional Design, Norman returns to some of his earlier ideas to elaborate what he had come to find as overly reductive.

### 5.2.2 Models and Approaches

The UCD process considers user requirements from the beginning and throughout the product cycle. Requirements are noted and refined through investigative methods including: ethnographic study, contextual inquiry, prototype testing, usability testing and other methods. Generative methods may also be used including: card sorting, affinity diagramming and participatory design sessions. In addition, user requirements can be inferred by careful analysis of usable products similar to the product being designed.

UCD takes inspiration from the following models:

- Cooperative design (a.k.a. co-design) which involves designers and users on an equal footing. This is the Scandinavian tradition of design of IT artifacts and it has been evolving since 1970.
- Participatory design (PD), a North American model inspired by cooperative design, with focus on the participation of users. Since 1990, bi-annual conferences have been held.
- Contextual design (CD, a.k.a. customer-centered design) involves gathering data from actual customers in real-world situations and applying findings to the final design.

The following principles help in ensuring a design is user-centered:

- Design is based upon an explicit understanding of users, tasks and environments.
- Users are involved throughout design and development.
- Design is driven and refined by user-centered evaluation.
- Process is iterative.
- Design addresses the whole user experience.
- Design team includes multidisciplinary skills and perspectives.

### 5.2.3 User-Centered Design Process

The goal of UCD is to make products with a high degree of usability (i.e., convenience of use, manageability, effectiveness, and meeting the user's requirements). The general phases of the UCD process are:

- **Specify Context of Use:** Identify the primary users of the product and their reasons, requirements and environment for product use.
- **Specify Requirements:** Identified the detailed technical requirements of the product. This can aid designers in planning development and setting goals.
- **Create Design Solutions and Development:** Based on product goals and requirements, create an iterative cycle of product testing and refinement.
- **Evaluate Product:** Perform usability testing and collect user feedback at every design stage.

The procedure is repeated to further refine the product. These phases are general approaches and factors such as design goals, team and their timeline, and environment in which the product is developed, determine the appropriate phases for a project and their order. Practical models include the waterfall model, agile model or any other software engineering practice.

### 5.2.4 Analysis Tools

There are a number of tools that are used in the analysis of UCD, mainly: personas, scenarios, and essential use cases.

#### Persona

During the UCD process, the design team may create a persona, an archetype representing a product user which helps guide decisions about product features, navigation, interactions, and aesthetics. In most cases, personas are synthesized from a series of ethnographic interviews with real people, then captured in one- or two-page descriptions that include behavior patterns, goals, skills, attitudes, and environment, and possibly fictional personal details to give it more character.

### 5.2.5 Designing Explanations for Non-Technical Audiences

Artificial Intelligence (AI) and machine learning are becoming increasingly integrated into various aspects of daily life, from healthcare to finance and education. While these technologies bring significant benefits, they also introduce complexity that can be difficult for non-technical users to understand. Explainable AI (XAI) aims to bridge this gap by making AI systems transparent and their decisions interpretable. Designing explanations for non-technical audiences requires a careful balance between clarity, accuracy, and accessibility to ensure that AI-driven insights are understandable and actionable.

Designing AI explanations for non-technical audiences is essential for ensuring that AI technologies are used effectively, ethically, and responsibly. By prioritizing clarity, relevance, visualization, and adaptability, AI developers can create explanations that are both understandable and useful. Addressing challenges such as balancing transparency with simplicity and accommodating diverse user knowledge levels will be crucial in making AI-driven decision-making more accessible. As AI continues to shape various industries, enhancing explainability for non-technical users will remain a fundamental goal in the pursuit of responsible AI deployment.

## The Importance of Explainability for Non-Technical Users

Explainability in AI is crucial for building trust and ensuring that end users—who may not have a technical background—can make informed decisions based on AI-generated outputs. Whether it is a doctor interpreting AI-assisted diagnoses, a financial analyst using AI-driven risk assessments, or a teacher understanding AI-recommended learning strategies, clear and comprehensible explanations are essential. Without proper explainability, users may either blindly trust AI decisions or dismiss them entirely due to a lack of understanding, reducing the effectiveness of AI applications.

## Principles of Effective AI Explanations

Effective AI explanations for non-technical audiences should adhere to several key principles. First, simplicity is vital. Explanations should avoid technical jargon and instead use relatable analogies and everyday language. Second, relevance matters. Users should only receive information that is directly applicable to their context, preventing information overload. Third, interactivity enhances understanding. Providing users with options to explore explanations at different levels of detail allows them to engage with the information in a way that suits their needs. Lastly, consistency ensures that explanations follow a predictable structure, making it easier for users to interpret AI outputs over time.

## Tailoring Explanations to Different Audiences

Different non-technical audiences require different types of explanations. A medical professional may need an AI explanation framed in terms of patient health and treatment outcomes, whereas a business executive may require an explanation that focuses on financial impact and risk assessment. Designing AI explanations should involve user research to understand the specific concerns, knowledge levels, and decision-making processes of the target audience. Customizing explanations ensures that users receive meaningful insights rather than generic information.

## Visualization as a Tool for Explainability

Visual elements such as charts, graphs, and interactive dashboards can significantly enhance the explainability of AI-driven insights. Many users find it easier to understand data through visual representation rather than text alone. For example, a risk assessment tool might use color-coded indicators to highlight areas of concern, making it immediately apparent where issues lie. Interactive elements allow users to explore AI decisions dynamically, such as adjusting input parameters to see how the model responds. Effective visualizations simplify complex information and make explanations more engaging.

### The Role of Analogies and Real-World Examples

Analogies and real-world examples are powerful tools for making AI explanations accessible to non-technical users. Comparing AI decision-making processes to familiar human activities—such as how a doctor diagnoses an illness or how a weather forecast predicts rain—can help users grasp abstract concepts. For instance, explaining a machine learning model's feature importance by comparing it to a recipe, where each ingredient contributes to the final dish, makes the concept more relatable. Thoughtful use of analogies enhances comprehension and reduces the perceived complexity of AI systems.

### Balancing Transparency with Simplicity

While it is important to make AI systems transparent, there is a fine line between providing enough information and overwhelming users with unnecessary complexity. Overly technical explanations can confuse non-experts, while overly simplified explanations may misrepresent AI processes. Striking a balance involves providing a clear overview while allowing users to access deeper layers of explanation if they choose. Layered explanations—where users can start with a high-level summary and drill down into details if needed—help maintain both accessibility and accuracy.

### Challenges in Designing Explanations for Non-Technical Users

Several challenges arise when designing AI explanations for non-technical audiences. One major challenge is variability in user knowledge levels. A single explanation approach may not work for all users, necessitating adaptive explanation techniques. Another challenge is avoiding biases in explanations. If AI explanations focus only on positive outcomes without addressing potential risks or uncertainties, users may develop an unrealistic perception of AI reliability. Additionally, some AI decisions are based on complex mathematical models that are inherently difficult to simplify without losing essential meaning. Overcoming these challenges requires iterative user testing and refinement.

### Best Practices for Communicating AI Decisions Effectively

Several best practices can improve the effectiveness of AI explanations. First, using plain language and avoiding unnecessary technical details ensures that explanations remain accessible. Second, breaking down explanations into step-by-step processes helps users follow the reasoning behind AI decisions. Third, incorporating user feedback allows AI systems to refine explanations based on real-world interactions. Finally, providing context-specific explanations—such as why an AI model made a particular recommendation in a given scenario—enhances the practical utility of AI insights for non-technical users.

### Future Directions in Explainability for Non-Technical Audiences

The future of explainable AI will likely involve advancements in user-friendly AI interfaces, natural language explanations, and interactive AI assistants. AI systems will become more conversational, allowing users to ask questions and receive explanations in a way that mimics human interactions. Additionally, regulatory frameworks may require standardized explanation formats to ensure transparency across industries. As AI continues to evolve, making explanations more accessible to non-technical users will remain a key focus to maximize AI's benefits while maintaining trust and accountability.

## 5.2.6 Balancing Simplicity and Completeness

Explainability in artificial intelligence (AI) has become a crucial aspect of AI development and deployment, especially as AI systems are increasingly integrated into decision-making processes in various industries. Ensuring that AI-generated decisions are understandable to users is essential for fostering trust, enabling oversight, and ensuring fairness. However, a fundamental challenge arises when attempting to balance simplicity and completeness in AI explanations. Simplicity ensures that explanations are accessible and comprehensible to diverse audiences, while completeness ensures that all necessary details about the AI model's decision-making process are included. Striking the right balance between these two aspects is essential to providing meaningful and actionable insights.

Balancing simplicity and completeness in AI explanations is essential for fostering trust, enabling informed decision-making, and ensuring compliance with ethical and regulatory standards. While simplicity makes AI insights accessible to a broader audience, completeness ensures that explanations remain meaningful and actionable. Achieving the right balance requires careful consideration of user needs, the implementation of adaptive and layered explanations, and the use of visualization techniques. As AI continues to evolve, advancing explainability frameworks and best practices will play a critical role in making AI systems more transparent, accountable, and user-friendly.

### The Need for Explainability in AI

Explainability in AI serves multiple purposes. First, it helps users build trust in AI systems by making their decision-making processes transparent. If an AI model provides predictions in high-stakes fields like healthcare, finance, or criminal justice, the users must understand how the model arrives at its conclusions. Second, explainability aids in identifying and mitigating biases, ensuring ethical AI deployment. If AI systems operate as "black boxes," unintended biases can go unnoticed, potentially leading to harmful outcomes. Finally, regulatory compliance often necessitates AI explainability, as organizations must justify AI-driven decisions to meet legal and ethical standards.

## Defining Simplicity in AI Explanations

Simplicity in AI explanations refers to the ability to convey the reasoning behind AI-generated decisions in a way that is easily understood by the target audience. Simple explanations avoid technical jargon, minimize unnecessary complexity, and focus on delivering key insights in an intuitive manner. For instance, a doctor using an AI-assisted diagnostic tool should be able to understand why the model suggests a particular diagnosis without needing a deep understanding of machine learning algorithms.

Achieving simplicity requires a user-centered approach. Explanations must be tailored to the knowledge level of the intended audience. For example, a medical AI system might provide different levels of explanation depending on whether the user is a physician, a medical student, or a patient. Simplicity ensures that AI systems remain accessible to non-technical users while retaining their practical utility.

## The Importance of Completeness in AI Explanations

Completeness in AI explanations ensures that all relevant information is included to provide a comprehensive understanding of an AI model's decision-making process. While simplicity focuses on clarity, completeness ensures that users receive sufficient detail to trust and verify AI outputs. For instance, in financial risk assessment, an AI system should not only provide a simple risk score but also offer details on the contributing factors, such as market trends, transaction history, and customer profiles. Complete explanations often include references to input data, the features that influenced a decision, the level of confidence in the prediction, and potential alternative outcomes. Without completeness, AI explanations may become oversimplified to the point where they lose their effectiveness. Users must be able to scrutinize AI-generated results and make informed decisions based on all relevant factors.

## Challenges in Balancing Simplicity and Completeness

Striking the right balance between simplicity and completeness presents several challenges. First, different users have varying levels of expertise and information needs. A data scientist might require a highly detailed breakdown of model weights and biases, whereas an end-user might only need a high-level summary. Second, overly simplified explanations can lead to a lack of trust if users feel they are not receiving the full picture. Conversely, excessively detailed explanations may overwhelm users and hinder effective decision-making. Third, technical limitations in AI models can sometimes make it difficult to provide meaningful explanations without reducing accuracy. For example, deep learning models with complex neural architectures may be inherently difficult to explain in a fully interpretable manner.

## Strategies for Achieving the Right Balance

Several strategies can help achieve an optimal balance between simplicity and completeness in AI explanations. One effective approach is layered explanations, where users are provided with a high-level summary first and then given the option to explore more detailed information as needed. For instance, a customer using an AI-based credit scoring system might receive a simple statement such as "Your loan application was declined due to a low credit score," followed by an option to view a breakdown of contributing factors.

Another strategy involves using visualization techniques to convey complex information in an intuitive way. Graphs, charts, and interactive dashboards can help users understand AI-generated insights without requiring extensive technical knowledge. For example, a heatmap displaying the influence of different variables on an AI decision can provide both simplicity and completeness in a single view.

AI systems can also be designed with adaptive explanations that adjust based on user preferences and expertise levels. A system that detects fraudulent transactions, for instance, could provide a summary explanation to a customer and a more detailed breakdown to a fraud investigator.

## The Role of Explainability Frameworks

Various explainability frameworks help AI developers balance simplicity and completeness. Model-agnostic methods, such as SHAP (Shapley Additive Explanations) and LIME (Local Interpretable Model-agnostic Explanations), allow users to explore AI decisions in an interpretable way without compromising too much on completeness. Model-specific techniques, such as decision trees and attention maps in neural networks, provide explanations tailored to the structure of specific AI models.

Regulatory bodies and ethical guidelines also influence the balance between simplicity and completeness. For example, the General Data Protection Regulation (GDPR) in the European Union mandates that users have the right to an explanation when AI impacts their legal rights or significant decisions. This legal requirement ensures that AI explanations are not only simple enough for consumers to understand but also complete enough to justify AI-driven actions.

### Future Directions in Explainability

As AI technology advances, new approaches to explainability will continue to emerge. One promising area is the use of natural language processing (NLP) to generate human-readable explanations that dynamically adjust based on user queries. AI-driven chatbots, for example, could explain AI decisions interactively, allowing users to ask follow-up questions and receive additional details when necessary.

Advancements in AI interpretability research are also leading to the development of hybrid models that integrate rule-based logic with machine learning to provide inherently interpretable AI systems. These models aim to retain predictive accuracy while offering transparency and detailed reasoning for AI-generated outcomes.

The future of AI explainability will also be shaped by industry collaboration. AI researchers, policymakers, and industry stakeholders must work together to establish best practices for balancing simplicity and completeness. Standardized guidelines and evaluation metrics for AI explanations can help ensure consistency across different domains and applications.

## 5.3 TECHNICAL BARRIERS

As artificial intelligence (AI) systems become increasingly sophisticated and influential across industries, the demand for explainability has grown. AI explainability refers to the ability to make AI decision-making processes transparent and understandable to humans. However, achieving explainability is not without challenges. Technical barriers often hinder the development and implementation of explainable AI (XAI), making it difficult for users to interpret the outputs of AI models accurately. These barriers stem from the complexity of AI algorithms, limitations in model interpretability, trade-offs with accuracy, and computational constraints. Addressing these challenges is essential to making AI more accountable, ethical, and trustworthy.

The technical barriers to AI explainability are multifaceted, encompassing challenges related to model complexity, accuracy trade-offs, computational constraints, feature attribution difficulties, and security concerns. Overcoming these barriers requires ongoing research, the development of standardized evaluation metrics, and advancements in AI model architectures. As AI continues to play a pivotal role in critical decision-making, ensuring that these systems are both powerful and interpretable is essential for fostering trust, accountability, and ethical deployment. Addressing these challenges will be key to making AI a more transparent and responsible tool for the future.

### 5.3.1 Complexity of AI Algorithms

One of the primary technical barriers to explainability in AI is the complexity of modern AI algorithms. Many state-of-the-art machine learning models, such as deep neural networks, employ thousands or even millions of parameters to process data and generate predictions. These models operate as "black boxes," meaning that even developers who build them often struggle to understand their internal workings fully. Unlike traditional rule-based systems, where logic can be explicitly traced, AI models learn patterns from data without predefined rules, making it difficult to extract straightforward explanations.

Deep learning models, particularly those used in natural language processing (NLP), image recognition, and reinforcement learning, further complicate explainability. Layers of artificial neurons transform inputs through nonlinear operations, making it challenging to determine which features contribute most to a decision. As a result, users and stakeholders often have to rely on post hoc interpretation techniques, which may not always provide complete or reliable explanations.

### 5.3.2 Trade-Off between Explainability and Accuracy

Another major technical challenge is the trade-off between explainability and accuracy. Many high-performing AI models are inherently complex, as they utilize deep layers, ensemble techniques, and advanced feature extraction methods to achieve superior accuracy. However, simplifying these models for better explainability often results in decreased predictive performance. For example, linear regression and decision trees offer clear interpretability, but they may not match the accuracy of deep learning models in complex tasks like medical diagnosis or financial forecasting.

This trade-off creates a dilemma for AI practitioners. Organizations that prioritize accuracy over explainability may deploy black-box models that deliver optimal results but lack transparency. Conversely, organizations that emphasize interpretability may settle for simpler models, which may not perform as well on complex datasets. Striking a balance between accuracy and explainability remains an ongoing challenge in AI research and application.

### 5.3.3 Model-Specific vs. Model-Agnostic Explanation Methods

Technical limitations also arise from the nature of explanation methods themselves. AI explainability approaches can be classified into two categories: model-specific and model-agnostic methods. Model-specific methods are designed to interpret particular types of models, such as attention visualization for deep learning or feature importance scores for decision trees. While these techniques provide valuable insights, they are often not generalizable across different AI architectures.

On the other hand, model-agnostic methods attempt to explain any AI model without modifying its structure. Techniques such as Local Interpretable Model-Agnostic Explanations (LIME) and SHapley Additive Explanations (SHAP) aim to provide post hoc explanations by approximating how a model behaves in different scenarios. However, these methods come with limitations, as they may not fully capture the decision-making logic of highly complex AI models. Furthermore, post hoc explanations can sometimes be misleading, creating the illusion of transparency without genuinely improving model interpretability.

### 5.3.4 Challenges in Feature Attribution

Feature attribution plays a crucial role in AI explainability by identifying which input variables contribute most to an AI model's prediction. However, attributing importance to features is technically challenging, especially in deep learning models that process vast amounts of data across multiple layers. For example, in image recognition tasks, convolutional neural networks (CNNs) extract hierarchical features from images, making it difficult to pinpoint which specific pixels led to a particular classification.

Additionally, some AI models operate on complex, high-dimensional data, making feature attribution even more problematic. In financial risk assessment, for instance, AI systems analyze large datasets that include customer demographics, transaction history, and market trends. Identifying which factors influenced a model's decision requires advanced interpretation techniques, but these methods are often computationally intensive and prone to errors.

### 5.3.5 Computational and Resource Constraints

Explainability in AI also faces technical barriers related to computational resources. Many explainability techniques, such as SHAP and LIME, require significant processing power, especially when applied to large-scale AI models. Generating explanations for complex models can demand substantial computational resources, increasing latency and making real-time explanations impractical.

For organizations deploying AI on edge devices or in low-power environments, computational limitations become a critical concern. AI explainability methods often involve running additional model simulations, perturbations, or reverse engineering, which can slow down decision-making processes. In sectors like healthcare, where real-time predictions are essential, computational inefficiencies can pose serious challenges.

### 5.3.6 Lack of Standardization in Explainability Metrics

Another significant technical barrier to AI explainability is the lack of standardized metrics for evaluating explanations. While various explainability techniques exist, there is no universally accepted method to measure how understandable an AI model's output is to different stakeholders. Different users—such as AI researchers, regulatory bodies, and end-users—may have varying expectations of what constitutes a good explanation.

Researchers have proposed multiple metrics, such as fidelity (how well an explanation aligns with model behavior), stability (how consistent explanations are across different instances), and user trust (how much a user believes the explanation). However, these metrics are often subjective and context-dependent, making it difficult to create a standardized framework for evaluating AI explainability across different domains.

### 5.3.7 Security and Privacy Concerns

Security and privacy issues further complicate AI explainability. Many AI models process sensitive data, including personal health records, financial transactions, and confidential business information. Providing detailed explanations about AI decisions may inadvertently expose sensitive data or create security vulnerabilities. For example, adversarial attacks can exploit AI explanations to manipulate models by learning how they weigh different features.

In privacy-sensitive applications, AI developers must balance the need for transparency with the need to protect user data. Techniques like differential privacy and federated learning attempt to mitigate these risks, but they can introduce additional complexity that may reduce explainability. Ensuring that AI explanations do not compromise security while remaining meaningful to users remains an ongoing challenge.

### 5.3.8 Future Directions and Potential Solutions

Despite these technical barriers, ongoing research and advancements in AI interpretability offer promising solutions. One approach is the development of inherently interpretable AI models, such as self-explaining neural networks, which integrate explanation mechanisms directly into their architecture. Another emerging area is the use of hybrid models that combine rule-based reasoning with machine learning, allowing for greater transparency without sacrificing accuracy.

Efforts are also being made to improve standardization in AI explainability. Organizations and regulatory bodies are working toward defining clear guidelines for AI transparency, which can help establish industry-wide best practices. Additionally, advances in explainability-as-a-service (XaaS) platforms are enabling organizations to integrate explainability tools more efficiently into their AI systems.

## 5.4 SOCIOCULTURAL AND ETHICAL IMPLICATIONS

Artificial Intelligence (AI) has transformed numerous sectors, ranging from healthcare and finance to law enforcement and education. However, as AI systems become more deeply embedded in society, concerns about their transparency and fairness have gained prominence. Explainability in AI is not just a technical necessity but also a sociocultural and ethical imperative. Ensuring that AI systems provide understandable and meaningful explanations is crucial for building trust, preventing bias, and safeguarding human rights. Sociocultural factors influence how different communities perceive AI explanations, while ethical considerations dictate the moral responsibilities of AI developers and users.

The sociocultural and ethical implications of AI explainability extend far beyond technical considerations. Explainable AI fosters trust, promotes fairness, and ensures accountability in automated decision-making. However, ethical challenges such as bias, privacy concerns, and regulatory complexities must be addressed to make AI transparency a reality. As AI continues to shape society, prioritizing explainability is essential for building ethical, inclusive, and socially responsible AI systems. Organizations, developers, and policymakers must collaborate to create AI frameworks that balance transparency with innovation, ensuring that AI serves humanity equitably and responsibly.

### 5.4.1 The Role of Explainability in Trust and Public Perception

Trust is a fundamental component of AI adoption and usability. If users cannot understand how an AI system arrives at its decisions, they may be hesitant to rely on it. The opacity of black-box AI models has led to widespread skepticism, particularly in sensitive areas such as healthcare and criminal justice. Explainability helps bridge the gap between technical complexity and user comprehension, thereby fostering public confidence in AI systems.

Different societies have varying levels of trust in technology, influenced by cultural factors such as historical experiences with automation, governmental regulation, and public education. In some cultures, technological advancements are embraced with enthusiasm, while in others, they are met with caution and resistance. The way AI explanations are framed and communicated must align with cultural expectations to ensure widespread acceptance. A failure to consider these sociocultural nuances can result in misunderstandings, misinformation, and reduced trust in AI-powered decision-making.

### 5.4.2 Bias, Fairness, and Social Justice

One of the most pressing ethical concerns in AI is the issue of bias. AI models are trained on historical data, which may contain systemic biases related to race, gender, socioeconomic status, and other demographic factors. If an AI system makes decisions without clear explanations, it becomes difficult to identify and address these biases, leading to discriminatory outcomes.

For example, in hiring processes, AI-powered recruitment tools have been criticized for favoring certain demographics over others. If these tools lack explainability, affected individuals have no way of contesting or understanding the reasoning behind their rejection. Similarly, in law enforcement, AI-driven predictive policing models have been found to disproportionately target minority communities. Without transparency, such biases remain unchecked, exacerbating social injustices.

Explainability in AI provides a means to detect and rectify biases. By making AI decision-making processes more transparent, developers and policymakers can implement corrective measures to ensure fairness. Ethical AI frameworks should prioritize explainability as a mechanism to uphold social justice and prevent discriminatory practices.

### 5.4.3 Ethical Responsibility of AI Developers and Organizations

AI developers and organizations have a moral obligation to design systems that are not only efficient but also ethically sound. The lack of explainability raises concerns about accountability, as it becomes difficult to determine responsibility when AI systems produce harmful or erroneous outcomes. Ethical AI development requires adherence to principles such as transparency, accountability, and inclusivity.

Developers should integrate explainability features into AI systems from the design stage rather than treating them as an afterthought. Organizations deploying AI should also ensure that users, regulators, and affected individuals have access to comprehensible explanations regarding how AI models function. This transparency is crucial for ethical decision-making and legal compliance.

Furthermore, AI ethics committees and interdisciplinary teams should be established to oversee the development and deployment of explainable AI models. These teams should include not only AI experts but also ethicists, sociologists, and legal professionals to ensure that multiple perspectives are considered.

### 5.4.4 The Impact of Explainability on Privacy and Security

While explainability is crucial for transparency, it also introduces privacy and security concerns. Providing detailed explanations of AI models can expose sensitive information, making systems vulnerable to adversarial attacks. For example, in the financial sector, revealing too much about an AI-driven fraud detection system may enable malicious actors to manipulate transactions in a way that avoids detection.

Striking a balance between transparency and privacy is a significant ethical challenge. AI developers must ensure that explanations are informative without compromising confidential data. Methods such as differential privacy and federated learning can help mitigate risks while maintaining an adequate level of explainability.

Additionally, data ownership and consent are ethical concerns in AI explainability. Individuals should have the right to understand how their data is being used in AI systems and whether they can opt out of automated decision-making processes. AI policies should mandate clear guidelines on user consent, ensuring that individuals have control over their personal information.

### 5.4.5 Regulatory and Legal Implications

The legal landscape surrounding AI explainability is still evolving, with different countries adopting various approaches to AI regulation. In the European Union, the General Data Protection Regulation (GDPR) includes a "right to explanation," granting individuals the ability to challenge and demand transparency in automated decision-making. Similar regulatory efforts are being explored in the United States, Canada, and other regions.

However, enforcing explainability through legal frameworks presents several challenges. Firstly, AI models differ in complexity, and a universal standard for explanations may not be feasible. Secondly, legal definitions of explainability remain ambiguous, making it difficult for organizations to comply effectively. Thirdly, regulatory requirements must strike a balance between innovation and ethical safeguards to avoid stifling technological advancements.

AI explainability laws must be adaptable, taking into account sector-specific needs. For example, in healthcare, patients should have access to clear explanations about AI-driven diagnoses, while in finance, consumers should receive understandable reasons for loan approvals or rejections. Policymakers should collaborate with AI researchers to develop legal frameworks that uphold both ethical standards and technological feasibility.

### 5.4.6 Societal Impact of AI Explanations in Different Fields

Explainability in AI carries significant societal implications across various industries. In healthcare, AI-assisted diagnostics and treatment recommendations must be interpretable for both doctors and patients. A lack of explainability in medical AI can lead to mistrust in automated systems, limiting their adoption and effectiveness.

In finance, AI-driven credit scoring and risk assessment must be transparent to ensure that consumers understand how their financial profiles are evaluated. Unexplained credit decisions can disproportionately impact certain demographics, contributing to financial exclusion. In criminal justice, AI explainability is essential for ensuring fair sentencing, bail decisions, and parole assessments. If judicial AI systems operate as black boxes, they risk perpetuating biases present in historical data. Transparent AI in legal settings can enhance due process and uphold the principles of justice.

### 5.4.7 Cultural Variations in AI Explainability Expectations

Different cultures have distinct expectations regarding AI explainability. In some societies, there is a high demand for AI systems to be fully transparent, while in others, users may prioritize efficiency over interpretability. For instance, Western nations, where individual rights and legal accountability are emphasized, may demand greater transparency in AI decision-making. Conversely, in some Asian countries where trust in centralized systems is higher, users may be more accepting of opaque AI models.

Understanding these cultural variations is crucial for designing AI systems that cater to diverse user needs. AI explanations should be tailored to align with cultural norms, ensuring that they are both accessible and meaningful to different populations.

CHAPTER 6

# Tools and Frameworks for XAI

## 6.1 OPEN-SOURCE LIBRARIES

As artificial intelligence (AI) continues to evolve, the need for transparency and interpretability in AI models has become a critical concern. Explainable AI (XAI) seeks to provide insights into how AI models arrive at their predictions, ensuring that decisions made by these systems can be understood and trusted by humans. Open-source libraries play a crucial role in advancing AI explainability by providing accessible tools that enable researchers, developers, and businesses to interpret and analyze AI-driven decision-making.

Open-source libraries for AI explainability have become indispensable tools for making AI systems more transparent, interpretable, and trustworthy. Libraries such as SHAP, LIME, Captum, ELI5, and AIX360 provide essential methodologies for understanding how AI models make decisions, contributing to ethical AI deployment and regulatory compliance. Despite challenges such as computational complexity and audience-specific interpretability needs, these libraries continue to evolve, ensuring that AI remains explainable and accessible to all stakeholders. Moving forward, continued collaboration and innovation in the open-source AI community will be key to advancing AI explainability and fostering responsible AI adoption worldwide.

### 6.1.1 The Importance of Open-Source Libraries in AI Explainability

Open-source libraries for AI explainability provide researchers and practitioners with standardized tools to interpret complex machine learning models. These libraries contribute to the democratization of AI by making powerful interpretability techniques accessible to a wide range of users. By leveraging these open-source tools, organizations can build more ethical, accountable, and regulatory-compliant AI systems. Furthermore, open-source libraries encourage collaboration among researchers and developers. The transparency of their codebases allows for peer review and improvement, ensuring that explainability techniques remain robust and up to date. Given that AI interpretability is a rapidly evolving field, the ability to refine and enhance existing methods through collective contributions is invaluable.

### 6.1.2 Popular Open-Source Libraries for AI Explainability

Several open-source libraries have been developed to provide explanations for AI models, each offering distinct methodologies and approaches. These libraries cater to different AI paradigms, including deep learning, tree-based models, and natural language processing.

#### SHapley Additive exPlanations (SHAP)

SHAP is one of the most widely used libraries for AI explainability. Based on Shapley values from cooperative game theory, SHAP provides a unified measure of feature importance for individual predictions. It helps users understand how different input features contribute to a model's output by assigning each feature a positive or negative impact score.

SHAP is particularly useful for high-stakes applications such as healthcare and finance, where understanding the reasoning behind AI-driven decisions is crucial. The library supports a variety of machine learning frameworks, including XGBoost, LightGBM, and deep learning models, making it highly versatile.

#### Local Interpretable Model-agnostic Explanations (LIME)

LIME is another prominent library designed to explain the predictions of complex black-box models. Unlike SHAP, which provides a global understanding of feature importance, LIME generates local approximations to explain individual predictions. It works by perturbing input data and training an interpretable model (such as a linear model) to approximate the behavior of the original complex model.

LIME is useful when users need an intuitive, instance-specific explanation of model predictions. It has been widely adopted in domains such as healthcare, finance, and criminal justice, where local interpretability is essential.

#### Captum

Captum is an open-source PyTorch library developed by Facebook AI that provides interpretability methods specifically for deep learning models. It includes various attribution techniques, such as Integrated Gradients, Layer Conductance, and Occlusion, which help explain how different layers and neurons contribute to model predictions.

Captum is particularly beneficial for neural networks, enabling researchers to understand which input features influence deep learning decisions. The library is seamlessly integrated with PyTorch, making it an excellent choice for AI practitioners using this framework.

#### ELI5 (Explain Like I'm 5)

ELI5 is a library focused on providing easy-to-understand explanations for a variety of machine learning models. It supports feature importance analysis, permutation importance, and visualization techniques. ELI5 is compatible with scikit-learn, XGBoost, and deep learning models, offering flexibility for different AI applications.

The simplicity and user-friendly nature of ELI5 make it ideal for users who require straightforward explanations without deep mathematical knowledge of interpretability methods.

### AI Explainability 360 (AIX360)

AIX360 is an open-source toolkit developed by IBM to support the explainability of AI models. The library provides a diverse set of algorithms tailored for both interpretable models and post-hoc explanations of black-box models. It includes rule-based explanations, prototype-based techniques, and feature importance methods, making it a comprehensive toolkit for AI interpretability.

AIX360 is designed to align with fairness and accountability considerations, ensuring that AI-driven decisions are both explainable and ethical. The toolkit is especially relevant for enterprise-level AI deployments that require adherence to regulatory standards.

## 6.1.3 Challenges and Limitations of Open-Source Explainability Libraries

While open-source libraries for AI explainability have significantly advanced the field, they also come with certain challenges and limitations. One major challenge is the computational cost of some explainability techniques. Methods like SHAP can be computationally expensive, particularly for large datasets and deep learning models, making them less practical for real-time applications.

Another challenge is the trade-off between accuracy and interpretability. Many high-performing AI models, such as deep neural networks, are inherently complex, and simplifying their decision-making processes may lead to loss of predictive power. Open-source libraries must balance providing meaningful explanations while maintaining model fidelity.

Additionally, the effectiveness of explainability methods depends on the audience. While researchers and developers may benefit from technical insights provided by these libraries, non-technical stakeholders (such as patients in a healthcare setting) may struggle to understand the outputs. More work is needed to create user-friendly explainability tools tailored to different audiences.

## 6.1.4 The Role of Open-Source Libraries in Ethical AI and Regulatory Compliance

Regulatory bodies around the world are increasingly emphasizing AI transparency and fairness. Open-source explainability libraries play a critical role in helping organizations comply with legal frameworks such as the General Data Protection Regulation (GDPR) and the AI Act proposed by the European Union. These regulations mandate that AI-driven decisions, especially in sensitive domains like healthcare and finance, must be explainable and non-discriminatory.

By using open-source explainability libraries, businesses can audit their AI models to ensure fairness and detect potential biases. This proactive approach helps prevent discriminatory outcomes and fosters ethical AI deployment.

Moreover, the open-source nature of these libraries promotes transparency by allowing independent researchers and regulators to verify the effectiveness of AI models. This openness ensures that AI systems remain accountable to the public and minimizes the risk of unethical AI practices.

### 6.1.5 Future Directions in Open-Source AI Explainability

The future of open-source AI explainability libraries lies in the integration of more sophisticated and efficient techniques. Researchers are working on developing faster, more scalable methods that can provide real-time explanations without compromising model performance. Additionally, advancements in visualization techniques will make AI explanations more accessible to non-technical users, improving AI adoption across diverse sectors.

Another promising direction is the integration of explainability tools directly into AI development pipelines. By embedding interpretability techniques into AI frameworks from the outset, developers can ensure that AI models remain transparent and accountable throughout their lifecycle.

Finally, greater interdisciplinary collaboration between AI researchers, ethicists, and legal experts will shape the development of explainability tools that align with societal values. Open-source communities will continue to play a vital role in driving this progress, fostering an environment of transparency, accountability, and responsible AI innovation.

### 6.1.6 LIME (Local Interpretable Model-Agnostic Explanations)

Artificial Intelligence (AI) models have increasingly become more complex, leading to challenges in understanding how they make decisions. As AI is integrated into critical sectors like healthcare, finance, and law enforcement, ensuring interpretability and transparency has become essential. One of the most widely used tools for AI explainability is LIME (Local Interpretable Model-Agnostic Explanations). LIME provides a way to understand complex machine learning models by approximating them with simpler, interpretable models for individual predictions. LIME is a powerful tool in the field of AI explainability, offering local, instance-specific insights into black-box models. Its model-agnostic nature, intuitive explanations, and ability to detect biases make it a valuable asset for AI practitioners across various industries. However, its limitations, such as sensitivity to perturbation techniques and reliance on surrogate models, must be carefully managed to ensure accurate interpretations.

As research in AI interpretability progresses, continuous improvements to LIME and its integration with other explainability methods will further enhance transparency and trust in AI systems. By leveraging tools like LIME, organizations can build more accountable and ethical AI solutions that align with user expectations and regulatory requirements.

### The Need for Model-Agnostic Explanations

Most high-performing machine learning models, such as deep neural networks and gradient-boosted decision trees, operate as black boxes, meaning their internal logic is not easily understandable. While these models provide high accuracy, their opacity makes it difficult to determine why they make specific predictions. This lack of transparency can lead to issues such as biased decision-making, lack of user trust, and regulatory non-compliance. Model-agnostic techniques like LIME help address this issue by offering explanations that work with any type of machine learning model. These explanations allow researchers, developers, and end-users to gain insights into model behavior, identify potential biases, and make informed decisions regarding AI deployments.

### How LIME Works

LIME operates on the principle of local interpretability, meaning it focuses on explaining individual predictions rather than the overall model. The key idea behind LIME is to approximate the complex black-box model with an interpretable surrogate model, such as a linear regression model, within a local region around the instance being analyzed. This is done using the following steps:

First, LIME perturbs the input data by making small modifications to the feature values and generating synthetic instances. These instances are then fed into the original black-box model to obtain predictions. By analyzing how slight changes in input affect the output, LIME constructs a local dataset. Next, LIME assigns weights to the perturbed samples based on their similarity to the original instance. This ensures that the surrogate model focuses more on the region of interest rather than making generalizations across the entire dataset.

Finally, LIME trains an interpretable model, such as a linear regression model, on the weighted dataset. This surrogate model approximates the decision boundary of the black-box model within the local region. The coefficients of this interpretable model are then used to explain the contribution of each feature to the final prediction.

### Strengths of LIME

LIME has several advantages that make it a powerful tool for AI explainability. One of its key strengths is its model-agnostic nature, meaning it can be applied to any machine learning model, regardless of its internal architecture. This flexibility allows it to be used across different domains and applications.

Another strength of LIME is its ability to provide intuitive explanations. By generating feature importance scores for individual predictions, LIME helps users understand which features are most influential in the decision-making process. This makes it particularly useful in high-stakes applications like healthcare, where doctors need to understand AI-driven diagnoses.

LIME is also valuable for identifying model biases. By analyzing explanations across different demographic groups, users can detect whether a model is making biased predictions. This capability is critical in ensuring fairness and compliance with ethical AI principles.

### Limitations and Challenges

Despite its strengths, LIME has certain limitations that must be considered when using it for AI explainability. One major challenge is the selection of the surrogate model. While LIME typically uses linear regression for interpretability, this approach may oversimplify the decision boundary of the black-box model, leading to inaccurate explanations. Choosing an appropriate surrogate model remains a challenge in ensuring faithful interpretations.

Another limitation is the sensitivity of LIME to perturbation techniques. Since LIME relies on generating synthetic data points, the way in which these perturbations are made can significantly influence the explanations. If the perturbations do not accurately represent the original data distribution, the resulting explanations may be misleading.

Additionally, LIME explanations are local rather than global. While this is useful for instance-specific analysis, it does not provide an overarching understanding of the model's behavior. Users who need insights into the overall decision-making process of a model may need to combine LIME with other explainability techniques.

### Applications of LIME in Various Industries

LIME has been widely adopted across different industries to enhance transparency and trust in AI systems. In healthcare, LIME is used to explain AI-generated medical diagnoses, allowing doctors to validate model predictions before making clinical decisions. For example, LIME can help highlight which patient features (e.g., symptoms, test results) contributed most to a model's decision regarding disease diagnosis.

In finance, LIME is applied to credit scoring and fraud detection models. By providing clear explanations of why a loan application was approved or rejected, LIME helps financial institutions comply with regulations such as the Fair Credit Reporting Act (FCRA). This improves customer trust and reduces potential legal liabilities.

In law enforcement and criminal justice, LIME is used to evaluate risk assessment models that predict recidivism rates. By understanding which factors contribute to a high-risk score, policymakers can ensure that AI-driven decisions align with ethical and legal standards.

### Future Directions and Enhancements

As AI explainability continues to evolve, researchers are exploring ways to improve LIME and address its limitations. One area of research involves enhancing the fidelity of surrogate models by experimenting with different interpretability techniques, such as decision trees and rule-based models, to better approximate black-box models.

Another direction is improving the robustness of perturbation methods. Researchers are developing techniques that generate more realistic perturbations to ensure that explanations remain faithful to the original data distribution. This can help reduce the risk of misleading interpretations.

Additionally, integrating LIME with other explainability techniques can provide more comprehensive insights. For example, combining LIME with SHAP (SHapley Additive exPlanations) can offer both local and global interpretability, giving users a more complete understanding of model behavior.

Furthermore, advancements in visualization tools can make LIME explanations more accessible to non-technical users. Interactive dashboards and visual representations of feature importance scores can help bridge the gap between AI developers and end-users.

## 6.1.7 SHAP (SHapley Additive exPlanations)

SHAP (SHapley Additive exPlanations) is a powerful tool for AI explainability that provides mathematically sound feature attributions based on game theory. Its ability to offer consistent, unbiased, and model-agnostic explanations makes it one of the most reliable interpretability techniques available today.

Despite its computational challenges, SHAP is widely used across various industries to enhance transparency, detect biases, and improve trust in AI decision-making. As research in AI interpretability advances, ongoing improvements to SHAP's efficiency and integration with other explainability methods will further strengthen its role in responsible AI development.

By leveraging SHAP, organizations can build more transparent and accountable AI systems, ensuring that AI-driven decisions align with ethical principles and societal expectations. As the demand for explainability grows, SHAP will continue to play a crucial role in making AI more interpretable, trustworthy, and fair.

## The Importance of SHAP in AI Explainability

SHAP is particularly valuable because it provides mathematically grounded explanations of how individual features contribute to a model's predictions. Many AI models operate as black boxes, making it challenging to identify the factors influencing their decisions. SHAP addresses this problem by assigning each feature a Shapley value, which quantifies its contribution to a given prediction. This helps stakeholders, including data scientists, policymakers, and end-users, understand model behavior, detect biases, and ensure fairness and accountability in AI systems.

## How SHAP Works

SHAP is derived from cooperative game theory, where each feature in a model is treated as a player in a coalition contributing to the final prediction. The method computes Shapley values by considering all possible feature combinations and calculating their marginal contributions to the prediction. This results in a fair and balanced distribution of credit among features.

SHAP follows these main steps:

- First, the method evaluates the model's output by considering subsets of features and measuring their impact on predictions. It does this by running the model multiple times with different feature combinations.
- Next, SHAP calculates the Shapley values for each feature by averaging its contributions across all possible feature subsets. This ensures that each feature receives an attribution based on its true impact rather than arbitrary importance scores.
- Finally, SHAP presents its results in the form of visual explanations, such as force plots, dependence plots, and summary plots, which provide users with clear and interpretable insights into the model's decision-making process.

## Strengths of SHAP

One of the primary advantages of SHAP is its theoretical foundation in game theory, which ensures that feature importance attributions are consistent and unbiased. Unlike heuristic-based methods that may provide inconsistent results, SHAP guarantees additive explanations, meaning the sum of individual feature contributions matches the model's total output.

Another strength of SHAP is its versatility. The method is model-agnostic, meaning it can be applied to any machine learning model, including tree-based algorithms, neural networks, and linear models. This flexibility makes SHAP widely applicable across different industries and AI applications.

Additionally, SHAP offers rich visualization tools that enhance interpretability. Summary plots help identify the most influential features across an entire dataset, while individual force plots illustrate how features drive a specific prediction. These visual explanations bridge the gap between technical and non-technical users, making AI decision-making more transparent.

### Limitations and Challenges

Despite its benefits, SHAP has certain limitations. One of the main challenges is its computational complexity. Since SHAP requires evaluating all possible feature subsets, calculating Shapley values can be computationally expensive, especially for models with a large number of features. This can lead to long processing times, making SHAP less practical for real-time applications.

Another challenge is the difficulty of interpreting SHAP values in high-dimensional datasets. While SHAP provides precise feature attributions, the sheer number of contributing factors can make it overwhelming to analyze results. Users must carefully design their analyses and choose appropriate visualization techniques to derive meaningful insights.

Additionally, SHAP relies on approximations in many cases to reduce computation time. While these approximations make the method more scalable, they can introduce slight inaccuracies in feature attributions. Researchers are actively working on improving SHAP's efficiency while maintaining its theoretical guarantees.

### Applications of SHAP in Various Industries

SHAP is widely used across different sectors to enhance AI transparency and trustworthiness. In healthcare, SHAP helps interpret AI models used for disease prediction, treatment recommendations, and medical diagnostics. By identifying the most influential patient features, such as symptoms and lab results, SHAP enables doctors to validate AI-generated recommendations and make informed clinical decisions.

In finance, SHAP plays a crucial role in credit scoring and fraud detection. Financial institutions use SHAP to explain why a customer was approved or denied a loan, ensuring compliance with regulatory requirements such as the Fair Credit Reporting Act (FCRA). Transparent credit decisions improve customer trust and reduce potential biases in lending practices.

In criminal justice, SHAP is used to interpret risk assessment models that predict recidivism rates. By highlighting the factors influencing a defendant's risk score, SHAP enables legal professionals to ensure that AI-driven decisions are fair and unbiased. This is critical for preventing discriminatory outcomes in sentencing and parole decisions.

In retail and e-commerce, SHAP helps companies understand customer behavior and optimize recommendation systems. By analyzing feature contributions to purchase predictions, businesses can personalize recommendations and improve customer experiences.

### Future Directions and Enhancements

As AI explainability continues to evolve, researchers are exploring ways to enhance SHAP's efficiency and usability. One promising direction is the development of faster approximation methods that maintain SHAP's theoretical guarantees while reducing computation time. Techniques such as TreeSHAP have already made SHAP more practical for tree-based models by significantly improving computational efficiency.

Another area of improvement is the integration of SHAP with other interpretability techniques. Combining SHAP with counterfactual explanations, for example, can provide both feature attributions and alternative decision paths, giving users a more holistic understanding of model behavior.

Furthermore, advancements in visualization tools can make SHAP explanations more accessible to non-technical users. Interactive dashboards that allow users to explore feature contributions dynamically can enhance transparency and trust in AI systems.

Finally, regulatory bodies and industry stakeholders are increasingly advocating for the adoption of SHAP and similar explainability tools to ensure fairness and accountability in AI applications. As AI regulations become more stringent, methods like SHAP will play a vital role in demonstrating compliance with ethical and legal standards.

## 6.1.8 ELI5 (Explain Like I'm 5)

ELI5 (Explain Like I'm 5) is a valuable tool for AI explainability that simplifies complex machine learning models and enhances transparency. By providing clear and accessible explanations, ELI5 helps data scientists, businesses, and regulatory bodies understand AI decision-making processes.

Despite some limitations, ELI5 remains a widely used interpretability tool across various industries, including healthcare, finance, law, and marketing. Its ability to provide feature importance scores, identify model biases, and debug predictions makes it a crucial component of responsible AI development. As research in AI interpretability advances, ELI5 will continue to play an essential role in making AI more transparent and trustworthy. By improving its computational efficiency, visualization capabilities, and deep learning compatibility, ELI5 can further enhance the explainability of AI models and drive ethical AI adoption across multiple sectors.

## Understanding AI Explainability and the Need for ELI5

AI explainability is crucial in building trust and ensuring that AI-driven decisions are fair and unbiased. If an AI model determines creditworthiness or medical diagnoses, stakeholders must understand how decisions are made to avoid biases and errors. Traditional machine learning models, such as decision trees, can be relatively easy to interpret. However, complex models like deep neural networks or ensemble methods require specialized tools like ELI5 to make their inner workings transparent. ELI5 provides simple and accessible explanations for AI models, making it easier for data scientists, domain experts, and even non-technical users to understand how predictions are generated. This interpretability enhances trust in AI applications and facilitates compliance with regulatory frameworks that mandate transparency in automated decision-making.

## How ELI5 Works

ELI5 functions as a model-agnostic explainability tool, meaning it can be applied to various machine learning models, including linear regression, random forests, gradient boosting machines, and deep learning models. It primarily works by breaking down complex models into comprehensible components and assigning importance scores to individual features.

ELI5 uses several techniques to explain AI models:

- Firstly, it provides feature importance scores, which help users understand which variables play the most significant role in a model's decision-making. By highlighting key features, ELI5 enables users to validate whether the model is focusing on the correct inputs.
- Secondly, it utilizes permutation importance, a method that shuffles feature values to assess their impact on predictions. This technique helps identify whether a particular feature is genuinely influential or if the model is overfitting to noise.
- Additionally, ELI5 can generate human-readable explanations for complex models. For instance, when used with deep learning frameworks like TensorFlow or PyTorch, it simplifies layer-wise attributions, making the decision-making process more transparent.

## Strengths of ELI5

One of ELI5's greatest strengths is its ability to make AI explanations accessible to both technical and non-technical audiences. Unlike highly technical methods that require an in-depth understanding of machine learning algorithms, ELI5 presents explanations in a simple and intuitive manner. This makes it an excellent tool for industries that require explainable AI, such as healthcare, finance, and criminal justice. Another advantage of ELI5 is its compatibility with multiple machine learning frameworks. Whether working with Scikit-learn, XGBoost, or deep learning libraries, ELI5 can be easily integrated to provide transparency across various models.

Moreover, ELI5 improves model debugging and refinement. By identifying which features contribute the most to a model's output, data scientists can detect potential biases, optimize feature selection, and improve model generalization. Additionally, ELI5 supports debugging by allowing users to inspect incorrectly classified instances. This feature is particularly useful in high-stakes applications where understanding prediction errors is essential for improving model accuracy and reliability.

## Limitations and Challenges

Despite its advantages, ELI5 has some limitations. One major challenge is that its explanations may still be too complex for complete AI novices. While it simplifies AI decision-making, some basic knowledge of machine learning concepts is necessary to fully interpret its outputs. Another limitation is that ELI5 works best with structured data and traditional machine learning models. While it can be applied to deep learning models, other explainability tools like SHAP (SHapley Additive Explanations) or LIME (Local Interpretable Model-Agnostic Explanations) may be more suitable for interpreting complex neural networks.

Additionally, ELI5's reliance on feature importance scores can sometimes lead to misleading interpretations if not used carefully. Feature correlations or interactions may not always be captured effectively, which can result in oversimplified explanations.

## Applications of ELI5 in Various Industries

ELI5 is widely used across different domains where AI transparency is essential. In healthcare, it helps doctors and medical professionals understand AI-driven diagnoses and treatment recommendations. For example, if an AI model predicts a high risk of a certain disease, ELI5 can highlight which symptoms or lab results contributed most to the prediction, making the decision more interpretable for healthcare providers.

In finance, ELI5 plays a critical role in explaining credit scoring models. Banks and lending institutions use AI to assess loan applications, and ELI5 ensures that customers understand why their applications were approved or denied. By providing clear explanations, it helps maintain compliance with regulatory standards that require transparency in financial decision-making.

In the legal and criminal justice sector, AI models are increasingly used to assess recidivism risks or automate legal document analysis. ELI5 aids legal professionals in understanding how these models arrive at decisions, reducing the risk of unfair or biased outcomes.

In e-commerce and marketing, businesses use AI to personalize product recommendations and optimize advertising strategies. ELI5 helps marketers understand which customer behaviors influence AI-generated recommendations, allowing them to refine their marketing strategies effectively.

### Future Directions and Enhancements

As AI continues to evolve, the demand for improved explainability tools like ELI5 will grow. Researchers are actively working on enhancing its capabilities to provide even more intuitive and interactive explanations.

One promising area of development is the integration of ELI5 with visualization tools. Interactive dashboards that allow users to explore feature attributions dynamically can make AI explanations even more accessible. By incorporating graphical interfaces, non-technical users can better understand AI models without relying solely on numerical outputs.

Another area of focus is improving ELI5's ability to handle deep learning models more effectively. While it currently supports certain neural networks, further advancements could make it more suitable for complex architectures like transformer models and convolutional neural networks (CNNs).

Additionally, combining ELI5 with other explainability techniques, such as SHAP and counterfactual explanations, can provide a more comprehensive understanding of AI behavior. Hybrid approaches that integrate multiple interpretability methods may offer deeper insights into model decision-making processes.

Finally, regulatory bodies and policymakers are increasingly advocating for the adoption of explainability tools like ELI5 to ensure responsible AI deployment. As AI regulations become more stringent, organizations will rely more heavily on tools like ELI5 to demonstrate compliance with ethical and legal standards.

## 6.2 PROPRIETARY XAI SOLUTIONS

Proprietary XAI solutions are crucial for enterprises that require scalable, secure, and regulatory-compliant AI explainability. These tools provide advanced features such as real-time explanations, bias detection, and model-agnostic interpretability, making them valuable assets in industries like healthcare, finance, and law enforcement.

While proprietary XAI solutions offer significant advantages, such as scalability, security, and professional support, they also come with challenges, including high costs and potential transparency limitations. Despite these challenges, the future of proprietary XAI solutions looks promising, with ongoing advancements in natural language explanations, hybrid interpretability techniques, and regulatory compliance automation.

As AI continues to play a larger role in critical decision-making, proprietary XAI solutions will be essential in ensuring that AI-driven decisions remain transparent, fair, and accountable. Organizations must carefully evaluate their needs and select the most suitable proprietary XAI tools to enhance the trustworthiness and effectiveness of their AI systems.

### 6.2.1 The Need for Proprietary XAI Solutions

Many organizations rely on AI for critical decision-making processes, and explainability is essential to ensure trust, accountability, and compliance. Proprietary XAI solutions offer structured and customized interpretations of AI models, making them easier to deploy in business environments. They often come with advanced security features, compliance tools, and user-friendly dashboards that facilitate easier interpretation of complex machine learning models.

One of the primary reasons businesses opt for proprietary XAI solutions is regulatory compliance. Governments and regulatory bodies worldwide are increasingly enforcing transparency requirements for AI-driven decision-making, especially in industries like finance and healthcare. Proprietary solutions ensure that AI explanations meet these requirements while protecting sensitive proprietary data.

Another advantage of proprietary XAI tools is their ability to handle complex enterprise-level AI models. These solutions integrate seamlessly with business intelligence tools, cloud computing platforms, and large-scale AI deployments, making them more practical for organizations with high-volume data processing needs.

### 6.2.2 Features of Proprietary XAI Solutions

Proprietary XAI solutions offer a wide range of features that make them distinct from open-source alternatives. Many of these tools provide interactive and user-friendly interfaces that allow both technical and non-technical users to interpret AI models effectively. They also incorporate state-of-the-art visualization techniques to present model insights in an intuitive manner.

One key feature of proprietary XAI solutions is model-agnostic explainability. These tools can be applied to various types of AI models, including deep learning networks, gradient boosting machines, and traditional machine learning algorithms. By offering model-agnostic explanations, proprietary solutions enable businesses to maintain flexibility in their AI strategy while ensuring transparency.

Another important feature is real-time explainability. Many proprietary XAI solutions provide instant explanations of AI decisions, which is particularly valuable in high-risk applications like fraud detection, medical diagnostics, and automated trading. Real-time explainability allows organizations to intervene when necessary and make data-driven adjustments to their AI models.

Additionally, proprietary XAI solutions often include bias detection and mitigation features. AI models can sometimes produce biased outputs due to imbalances in training data. Proprietary tools help organizations identify and address biases to ensure fair and ethical AI decision-making.

### 6.2.3 Leading Proprietary XAI Solutions

Several technology companies and AI firms have developed proprietary XAI solutions that cater to enterprise needs. These solutions provide tailored explainability features that integrate seamlessly with existing AI and analytics workflows.

IBM Watson OpenScale is one of the most well-known proprietary XAI solutions. It provides model explainability, fairness detection, and bias mitigation capabilities. Watson OpenScale allows businesses to monitor AI models in real time and ensure compliance with industry regulations.

Google's Explainable AI (XAI) is another prominent proprietary solution. Integrated into Google Cloud AI, it provides tools for understanding feature attributions, detecting biases, and explaining model predictions in a way that is accessible to both developers and business users.

Microsoft's InterpretML is a proprietary tool that enables businesses to apply interpretable AI techniques to their models. It supports both local and global explainability methods, helping organizations understand how AI-driven decisions are made.

Other notable proprietary XAI solutions include Fiddler AI, H2O.ai's Driverless AI, and SAS Visual Data Mining and Machine Learning. These platforms provide various explainability and fairness auditing features that enhance trust in AI applications.

### 6.2.4 Advantages of Proprietary XAI Solutions

One of the primary advantages of proprietary XAI solutions is scalability. These tools are designed for enterprise use, meaning they can handle large volumes of data and complex AI models efficiently. This makes them particularly useful for industries that require high-throughput AI decision-making.

Another significant advantage is security. Proprietary solutions often come with enhanced security features that protect sensitive business data from unauthorized access. This is crucial for industries like healthcare, finance, and government applications, where data privacy is a top priority.

Proprietary XAI solutions also offer dedicated support and updates. Unlike open-source tools that rely on community support, proprietary solutions come with professional technical support, ensuring that businesses can resolve issues quickly and effectively. Regular updates and enhancements also mean that these solutions keep up with the latest advancements in AI explainability.

### 6.2.5 Limitations and Challenges

Despite their benefits, proprietary XAI solutions also have some limitations. One of the primary drawbacks is cost. These solutions often require substantial investment, making them less accessible to smaller organizations and startups. Licensing fees, infrastructure costs, and subscription models can make proprietary XAI solutions expensive compared to open-source alternatives.

Another challenge is the potential lack of transparency. While these tools are designed to improve AI explainability, they themselves can sometimes function as "black boxes." Organizations using proprietary XAI solutions may not always have full visibility into how the explanation models work, which could reduce trust in the system.

Additionally, some proprietary XAI solutions may have limited customization options. Unlike open-source tools, which allow users to modify and extend their functionality, proprietary solutions often come with predefined explainability features that may not be flexible enough for specific business needs.

### 6.2.6 Future Trends in Proprietary XAI Solutions

As AI technology continues to evolve, proprietary XAI solutions are likely to become more sophisticated. One emerging trend is the integration of natural language explanations. Instead of presenting raw feature importance scores or statistical attributions, future XAI solutions may generate human-like explanations that make AI decision-making even more accessible to non-technical users.

Another trend is the development of hybrid XAI approaches. Future proprietary tools may combine multiple explainability techniques, such as SHAP, LIME, and counterfactual explanations, to provide a more comprehensive understanding of AI models. Regulatory compliance will also play a major role in shaping the future of proprietary XAI solutions. With increasing global regulations around

AI transparency and ethics, businesses will need advanced explainability tools to ensure compliance. Future solutions may incorporate automated regulatory auditing features to help organizations meet transparency standards effortlessly.

Furthermore, advancements in AI fairness and bias detection will continue to be a focus for proprietary XAI developers. As concerns about algorithmic discrimination grow, these tools will integrate more robust fairness assessment frameworks to ensure that AI systems operate equitably across different demographics.

## 6.3 EMERGING TOOLS

Emerging XAI tools play a crucial role in addressing the challenges associated with AI transparency and trustworthiness. These tools help businesses and researchers interpret complex AI models, ensuring fairness, accountability, and regulatory compliance. With ongoing advancements in explainability techniques, the future of AI promises greater transparency and more ethical decision-making processes. As organizations increasingly adopt AI-driven solutions, integrating state-of-the-art XAI tools will be essential for fostering trust and ensuring responsible AI deployment.

### 6.3.1 The Need for Emerging XAI Tools

With AI being widely deployed in sectors such as healthcare, finance, law enforcement, and autonomous systems, the consequences of opaque AI decision-making can be significant. Regulatory bodies worldwide are enforcing stricter AI transparency requirements, leading to a surge in demand for explainability tools that can provide insights into model predictions without compromising performance. Additionally, organizations seek to ensure ethical AI deployment by mitigating biases and improving user trust through transparent explanations. Emerging XAI tools address these concerns by integrating explainability mechanisms directly into AI workflows, helping businesses maintain regulatory compliance and ethical AI practices.

### 6.3.2 Categories of Emerging XAI Tools

Emerging XAI tools can be categorized into model-specific, model-agnostic, and hybrid methods. Model-specific tools are designed to explain particular AI architectures, such as convolutional neural networks (CNNs) for image processing or transformer-based models for natural language processing (NLP). These tools offer insights into feature importance, attention mechanisms, and decision pathways. Model-agnostic tools, on the other hand, can be applied to various machine learning models without requiring modifications. They typically rely on perturbation-based techniques or surrogate models to approximate decision boundaries. Hybrid XAI tools combine multiple explainability approaches to provide more comprehensive insights while balancing interpretability and accuracy.

### 6.3.3 Key Emerging XAI Tools

#### SHAP (SHapley Additive Explanations)

SHAP is an advanced model-agnostic tool that leverages game-theoretic principles to assign importance scores to individual features in an AI model. It helps users understand how each feature contributes to a prediction, making it widely used in finance, healthcare, and fraud detection applications. SHAP provides both local and global explanations, allowing users to interpret individual predictions as well as broader model behavior.

#### LIME (Local Interpretable Model-Agnostic Explanations)

LIME is a powerful explainability tool that generates interpretable approximations of complex AI models by perturbing input data and observing the changes in predictions. It creates locally interpretable models that help users understand specific instances of AI decision-making. LIME is particularly useful in cases where transparency is required for high-stakes applications, such as loan approvals or medical diagnoses.

#### Integrated Gradients

Integrated Gradients is a technique designed for deep learning models, particularly those used in computer vision and NLP. It helps explain neural network predictions by calculating the contribution of each input feature to the final output. This method is particularly effective in scenarios where deep learning models are used for high-risk decision-making processes.

#### Captum

Developed by Facebook AI, Captum is an open-source XAI tool that provides interpretability methods specifically for PyTorch-based deep learning models. It offers multiple techniques, including feature attribution, layer-wise relevance propagation, and integrated gradients, enabling users to analyze how different layers in a neural network contribute to a decision.

#### Fiddler AI

Fiddler AI is a proprietary XAI platform that provides real-time explainability for enterprise AI models. It integrates bias detection, fairness auditing, and monitoring features, making it an ideal solution for organizations that require high transparency in AI-driven decision-making. Fiddler AI allows businesses to deploy explainable AI models with confidence, ensuring regulatory compliance and trustworthiness.

#### Google Explainable AI

Google's Explainable AI service provides model interpretability tools for AI applications running on Google Cloud. It includes feature importance analysis, fairness testing, and bias detection, helping businesses deploy more transparent and accountable AI systems. The tool is particularly beneficial for enterprises that use machine learning models for high-impact applications such as medical diagnostics and financial risk assessment.

#### IBM Watson OpenScale

IBM Watson OpenScale is an enterprise-grade XAI platform that helps organizations track and explain AI decisions while ensuring fairness and regulatory compliance. It provides bias detection, real-time explainability, and monitoring capabilities, making it a valuable tool for businesses deploying AI solutions in sensitive domains such as healthcare and finance.

#### H2O.ai Driverless AI

H2O.ai's Driverless AI is an automated machine learning (AutoML) platform that incorporates built-in explainability features. It enables users to interpret AI models through visualizations, feature importance analysis, and model documentation. The tool is particularly useful for organizations seeking to balance automation with explainability in AI workflows.

#### DeepLIFT (Deep Learning Important FeaTures)

DeepLIFT is an interpretability tool specifically designed for deep learning models. It compares the activation of neurons in a neural network to a reference activation, helping users understand how different inputs influence predictions. DeepLIFT is particularly useful in analyzing the decision-making processes of complex deep learning architectures.

#### Alibi Explain

Alibi Explain is an open-source XAI library designed to provide interpretable explanations for machine learning models. It includes a range of explainability techniques, such as counterfactual explanations, adversarial detection, and contrastive explanations, making it a versatile tool for various AI applications.

### 6.3.4 Challenges and Future Directions

While emerging XAI tools offer significant advancements in explainability, challenges remain in balancing transparency with model accuracy. Some explainability methods can reduce predictive performance, leading to trade-offs between interpretability and effectiveness. Additionally, certain XAI techniques generate explanations that may be too complex for non-technical users to understand, limiting their practicality in real-world applications. Future developments in XAI are expected to focus on enhancing usability, improving real-time interpretability, and integrating AI ethics considerations into explainability tools. Researchers are exploring hybrid models that combine multiple interpretability techniques to create more robust and user-friendly XAI solutions. Moreover, advancements in natural language explanations will enable AI systems to generate human-like descriptions of their decision-making processes, making explainability more accessible to non-technical stakeholders.

CHAPTER 7

# Best Practices for Implementing Explainable AI

## 7.1 ALIGNING EXPLANATIONS WITH STAKEHOLDER NEEDS

Aligning AI explanations with stakeholder needs is essential for fostering trust, accountability, and usability in AI-driven systems. Different stakeholders—ranging from technical teams to regulatory bodies and end-users—require tailored explanations that match their level of expertise and objectives. By adopting layered explanations, interactive dashboards, visual storytelling, and balanced fidelity, organizations can enhance AI transparency while maintaining clarity. Overcoming challenges such as transparency vs. proprietary concerns, bias in explanations, and AI literacy gaps will be key to advancing explainability efforts. As AI continues to evolve, the future of XAI will involve more adaptive, personalized, and regulatory-compliant explanation frameworks that empower stakeholders to engage confidently with AI systems.

### 7.1.1 Understanding Stakeholder Categories and Their Needs

To align explanations effectively, it is important to identify key stakeholder groups and their specific requirements. Broadly, stakeholders in AI-driven systems can be categorized into technical stakeholders, business stakeholders, regulatory and compliance authorities, and general end-users. Each group has a different level of technical expertise and distinct concerns regarding AI decision-making.

#### Technical Stakeholders

Technical stakeholders include data scientists, AI engineers, and researchers who develop, train, and optimize AI models. Their primary concern is ensuring model performance, robustness, and interpretability. For this group, explanations should be detailed and data-driven, offering insights into model architecture, feature importance, and algorithmic behavior. Tools like SHAP (SHapley Additive Explanations), LIME (Local Interpretable Model-agnostic Explanations), and Integrated Gradients help these professionals understand how different inputs contribute to AI decisions. Debugging and troubleshooting AI models also require deeper interpretability to diagnose potential biases, adversarial vulnerabilities, and overfitting issues.

### Business Stakeholders

Business stakeholders, including executives, product managers, and decision-makers, are primarily concerned with how AI impacts organizational goals, operations, and profitability. They need explanations that translate AI insights into actionable business strategies. For this audience, AI explanations should be framed in terms of cost savings, efficiency improvements, and competitive advantages. Simplified visualizations, case studies, and predictive outcome reports are effective ways to present AI insights to business stakeholders. The goal is to bridge the gap between complex AI mechanics and real-world business applications.

### Regulatory and Compliance Authorities

Regulators and policymakers oversee AI compliance with ethical, legal, and industry-specific standards. Their focus is on accountability, bias detection, fairness, and adherence to governance frameworks such as GDPR (General Data Protection Regulation) and the AI Act. Explanations for this group should prioritize transparency, auditability, and documentation of AI decisions. Providing clear justifications for AI-driven outcomes, alongside bias mitigation strategies, ensures regulatory bodies can assess whether AI models comply with legal and ethical requirements. Regulatory authorities may also require access to traceability logs, model version histories, and decision rationales to evaluate AI systems' adherence to fairness principles.

### General End-Users

General end-users interact with AI systems without deep technical expertise. Their concerns revolve around trust, usability, and the fairness of AI-driven outcomes. Whether using AI-powered loan approval systems, medical diagnosis tools, or automated hiring platforms, end-users need explanations that are intuitive and non-technical. Clear, plain-language explanations with relatable analogies, visual cues, and step-by-step justifications help build user confidence. Ensuring AI-generated decisions are comprehensible enhances user engagement and minimizes skepticism towards automated systems.

## 7.1.2 Customizing Explanation Methods for Different Stakeholders

A one-size-fits-all approach to AI explanations is ineffective, as different stakeholders require different levels of detail and forms of presentation. By tailoring explanation methods, organizations can ensure that AI insights are relevant, accessible, and actionable.

### Layered Explanations

A layered approach to AI explainability involves providing multiple levels of detail depending on the stakeholder's expertise. For instance, an AI explanation can start with a high-level summary suitable for executives, followed by interactive visualizations for regulators, and then an in-depth breakdown of model computations for technical teams. This multi-tiered approach ensures that each stakeholder can access information relevant to their needs without being overwhelmed by unnecessary complexity.

### Interactive Explainability Dashboards

Many organizations are adopting interactive dashboards that allow stakeholders to explore AI explanations dynamically. These dashboards can present different types of explanations based on the user's role, enabling them to customize the level of detail. For example, a compliance officer may access fairness reports and bias detection insights, while a data scientist can inspect model parameters and feature attributions. This adaptive approach enhances usability and ensures that AI transparency aligns with stakeholder expectations.

### Visual and Narrative-Based Explanations

For non-technical stakeholders, visual explanations such as heatmaps, flow diagrams, and interactive simulations make AI decisions more digestible. Narrative-based explanations, where AI outputs are translated into human-like storytelling, help convey complex AI reasoning in simple terms. For example, in healthcare AI, a system could provide a textual summary explaining why a particular diagnosis was suggested, using comparisons to past cases and medical literature.

### Explanation Fidelity vs. Simplicity

A key challenge in aligning explanations with stakeholder needs is balancing fidelity (the accuracy of the explanation) with simplicity (how easily the explanation can be understood). Highly detailed explanations may be useful for data scientists but can overwhelm business users. On the other hand, oversimplified explanations may fail to capture critical AI nuances required for technical validation. Organizations must find a middle ground, ensuring that explanations are both truthful and comprehensible.

## 7.1.3 Challenges in Aligning AI Explanations with Stakeholder Needs

Despite the growing emphasis on XAI, aligning explanations with diverse stakeholder needs presents several challenges. One major challenge is the trade-off between transparency and intellectual property concerns. Companies developing proprietary AI models may be reluctant to disclose too much information, fearing competitive risks. Striking a balance between transparency and business confidentiality is crucial.

Another challenge is addressing biases in AI explanations. If explanations are not carefully crafted, they may reinforce or obscure existing biases in the AI model.

Ensuring fairness in AI explanations requires continuous evaluation and refinement of interpretability methods.

Additionally, explainability efforts must account for varying levels of AI literacy among stakeholders. While data scientists can interpret complex statistical explanations, end-users may struggle to understand why an AI system made a specific decision. Designing explanations that accommodate varying levels of AI literacy enhances inclusivity and fosters broader acceptance of AI systems.

### 7.1.4 Future Directions in AI Explainability

The future of XAI will likely involve more personalized and context-aware explanations. AI systems will increasingly tailor their explanations based on user preferences, expertise levels, and specific use cases. Natural language processing (NLP) advancements will enable AI systems to generate human-like explanations dynamically, improving accessibility.

Regulatory frameworks will continue to evolve, shaping how AI explanations must be designed and presented. Organizations will need to integrate standardized explainability metrics and reporting frameworks to ensure compliance with emerging AI governance policies.

Additionally, explainability research will focus on integrating causal inference techniques, allowing AI models to provide more meaningful "what-if" scenarios. This will help stakeholders better understand how changes in input variables influence AI decisions, leading to greater trust in AI applications.

## 7.2 TESTING AND VALIDATING EXPLANATIONS

Testing and validating AI explanations is a critical step in ensuring that AI-driven decisions are transparent, accurate, and trustworthy. By employing various validation techniques such as ground-truth comparisons, adversarial testing, user studies, and automated checks, organizations can enhance the reliability of AI explanations. However, challenges such as complexity-interpretability trade-offs, subjective evaluation criteria, and the evolving nature of AI models must be addressed to ensure robust validation. Adopting best practices, including interdisciplinary collaboration, continuous auditing, and user education, can help improve the quality of AI explanations. As AI explainability continues to evolve, future advancements in causal inference, benchmarking, and self-explaining models will further strengthen the validation process, fostering greater trust and accountability in AI systems.

### 7.2.1 Importance of Testing AI Explanations

Testing AI explanations is essential for multiple reasons. First, it ensures that explanations correctly reflect the AI model's decision-making process. If explanations are misleading or incorrect, they can create a false sense of trust or lead to incorrect conclusions. Second, validation ensures consistency across different AI outputs. Variability in explanations for similar inputs can signal instability in the AI model. Third, validated explanations improve stakeholder confidence, making AI-driven systems more acceptable to regulators, business leaders, and end-users. Without robust testing, explanations risk becoming arbitrary, overly simplified, or even deceptive.

### 7.2.2 Key Metrics for Validating AI Explanations

Several metrics can be used to evaluate the quality of AI explanations. Fidelity measures how accurately an explanation reflects the model's internal reasoning. High-fidelity explanations are essential for technical users, such as data scientists and developers. Consistency ensures that similar inputs yield similar explanations, reinforcing reliability. Comprehensibility assesses whether explanations are understandable to non-technical stakeholders, such as business executives and general users. Actionability determines whether explanations provide meaningful insights that allow users to adjust inputs, correct biases, or improve decision-making. Fairness validation examines whether explanations expose or mitigate biases in AI predictions, ensuring ethical AI deployment.

### 7.2.3 Techniques for Testing AI Explanations

Different testing techniques are used to assess the validity and reliability of AI explanations. One common approach is the ground-truth comparison method, where explanations are compared against known causal relationships or expert domain knowledge. If an AI system's explanation deviates significantly from what domain experts expect, it may indicate a flaw in either the model or its interpretability method. Another method is adversarial testing, where inputs are deliberately altered to see if explanations change in a logical and predictable manner. This technique helps detect biases and inconsistencies in AI-generated explanations.

Additionally, user studies are crucial for validating explanations from a human-centered perspective. Stakeholders interact with AI explanations and provide feedback on their clarity, usefulness, and trustworthiness. A/B testing is also employed to compare different explanation methods and determine which approach is most effective for specific audiences. Automated validation frameworks, such as LIME and SHAP consistency checks, can help assess whether feature importance rankings remain stable across different runs of the model.

### 7.2.4 Challenges in Validating AI Explanations

Validating AI explanations comes with several challenges. One major challenge is the trade-off between complexity and interpretability. Highly complex models, such as deep neural networks, generate intricate decision patterns that are difficult to explain in human terms. Simplifying explanations too much can result in a loss of accuracy, while overly technical explanations may be incomprehensible to non-experts. Another challenge is subjectivity in evaluating explanations. Different stakeholders may have different expectations regarding what constitutes a "good" explanation. Regulators may prioritize transparency and fairness, while business leaders may focus on operational impact. Balancing these varying needs is essential for effective validation.

Furthermore, the dynamic nature of AI models presents another hurdle. Many AI systems continuously learn and evolve based on new data. As models change, explanations may need to be revalidated to ensure they remain accurate and consistent. Without continuous testing, explanations may become outdated or misaligned with the AI system's evolving decision logic.

### 7.2.5 Best Practices for Robust Explanation Validation

To ensure effective validation of AI explanations, organizations should adopt best practices. First, explanations should be tested using multiple validation methods, including empirical evaluations, statistical tests, and user feedback. No single metric or technique is sufficient on its own. Second, interdisciplinary collaboration is crucial. AI engineers, domain experts, ethicists, and end-users should all be involved in validating explanations to ensure they are accurate, fair, and useful across different contexts. Third, organizations should maintain transparency by documenting explanation validation results, including any biases detected and corrective measures taken. This documentation helps establish accountability and trust.

Additionally, organizations should consider explainability as an ongoing process rather than a one-time effort. Regular audits and updates should be conducted to ensure explanations remain relevant and effective as AI models and regulatory requirements evolve. Lastly, investing in user education is vital. Even the best AI explanations can be misinterpreted if stakeholders do not have the necessary knowledge to understand them. Providing training sessions and documentation on how to interpret AI explanations enhances user trust and confidence.

### 7.2.6 Future Directions in Testing AI Explanations

As AI continues to advance, new methods for testing and validating explanations will emerge. One promising direction is the integration of causal inference techniques, which help assess whether explanations truly capture cause-and-effect relationships within AI models. Another emerging trend is explainability benchmarking, where standardized tests and datasets are developed to evaluate the quality of AI explanations across different models and use cases. Additionally, advances in natural language processing (NLP) will enable AI systems to generate human-like explanations tailored to individual users' needs and comprehension levels.

Regulatory bodies are also expected to introduce stricter guidelines for AI explainability. Organizations will need to align their validation processes with evolving legal and ethical standards to ensure compliance. Moreover, AI systems will increasingly incorporate self-explaining mechanisms, where models generate built-in explanations during decision-making rather than relying on post-hoc interpretability methods. This shift will enhance the reliability and transparency of AI explanations.

## 7.3 DOCUMENTATION AND COMMUNICATION

Documentation and communication are fundamental pillars of Explainable AI, ensuring that AI systems remain transparent, trustworthy, and accountable. Proper documentation captures the inner workings of AI models, while effective communication tailors explanations to different stakeholders, improving comprehension and usability. Addressing challenges such as complexity, subjectivity, and uncertainty is essential for advancing explainability efforts. By adopting best practices, leveraging visual and interactive communication methods, and continuously refining AI explanations, organizations can foster greater trust in AI-driven decision-making. As AI technologies evolve, innovative approaches to documentation and communication will further enhance explainability, paving the way for responsible and ethical AI deployment.

### 7.3.1 Understanding the Documentation

Documentation is any communicable material that is used to describe, explain or instruct regarding some attributes of an object, system or procedure, such as its parts, assembly, installation, maintenance, and use. As a form of knowledge management and knowledge organization, documentation can be provided on paper, online, or on digital or analog media, such as audio tape or CDs. Examples are user guides, white papers, online help, and quick-reference guides. Paper or hard-copy documentation has become less common. Documentation is often distributed via websites, software products, and other online applications. Documentation as a set of instructional materials shouldn't be confused with documentation science, the study of the recording and retrieval of information.

#### Principles for Producing Documentation

While associated International Organization for Standardization (ISO) standards are not easily available publicly, a guide from other sources for this topic may serve the purpose. Documentation development may involve document drafting, formatting, submitting, reviewing, approving, distributing, reposting and tracking, etc., and are convened by associated standard operating procedure in a regulatory industry. It could also involve creating content from scratch. Documentation should be easy to read and understand. If it is too long and too wordy, it may be misunderstood or ignored. Clear, concise words should be used, and sentences should be limited to a maximum of 15 words. Documentation intended for a general audience should avoid gender-specific terms and cultural biases. In a series of procedures, steps should be clearly numbered.

### Producing Documentation

Technical writers and corporate communicators are professionals whose field and work is documentation. Ideally, technical writers have a background in both the subject matter and also in writing, managing content, and information architecture. Technical writers more commonly collaborate with subject-matter experts, such as engineers, technical experts, medical professionals, etc. to define and then create documentation to meet the user's needs. Corporate communications includes other types of written documentation, for example:

- **Market Communications (MarCom):** MarCom writers endeavor to convey the company's value proposition through a variety of print, electronic, and social media. This area of corporate writing is often engaged in responding to proposals.
- **Technical Communication (TechCom):** Technical writers document a company's product or service. Technical publications can include user guides, installation and configuration manuals, and troubleshooting and repair procedures.
- **Legal Writing:** This type of documentation is often prepared by attorneys or paralegals.
- **Compliance Documentation:** This type of documentation codifies standard operating procedures, for any regulatory compliance needs, as for safety approval, taxation, financing, and technical approval.
- **Healthcare Documentation:** This field of documentation encompasses the timely recording and validation of events that have occurred during the course of providing health care.

## 7.3.2 Understanding the Communication

Communication is commonly defined as the transmission of information. Its precise definition is disputed and there are disagreements about whether unintentional or failed transmissions are included and whether communication not only transmits meaning but also creates it. Models of communication are simplified overviews of its main components and their interactions. Many models include the idea that a source uses a coding system to express information in the form of a message. The message is sent through a channel to a receiver who has to decode it to understand it. The main field of inquiry investigating communication is called communication studies.

A common way to classify communication is by whether information is exchanged between humans, members of other species, or non-living entities such as computers. For human communication, a central contrast is between verbal and non-verbal communication. Verbal communication involves the exchange of messages in linguistic form, including spoken and written messages as well as sign language.

Non-verbal communication happens without the use of a linguistic system, for example, using body language, touch, and facial expressions. Another distinction is between interpersonal communication, which happens between distinct persons, and intrapersonal communication, which is communication with oneself. Communicative competence is the ability to communicate well and applies to the skills of formulating messages and understanding them.

Non-human forms of communication include animal and plant communication. Researchers in this field often refine their definition of communicative behavior by including the criteria that observable responses are present and that the participants benefit from the exchange. Animal communication is used in areas like courtship and mating, parent–offspring relations, navigation, and self-defense. Communication through chemicals is particularly important for the relatively immobile plants.

For example, maple trees release so-called volatile organic compounds into the air to warn other plants of a herbivore attack. Most communication takes place between members of the same species. The reason is that its purpose is usually some form of cooperation, which is not as common between different species. Interspecies communication happens mainly in cases of symbiotic relationships. For instance, many flowers use symmetrical shapes and distinctive colors to signal to insects where nectar is located. Humans engage in interspecies communication when interacting with pets and working animals.

Human communication has a long history and how people exchange information has changed over time. These changes were usually triggered by the development of new communication technologies. Examples are the invention of writing systems, the development of mass printing, the use of radio and television, and the invention of the internet. The technological advances also led to new forms of communication, such as the exchange of data between computers.

## Definitions

The word communication has its root in the Latin verb communicare, which means 'to share' or 'to make common'. Communication is usually understood as the transmission of information: a message is conveyed from a sender to a receiver using some medium, such as sound, written signs, bodily movements, or electricity. Sender and receiver are often distinct individuals but it is also possible for an individual to communicate with themselves. In some cases, sender and receiver are not individuals but groups like organizations, social classes, or nations. In a different sense, the term communication refers to the message that is being communicated or to the field of inquiry studying communicational phenomena.

The precise characterization of communication is disputed. Many scholars have raised doubts that any single definition can capture the term accurately. These difficulties come from the fact that the term is applied to diverse phenomena in different contexts, often with slightly different meanings. The issue of the right definition affects the research process on many levels. This includes issues like which empirical phenomena are observed, how they are categorized, which hypotheses and laws are formulated as well as how systematic theories based on these steps are articulated.

Some definitions are broad and encompass unconscious and non-human behavior. Under a broad definition, many animals communicate within their own species and flowers communicate by signaling the location of nectar to bees through their colors and shapes. Other definitions restrict communication to conscious interactions among human beings. Some approaches focus on the use of symbols and signs while others stress the role of understanding, interaction, power, or transmission of ideas. Various characterizations see the communicator's intent to send a message as a central component. In this view, the transmission of information is not sufficient for communication if it happens unintentionally. A version of this view is given by philosopher Paul Grice, who identifies communication with actions that aim to make the recipient aware of the communicator's intention. One question in this regard is whether only successful transmissions of information should be regarded as communication. For example, distortion may interfere with and change the actual message from what was originally intended. A closely related problem is whether acts of deliberate deception constitute communication.

According to a broad definition by literary critic I. A. Richards, communication happens when one mind acts upon its environment to transmit its own experience to another mind. Another interpretation is given by communication theorists Claude Shannon and Warren Weaver, who characterize communication as a transmission of information brought about by the interaction of several components, such as a source, a message, an encoder, a channel, a decoder, and a receiver. The transmission view is rejected by transactional and constitutive views, which hold that communication is not just about the transmission of information but also about the creation of meaning. Transactional and constitutive perspectives hold that communication shapes the participant's experience by conceptualizing the world and making sense of their environment and themselves. Researchers studying animal and plant communication focus less on meaning-making. Instead, they often define communicative behavior as having other features, such as playing a beneficial role in survival and reproduction, or having an observable response.

## Models of Communication

Models of communication are conceptual representations of the process of communication. Their goal is to provide a simplified overview of its main components. This makes it easier for researchers to formulate hypotheses, apply communication-related concepts to real-world cases, and test predictions. Due to their simplified presentation, they may lack the conceptual complexity needed for a comprehensive understanding of all the essential aspects of communication. They are usually presented visually in the form of diagrams showing the basic components and their interaction.

Models of communication are often categorized based on their intended applications and how they conceptualize communication. Some models are general in the sense that they are intended for all forms of communication. Specialized models aim to describe specific forms, such as models of mass communication.

One influential way to classify communication is to distinguish between linear transmission, interaction, and transaction models. Linear transmission models focus on how a sender transmits information to a receiver. They are linear because this flow of information only goes in a single direction. This view is rejected by interaction models, which include a feedback loop.

Feedback is needed to describe many forms of communication, such as a conversation, where the listener may respond to a speaker by expressing their opinion or by asking for clarification. Interaction models represent the process as a form of two-way communication in which the communicators take turns sending and receiving messages.

Transaction models further refine this picture by allowing representations of sending and responding at the same time. This modification is needed to describe how the listener can give feedback in a face-to-face conversation while the other person is talking. Examples are non-verbal feedback through body posture and facial expression. Transaction models also hold that meaning is produced during communication and does not exist independently of it.

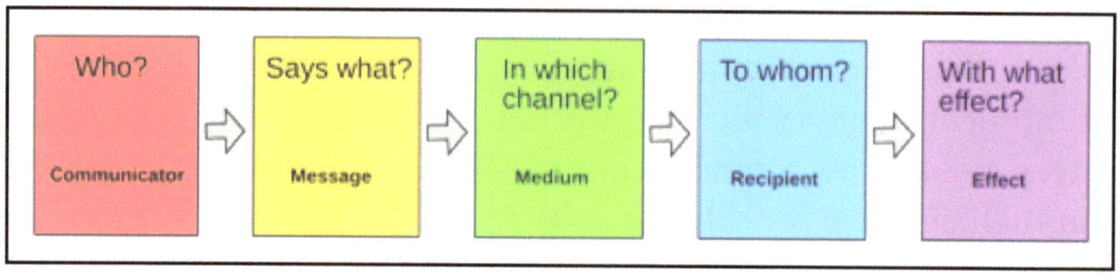


**Fig: Lasswell's model of communication, which is based on five questions corresponding to five basic components**

All the early models, developed in the middle of the 20th century, are linear transmission models. Lasswell's model, for example, is based on five fundamental questions: "Who?", "Says what?", "In which channel?", "To whom?", and "With what effect?". The goal of these questions is to identify the basic components involved in the communicative process: the sender, the message, the channel, the receiver, and the effect. Lasswell's model was initially only conceived as a model of mass communication, but it has been applied to other fields as well. Some communication theorists, like Richard Braddock, have expanded it by including additional questions, like "Under what circumstances?" and "For what purpose?".

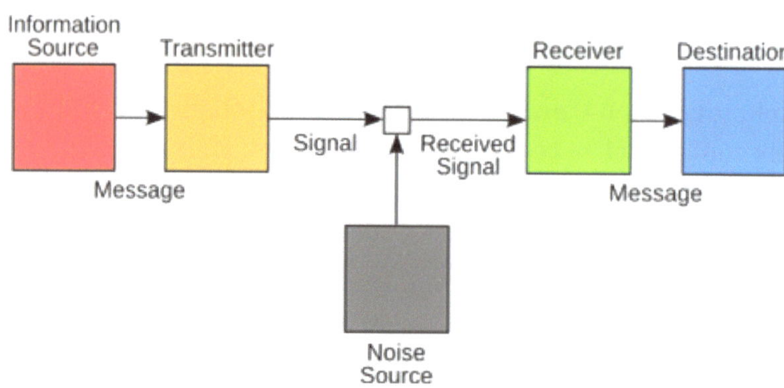


**Fig: Shannon–Weaver model of communication, which focuses on how a message is first translated into a signal and then back into a message**

The Shannon–Weaver model is another influential linear transmission model. It is based on the idea that a source creates a message, which is then translated into a signal by a transmitter. Noise may interfere with and distort the signal. Once the signal reaches the receiver, it is translated back into a message and made available to the destination. For a landline telephone call, the person calling is the source and their telephone is the transmitter. The transmitter translates the message into an electrical signal that travels through the wire, which acts as the channel. The person taking the call is the destination and their telephone is the receiver. The Shannon–Weaver model includes an in-depth discussion of how noise can distort the signal and how successful communication can be achieved despite noise. This can happen by making the message partially redundant so that decoding is possible nonetheless. Other influential linear transmission models include Gerbner's model and Berlo's model.

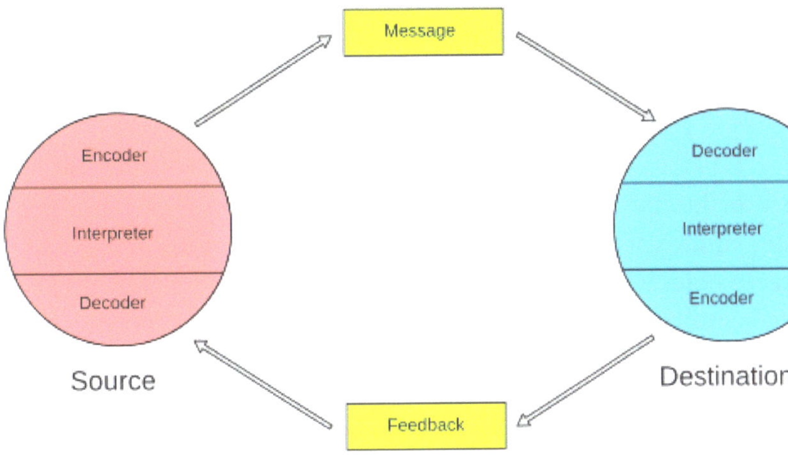


**Fig: Schramm's model of communication, which focuses on the processes of encoding and decoding as well as feedback**

The earliest interaction model was developed by communication theorist Wilbur Schramm. He states that communication starts when a source has an idea and expresses it in the form of a message. This process is called encoding and happens using a code, i.e. a sign system that is able to express the idea, for instance, through visual or auditory signs. The message is sent to a destination, who has to decode and interpret it to understand it. In response, they formulate their own idea, encode it into a message, and send it back as a form of feedback. Another innovation of Schramm's model is that previous experience is necessary to be able to encode and decode messages. For communication to be successful, the fields of experience of source and destination have to overlap.

The first transactional model was proposed by communication theorist Dean Barnlund in 1970. He understands communication as "the production of meaning, rather than the production of messages". Its goal is to decrease uncertainty and arrive at a shared understanding. This happens in response to external and internal cues. Decoding is the process of ascribing meaning to them and encoding consists in producing new behavioral cues as a response.

## Verbal

Verbal communication is the exchange of messages in linguistic form, i.e., by means of language. In colloquial usage, verbal communication is sometimes restricted to oral communication and may exclude writing and sign language. However, in academic discourse, the term is usually used in a wider sense, encompassing any form of linguistic communication, whether through speech, writing, or gestures.

Some of the challenges in distinguishing verbal from non-verbal communication come from the difficulties in defining what exactly language means. Language is usually understood as a conventional system of symbols and rules used for communication. Such systems are based on a set of simple units of meaning that can be combined to express more complex ideas. The rules for combining the units into compound expressions are called grammar. Words are combined to form sentences.

One hallmark of human language, in contrast to animal communication, lies in its complexity and expressive power. Human language can be used to refer not just to concrete objects in the here-and-now but also to spatially and temporally distant objects and to abstract ideas. Humans have a natural tendency to acquire their native language in childhood. They are also able to learn other languages later in life as second languages. However, this process is less intuitive and often does not result in the same level of linguistic competence. The academic discipline studying language is called linguistics. Its subfields include semantics (the study of meaning), morphology (the study of word formation), syntax (the study of sentence structure), pragmatics (the study of language use), and phonetics (the study of basic sounds).

A central contrast among languages is between natural and artificial or constructed languages. Natural languages, like English, Spanish, and Japanese, developed naturally and for the most part unplanned in the course of history. Artificial languages, like Esperanto, Quenya, C++, and the language of first-order logic, are purposefully designed from the ground up. Most everyday verbal communication happens using natural languages. Central forms of verbal communication are speech and writing together with their counterparts of listening and reading. Spoken languages use sounds to produce signs and transmit meaning while for writing, the signs are physically inscribed on a surface. Sign languages, like American Sign Language and Nicaraguan Sign Language, are another form of verbal communication. They rely on visual means, mostly by using gestures with hands and arms, to form sentences and convey meaning.

Verbal communication serves various functions. One key function is to exchange information, i.e. an attempt by the speaker to make the audience aware of something, usually of an external event. But language can also be used to express the speaker's feelings and attitudes. A closely related role is to establish and maintain social relations with other people. Verbal communication is also utilized to coordinate one's behavior with others and influence them. In some cases, language is not employed for an external purpose but only for entertainment or personal enjoyment. Verbal communication further helps individuals conceptualize the world around them and themselves. This affects how perceptions of external events are interpreted, how things are categorized, and how ideas are organized and related to each other.

### Non-Verbal

Non-verbal communication is the exchange of information through non-linguistic modes, like facial expressions, gestures, and postures. However, not every form of non-verbal behavior constitutes non-verbal communication.

Some theorists, like Judee Burgoon, hold that it depends on the existence of a socially shared coding system that is used to interpret the meaning of non-verbal behavior. Non-verbal communication has many functions. It frequently contains information about emotions, attitudes, personality, interpersonal relations, and private thoughts.

Non-verbal communication often happens unintentionally and unconsciously, like sweating or blushing, but there are also conscious intentional forms, like shaking hands or raising a thumb. It often happens simultaneously with verbal communication and helps optimize the exchange through emphasis and illustration or by adding additional information. Non-verbal cues can clarify the intent behind a verbal message. Using multiple modalities of communication in this way usually makes communication more effective if the messages of each modality are consistent. However, in some cases different modalities can contain conflicting messages. For example, a person may verbally agree with a statement but press their lips together, thereby indicating disagreement non-verbally.

There are many forms of non-verbal communication. They include kinesics, proxemics, haptics, paralanguage, chronemics, and physical appearance. Kinesics studies the role of bodily behavior in conveying information. It is commonly referred to as body language, even though it is, strictly speaking, not a language but rather non-verbal communication. It includes many forms, like gestures, postures, walking styles, and dance. Facial expressions, like laughing, smiling, and frowning, all belong to kinesics and are expressive and flexible forms of communication.

Oculesics is another subcategory of kinesics in regard to the eyes. It covers questions like how eye contact, gaze, blink rate, and pupil dilation form part of communication. Some kinesic patterns are inborn and involuntary, like blinking, while others are learned and voluntary, like giving a military salute.

Proxemics studies how personal space is used in communication. The distance between the speakers reflects their degree of familiarity and intimacy with each other as well as their social status. Haptics examines how information is conveyed using touching behavior, like handshakes, holding hands, kissing, or slapping. Meanings linked to haptics include care, concern, anger, and violence. For instance, handshaking is often seen as a symbol of equality and fairness, while refusing to shake hands can indicate aggressiveness. Kissing is another form often used to show affection and erotic closeness.

Paralanguage, also known as vocalics, encompasses non-verbal elements in speech that convey information. Paralanguage is often used to express the feelings and emotions that the speaker has but does not explicitly stated in the verbal part of the message. It is not concerned with the words used but with how they are expressed. This includes elements like articulation, lip control, rhythm, intensity, pitch, fluency, and loudness. For example, saying something loudly and in a high pitch conveys a different meaning on the non-verbal level than whispering the same words. Paralanguage is mainly concerned with spoken language but also includes aspects of written language, like the use of colors and fonts as well as spatial arrangement in paragraphs and tables. Non-linguistic sounds may also convey information; crying indicates that an infant is distressed, and babbling conveys information about infant health and well-being.

Chronemics concerns the use of time, such as what messages are sent by being on time versus late for a meeting. The physical appearance of the communicator, such as height, weight, hair, skin color, gender, clothing, tattooing, and piercing, also carries information. Appearance is an important factor for first impressions but is more limited as a mode of communication since it is less changeable. Some forms of non-verbal communication happen using such artifacts as drums, smoke, batons, traffic lights, and flags.

Non-verbal communication can also happen through visual media like paintings and drawings. They can express what a person or an object looks like and can also convey other ideas and emotions. In some cases, this type of non-verbal communication is used in combination with verbal communication, for example, when diagrams or maps employ labels to include additional linguistic information.

Traditionally, most research focused on verbal communication. However, this paradigm began to shift in the 1950s when research interest in non-verbal communication increased and emphasized its influence. For example, many judgments about the nature and behavior of other people are based on non-verbal cues. It is further present in almost every communicative act to some extent and certain parts of it are universally understood. These considerations have prompted some communication theorists, like Ray Birdwhistell, to claim that the majority of ideas and information is conveyed this way. It has also been suggested that human communication is at its core non-verbal and that words can only acquire meaning because of non-verbal communication. The earliest forms of human communication, such as crying and babbling, are non-verbal. Some basic forms of communication happen even before birth between mother and embryo and include information about nutrition and emotions. Non-verbal communication is studied in various fields besides communication studies, like linguistics, semiotics, anthropology, and social psychology.

## Interpersonal

Interpersonal communication is communication between distinct people. Its typical form is dyadic communication, i.e. between two people, but it can also refer to communication within groups. It can be planned or unplanned and occurs in many forms, like when greeting someone, during salary negotiations, or when making a phone call. Some communication theorists, like Virginia M. McDermott, understand interpersonal communication as a fuzzy concept that manifests in degrees. In this view, an exchange varies in how interpersonal it is based on several factors. It depends on how many people are present, and whether it happens face-to-face rather than through telephone or email. A further factor concerns the relation between the communicators: group communication and mass communication are less typical forms of interpersonal communication and some theorists treat them as distinct types.

Interpersonal communication can be synchronous or asynchronous. For asynchronous communication, the parties take turns in sending and receiving messages. This occurs when exchanging letters or emails. For synchronous communication, both parties send messages at the same time. This happens when one person is talking while the other person sends non-verbal messages in response signaling whether they agree with what is being said. Some communication theorists, like Sarah Trenholm and Arthur Jensen, distinguish between content messages and relational messages. Content messages express the speaker's feelings toward the topic of discussion. Relational messages, on the other hand, demonstrate the speaker's feelings toward their relation with the other participants.

Various theories of the function of interpersonal communication have been proposed. Some focus on how it helps people make sense of their world and create society. Others hold that its primary purpose is to understand why other people act the way they do and to adjust one's behavior accordingly. A closely related approach is to focus on information and see interpersonal communication as an attempt to reduce uncertainty about others and external events. Other explanations understand it in terms of the needs it satisfies. This includes the needs of belonging somewhere, being included, being liked, maintaining relationships, and influencing the behavior of others.

On a practical level, interpersonal communication is used to coordinate one's actions with the actions of others to get things done. Research on interpersonal communication includes topics like how people build, maintain, and dissolve relationships through communication. Other questions are why people choose one message rather than another and what effects these messages have on the communicators and their relation. A further topic is how to predict whether two people would like each other.

### Intrapersonal

Intrapersonal communication is communication with oneself. In some cases this manifests externally, such as when engaged in a monologue, taking notes, highlighting a passage, and writing a diary or a shopping list. But many forms of intrapersonal communication happen internally in the form of an inner exchange with oneself, as when thinking about something or daydreaming. Closely related to intrapersonal communication is communication that takes place within an organism below the personal level, such as exchange of information between organs or cells.

Intrapersonal communication can be triggered by internal and external stimuli. It may happen in the form of articulating a phrase before expressing it externally. Other forms are to make plans for the future and to attempt to process emotions to calm oneself down in stressful situations. It can help regulate one's own mental activity and outward behavior as well as internalize cultural norms and ways of thinking. External forms of intrapersonal communication can aid one's memory. This happens, for example, when making a shopping list. Another use is to unravel difficult problems, as when solving a complex mathematical equation line by line. New knowledge can also be internalized this way, such as when repeating new vocabulary to oneself. Because of these functions, intrapersonal communication can be understood as "an exceptionally powerful and pervasive tool for thinking."

Based on its role in self-regulation, some theorists have suggested that intrapersonal communication is more basic than interpersonal communication. Young children sometimes use egocentric speech while playing in an attempt to direct their own behavior. In this view, interpersonal communication only develops later when the child moves from their early egocentric perspective to a more social perspective. A different explanation holds that interpersonal communication is more basic since it is first used by parents to regulate what their child does. Once the child has learned this, they can apply the same technique to themselves to get more control over their own behavior.

### Channels

For communication to be successful, the message has to travel from the sender to the receiver. The channel is the way this is accomplished. It is not concerned with the meaning of the message but only with the technical means of how the meaning is conveyed. Channels are often understood in terms of the senses used to perceive the message, i.e. hearing, seeing, smelling, touching, and tasting. But in the widest sense, channels encompass any form of transmission, including technological means like books, cables, radio waves, telephones, or television. Naturally transmitted messages usually fade rapidly whereas some messages using artificial channels have a much longer lifespan, as in the case of books or sculptures.

The physical characteristics of a channel have an impact on the code and cues that can be used to express information. For example, typical telephone calls are restricted to the use of verbal language and paralanguage but exclude facial expressions. It is often possible to translate messages from one code into another to make them available to a different channel. An example is writing down a spoken message or expressing it using sign language.

The transmission of information can occur through multiple channels at once. For example, face-to-face communication often combines the auditory channel to convey verbal information with the visual channel to transmit non-verbal information using gestures and facial expressions. Employing multiple channels can enhance the effectiveness of communication by helping the receiver better understand the subject matter.

The choice of channels often matters since the receiver's ability to understand may vary depending on the chosen channel. For instance, a teacher may decide to present some information orally and other information visually, depending on the content and the student's preferred learning style. This underlines the role of a media-adequate approach.

### Communicative Competence

Communicative competence is the ability to communicate effectively or to choose the appropriate communicative behavior in a given situation. It concerns what to say, when to say it, and how to say it. It further includes the ability to receive and understand messages. Competence is often contrasted with performance since competence can be present even if it is not exercised, while performance consists in the realization of this competence. However, some theorists reject a stark contrast and hold that performance is the observable part and is used to infer competence in relation to future performances.

Two central components of communicative competence are effectiveness and appropriateness. Effectiveness is the degree to which the speaker achieves their desired outcomes or the degree to which preferred alternatives are realized. This means that whether a communicative behavior is effective does not just depend on the actual outcome but also on the speaker's intention, i.e. whether this outcome was what they intended to achieve. Because of this, some theorists additionally require that the speaker be able to give an explanation of why they engaged in one behavior rather than another. Effectiveness is closely related to efficiency, the difference being that effectiveness is about achieving goals while efficiency is about using few resources (such as time, effort, and money) in the process.

Appropriateness means that the communicative behavior meets social standards and expectations. Communication theorist Brian H. Spitzberg defines it as "the perceived legitimacy or acceptability of behavior or enactments in a given context". This means that the speaker is aware of the social and cultural context in order to adapt and express the message in a way that is considered acceptable in the given situation. For example, to bid farewell to their teacher, a student may use the expression "Goodbye, sir" but not the expression "I gotta split, man", which they may use when talking to a peer. To be both effective and appropriate means to achieve one's preferred outcomes in a way that follows social standards and expectations. Some definitions of communicative competence put their main emphasis on either effectiveness or appropriateness while others combine both features.

Many additional components of communicative competence have been suggested, such as empathy, control, flexibility, sensitivity, and knowledge. It is often discussed in terms of the individual skills employed in the process, i.e. the specific behavioral components that make up communicative competence. Message production skills include reading and writing. They are correlated with the reception skills of listening and reading. There are both verbal and non-verbal communication skills. For example, verbal communication skills involve the proper understanding of a language, including its phonology, orthography, syntax, lexicon, and semantics.

Many aspects of human life depend on successful communication, from ensuring basic necessities of survival to building and maintaining relationships. Communicative competence is a key factor regarding whether a person is able to reach their goals in social life, like having a successful career and finding a suitable spouse. Because of this, it can have a large impact on the individual's well-being. The lack of communicative competence can cause problems both on the individual and the societal level, including professional, academic, and health problems.

Barriers to effective communication can distort the message. They may result in failed communication and cause undesirable effects. This can happen if the message is poorly expressed because it uses terms with which the receiver is not familiar, or because it is not relevant to the receiver's needs, or because it contains too little or too much information. Distraction, selective perception, and lack of attention to feedback may also be responsible. Noise is another negative factor. It concerns influences that interfere with the message on its way to the receiver and distort it. Crackling sounds during a telephone call are one form of noise. Ambiguous expressions can also inhibit effective communication and make it necessary to disambiguate between possible interpretations to discern the sender's intention.

These interpretations depend also on the cultural background of the participants. Significant cultural differences constitute an additional obstacle and make it more likely that messages are misinterpreted.

## Computer

**Fig: Example of computer communication: modems act as transmitter and receiver while the public telephone network is used as a transmission system**

Computer communication concerns the exchange of data between computers and similar devices. For this to be possible, the devices have to be connected through a transmission system that forms a network between them. A transmitter is needed to send messages and a receiver is needed to receive them. A personal computer may use a modem as a transmitter to send information to a server through the public telephone network as the transmission system. The server may use a modem as its receiver. To transmit the data, it has to be converted into an electric signal. Communication channels used for transmission are either analog or digital and are characterized by features like bandwidth and latency.

There are many forms of computer networks. The most commonly discussed ones are LANs and WANs. LAN stands for local area network, which is a computer network within a limited area, usually with a distance of less than one kilometer. This is the case when connecting two computers within a home or an office building. LANs can be set up using a wired connection, like Ethernet, or a wireless connection, like Wi-Fi. WANs, on the other hand, are wide area networks that span large geographical regions, like the internet. Their networks are more complex and may use several intermediate connection nodes to transfer information between endpoints. Further types of computer networks include PANs (personal area networks), CANs (campus area networks), and MANs (metropolitan area networks).

For computer communication to be successful, the involved devices have to follow a common set of conventions governing their exchange. These conventions are known as the communication protocol. They concern various aspects of the exchange, like the format of messages and how to respond to transmission errors. They also cover how the two systems are synchronized, for example, how the receiver identifies the start and end of a signal.

Based on the flow of informations, systems are categorized as simplex, half-duplex, and full-duplex. For simplex systems, signals flow only in one direction from the sender to the receiver, like in radio, cable television, and screens displaying arrivals and departures at airports. Half-duplex systems allow two-way exchanges but signals can only flow in one direction at a time, like walkie-talkies and police radios. In the case of full-duplex systems, signals can flow in both directions at the same time, like regular telephone and internet. In either case, it is often important for successful communication that the connection is secure to ensure that the transmitted data reaches only the intended destination and is not intercepted by an unauthorized third party. This can be achieved by using cryptography, which changes the format of the transmitted information to make it unintelligible to potential interceptors.

Human-computer communication is a closely related field that concerns topics like how humans interact with computers and how data in the form of inputs and outputs is exchanged. This happens through a user interface, which includes the hardware used to interact with the computer, like a mouse, a keyboard, and a monitor, as well as the software used in the process. On the software side, most early user interfaces were command-line interfaces in which the user must type a command to interact with the computer. Most modern user interfaces are graphical user interfaces, like Microsoft Windows and macOS, which are usually much easier to use for non-experts.

They involve graphical elements through which the user can interact with the computer, commonly using a design concept known as skeumorphism to make a new concept feel familiar and speed up understanding by mimicking the real-world equivalent of the interface object. Examples include the typical computer folder icon and recycle bin used for discarding files. One aim when designing user interfaces is to simplify the interaction with computers. This helps make them more user-friendly and accessible to a wider audience while also increasing productivity.

### 7.3.3 Importance of Documentation in Explainable AI

Documentation in XAI is crucial for several reasons. It provides a structured approach to recording the development, deployment, and operation of AI systems, ensuring that stakeholders can understand the model's behavior over time. Proper documentation also aids in regulatory compliance by providing evidence of fairness, transparency, and bias mitigation. Additionally, it serves as a reference for developers and data scientists to debug and improve AI models.

A well-documented AI system includes details on model architecture, data sources, feature selection, training processes, evaluation metrics, and any explainability techniques applied. It also records known limitations and potential biases, enabling users to make informed decisions about the AI system's reliability. Without comprehensive documentation, AI systems risk being seen as black boxes, eroding user confidence and limiting their adoption in critical applications such as healthcare, finance, and criminal justice.

### 7.3.4 Key Components of XAI Documentation

Effective XAI documentation should include several key components. Model documentation should outline the algorithm used, data preprocessing techniques, and training parameters. Explanation documentation should describe the methods employed to generate interpretable outputs, such as SHAP, LIME, or counterfactual explanations. Ethical considerations should highlight efforts to mitigate bias and ensure fairness. User guides should provide instructions on interpreting AI-generated explanations for both technical and non-technical users.

Audit logs are another essential component, capturing changes made to the AI system over time. These logs help track the impact of modifications on model performance and explainability. Additionally, regulatory compliance documentation should address how the AI system aligns with relevant laws and industry standards. By maintaining detailed documentation, organizations can improve transparency, accountability, and continuous improvement in AI explainability.

### 7.3.5 Challenges in AI Documentation

Despite its importance, AI documentation faces several challenges. One of the main difficulties is the complexity of AI models, especially deep learning systems. Documenting the intricate decision-making processes of these models in a human-readable manner is a significant challenge. Additionally, AI systems evolve over time, requiring continuous updates to documentation. Failing to keep documentation current can lead to discrepancies between the model's actual behavior and its recorded explanations.

Another challenge is striking a balance between technical depth and accessibility. Overly complex documentation may be useful for AI developers but difficult for business leaders, regulators, or end-users to comprehend. Conversely, overly simplified documentation may lack the necessary detail for debugging or regulatory scrutiny. Standardizing documentation practices across industries can help address this challenge, but widespread adoption remains a work in progress.

### 7.3.6 Effective Communication of AI Explanations

In addition to thorough documentation, effective communication is essential for making AI explanations useful to different audiences. AI-generated explanations should be tailored to the needs of stakeholders, ranging from data scientists and engineers to policymakers and end-users. Communication strategies should ensure that explanations are clear, concise, and actionable, enabling users to trust and understand AI decisions.

One effective approach is using visual aids to communicate AI explanations. Graphs, heatmaps, and feature importance plots can help users visualize how the AI model arrived at its decisions. Natural language generation (NLG) techniques can also be employed to create human-readable explanations, translating complex AI logic into easily digestible insights. Interactive dashboards that allow users to explore AI decisions dynamically can further enhance explainability.

### 7.3.7 Customizing Explanations for Different Audiences

Different stakeholders require different levels of detail in AI explanations. For technical users, such as AI engineers and data scientists, detailed algorithmic explanations, model weights, and performance metrics are necessary. These users benefit from access to raw data, model code, and explainability tool outputs such as SHAP values or decision trees.

For business leaders and decision-makers, explanations should focus on the impact of AI decisions on business outcomes. These users require high-level insights that highlight key factors influencing AI predictions without diving into technical intricacies. Regulatory bodies and compliance officers need explanations that demonstrate adherence to fairness, transparency, and accountability principles, often requiring a mix of technical and ethical documentation.

For general users, AI explanations should prioritize simplicity and clarity. These explanations should avoid jargon and use analogies or everyday language to illustrate AI decision-making. Providing users with the ability to ask follow-up questions or receive alternative explanations can further improve their understanding.

### 7.3.8 Communicating Limitations and Uncertainty

One of the most critical aspects of AI communication is conveying the limitations and uncertainties associated with AI-generated explanations. No AI model is perfect, and all explanations carry some degree of uncertainty. Clearly communicating confidence levels, potential biases, and areas where the model may struggle ensures that users do not over-rely on AI predictions.

Uncertainty can be communicated using probabilistic scores, confidence intervals, or qualitative statements. For example, a medical AI system predicting disease risk should indicate whether its confidence level is high, moderate, or low. In finance, risk assessment models should highlight potential margin of error in credit scoring. By transparently communicating limitations, organizations can manage expectations and encourage responsible AI usage.

### 7.3.9 Best Practices for AI Documentation and Communication

To ensure effective documentation and communication of AI explanations, organizations should follow best practices. First, documentation should be maintained throughout the AI lifecycle, from development to deployment and continuous monitoring. Using standardized documentation frameworks, such as Model Cards or FactSheets, can help ensure consistency across AI projects.

Second, AI explanations should be tested with target audiences to gauge their clarity and effectiveness. User feedback should be collected to refine explanations and address gaps in understanding. Third, organizations should invest in AI literacy programs to educate stakeholders on interpreting AI explanations. Providing training sessions, interactive tools, and user-friendly documentation can improve AI adoption and trust.

Fourth, explainability efforts should be integrated into governance frameworks. Organizations should establish clear policies for documenting and communicating AI decisions, ensuring compliance with industry regulations and ethical guidelines. AI explanation audits should be conducted periodically to identify areas for improvement.

### 7.3.10 Future Directions in AI Documentation and Communication

As AI continues to evolve, the field of explainability documentation and communication will also progress. Automated documentation generation tools will play a significant role in streamlining the process. AI systems will increasingly be able to generate self-explanatory reports, summarizing model behavior and key decision-making factors without requiring manual intervention.

Advancements in interactive AI explanations will also enhance communication. Future AI systems may allow users to ask natural language questions about AI decisions and receive context-aware responses. Multimodal explanations, combining text, visuals, and interactive elements, will improve user engagement and understanding.

Regulatory advancements will also shape the future of AI documentation. As explainability requirements become more standardized, organizations will need to align their documentation and communication strategies with legal and ethical guidelines. Increased collaboration between AI researchers, policymakers, and industry leaders will drive the development of best practices for AI documentation.

CHAPTER 8

# Emerging Trends and Future Directions

## 8.1 XAI FOR GENERATIVE AI SYSTEMS

Explainability in generative AI is a complex but essential challenge. As these models generate increasingly realistic and impactful content, understanding their decision-making processes becomes critical for trust, fairness, and accountability. Techniques such as latent space visualization, feature attribution, counterfactual explanations, and model distillation provide valuable insights into generative AI behavior. Ensuring explainability across different applications—from text and image generation to drug discovery—enhances transparency and user confidence. Moving forward, integrating explainability into generative AI systems at the design level will be key to building more interpretable and responsible AI models. By prioritizing XAI, we can harness the creative power of generative AI while maintaining ethical and societal safeguards.

### 8.1.1 The Need for Explainability in Generative AI

Generative AI models differ from traditional AI systems in that they produce novel content rather than making predictions or classifications. This creative ability makes their inner workings even more challenging to interpret. The lack of explainability in these models can lead to issues such as biased content generation, lack of reproducibility, and security vulnerabilities, including adversarial attacks. Explainable AI techniques can help mitigate these risks by offering a clearer understanding of how inputs influence outputs, identifying biases in training data, and providing users with confidence in the system's reliability.

In high-stakes applications, such as AI-generated medical imaging or automated content moderation, explainability becomes even more critical. Without clear explanations, it is difficult to assess whether the generated output is safe, ethical, or aligned with user expectations. Furthermore, explainability helps developers refine generative AI models by pinpointing problematic areas and improving their training methodologies.

### 8.1.2 Challenges in Applying XAI to Generative AI Systems

Explaining generative AI models presents unique challenges compared to other AI systems. First, generative models are typically high-dimensional and non-linear, making it difficult to trace specific input-output relationships. Unlike decision trees or linear regression models, where outputs can be clearly linked to input features, generative models often work in latent spaces that lack direct human interpretability.

Another challenge lies in evaluating explanations. Traditional XAI techniques such as SHAP and LIME are well-suited for predictive models but may struggle to explain generative models' creative outputs. The stochastic nature of generative AI means that the same input can yield different outputs, adding complexity to interpretability efforts. Additionally, many generative models involve adversarial training, further complicating their explainability due to the interplay between competing neural networks.

### 8.1.3 Techniques for Enhancing Explainability in Generative AI

Several techniques have been proposed to improve the explainability of generative AI models. One approach is latent space visualization, which helps users understand how different parts of the model contribute to generated outputs. By mapping latent variables to interpretable features, researchers can analyze how changes in input conditions affect the generated content.

Another technique involves feature attribution methods. By applying perturbation-based approaches, researchers can identify which features in the input data have the most significant impact on the output. For example, in AI-generated images, attention maps can highlight which areas of the input image influence the generated version most.

Counterfactual explanations provide another means of enhancing generative AI explainability. These methods generate alternative outputs by modifying certain input parameters, allowing users to explore how small changes affect the model's decisions. In text generation, counterfactual explanations can help identify which words influence the model's response most strongly.

Model distillation is another promising approach. By training simpler, more interpretable models to approximate the behavior of complex generative AI systems, researchers can gain insights into decision-making patterns. This method sacrifices some accuracy but provides a more transparent understanding of how the generative model operates.

### 8.1.4 Explainability in Specific Generative AI Domains

#### Text Generation and Explainability

AI-powered text generators, such as OpenAI's GPT models, have shown remarkable fluency and coherence. However, their decision-making remains largely a black box. Explainability in text generation involves analyzing token importance, sequence dependency, and the impact of training data on outputs. Techniques like attention visualization can help illustrate which words the model prioritizes when generating responses. Additionally, rule-based evaluations can assess whether generated text aligns with ethical guidelines, reducing bias and misinformation risks.

### Image and Video Synthesis

Generative AI has significantly advanced image and video synthesis, with applications in art, design, and entertainment. However, the potential for deepfake misuse raises concerns about transparency. Explainability techniques such as class activation maps and adversarial interpretability methods can help identify which features contribute to AI-generated images. Understanding how models manipulate facial expressions or object placements can improve ethical AI implementation and prevent malicious use cases.

### Drug Discovery and Scientific Research

In healthcare and scientific research, generative AI is used to design new molecules and optimize chemical structures. Explainability in these applications ensures that generated compounds adhere to known scientific principles. Feature attribution techniques, such as gradient-based saliency maps, help researchers understand why a model proposes a particular molecular structure. By making generative models more interpretable, scientists can ensure AI-generated solutions align with established knowledge and safety standards.

## 8.1.5 Trust and User Confidence in Generative AI

One of the primary goals of applying XAI to generative AI is fostering user trust. When users understand why an AI-generated output appears a certain way, they are more likely to trust and adopt these systems. Providing interpretable explanations improves transparency, helping stakeholders make informed decisions about the reliability of AI-generated content.

Regulatory bodies and policymakers also benefit from enhanced explainability. AI-generated content in legal, financial, and healthcare applications requires clear justifications to comply with industry regulations. Explainability frameworks help organizations meet compliance standards by documenting how generative AI models function and identifying potential risks.

Human-in-the-loop (HITL) systems further enhance trust by integrating expert review mechanisms. In applications where generative AI suggests creative or scientific outputs, human oversight ensures that the final content meets quality and ethical standards. Combining AI explainability with human expertise creates a balanced approach that leverages AI's capabilities while maintaining accountability.

### 8.1.6 The Future of XAI in Generative AI

As generative AI continues to evolve, so will the methods for making these models interpretable. Future advancements in XAI for generative AI may include improved visualization techniques, real-time explanation generation, and adaptive interpretability frameworks that tailor explanations to different user needs.

One promising direction is integrating explainability directly into generative AI training. By designing models that inherently generate interpretable outputs, researchers can reduce the need for post hoc explanations. Hybrid models that combine rule-based systems with deep learning architectures may also improve interpretability without sacrificing creativity.

Collaborative efforts between AI researchers, ethicists, and regulatory agencies will be crucial in shaping the future of explainable generative AI. By establishing industry-wide best practices and standardizing evaluation metrics for interpretability, the AI community can ensure that generative models remain both powerful and responsible.

## 8.2 CAUSAL INFERENCE IN EXPLAINABILITY

Causal inference plays a crucial role in enhancing explainability in AI. By distinguishing between correlation and causation, causal inference techniques provide deeper insights into how AI models make decisions. Methods such as Structural Causal Models, do-calculus, counterfactual explanations, and mediation analysis enable AI systems to generate more reliable and actionable explanations. Applications in healthcare, finance, and criminal justice demonstrate the importance of causal reasoning in ensuring fairness and trust in AI-driven decisions. As research progresses, integrating causal inference into AI models will be key to making AI systems more interpretable, transparent, and accountable.

### 8.2.1 Understanding the Causal Inference

Causal inference is the process of determining the independent, actual effect of a particular phenomenon that is a component of a larger system. The main difference between causal inference and inference of association is that causal inference analyzes the response of an effect variable when a cause of the effect variable is changed. The study of why things occur is called etiology, and can be described using the language of scientific causal notation. Causal inference is said to provide the evidence of causality theorized by causal reasoning.

Causal inference is widely studied across all sciences. Several innovations in the development and implementation of methodology designed to determine causality have proliferated in recent decades. Causal inference remains especially difficult where experimentation is difficult or impossible, which is common throughout most sciences.

The approaches to causal inference are broadly applicable across all types of scientific disciplines, and many methods of causal inference that were designed for certain disciplines have found use in other disciplines.

Causal inference is difficult to perform and there is significant debate amongst scientists about the proper way to determine causality. Despite other innovations, there remain concerns of misattribution by scientists of correlative results as causal, of the usage of incorrect methodologies by scientists, and of deliberate manipulation by scientists of analytical results in order to obtain statistically significant estimates. Particular concern is raised in the use of regression models, especially linear regression models.

## Definition

Inferring the cause of something has been described as:

- "...reason[ing] to the conclusion that something is, or is likely to be, the cause of something else".
- "Identification of the cause or causes of a phenomenon, by establishing covariation of cause and effect, a time-order relationship with the cause preceding the effect, and the elimination of plausible alternative causes."

## Methodology

### General

Causal inference is conducted via the study of systems where the measure of one variable is suspected to affect the measure of another. Causal inference is conducted with regard to the scientific method. The first step of causal inference is to formulate a falsifiable null hypothesis, which is subsequently tested with statistical methods.

Frequentist statistical inference is the use of statistical methods to determine the probability that the data occur under the null hypothesis by chance; Bayesian inference is used to determine the effect of an independent variable. Statistical inference is generally used to determine the difference between variations in the original data that are random variation or the effect of a well-specified causal mechanism. Notably, correlation does not imply causation, so the study of causality is as concerned with the study of potential causal mechanisms as it is with variation amongst the data. A frequently sought after standard of causal inference is an experiment wherein treatment is randomly assigned but all other confounding factors are held constant. Most of the efforts in causal inference are in the attempt to replicate experimental conditions.

Epidemiological studies employ different epidemiological methods of collecting and measuring evidence of risk factors and effect and different ways of measuring association between the two. Results of a 2020 review of methods for causal inference found that using existing literature for clinical training programs can be challenging.

Common frameworks for causal inference include the causal pie model (component-cause), Pearl's structural causal model (causal diagram + do-calculus), structural equation modeling, and Rubin causal model (potential-outcome), which are often used in areas such as social sciences and epidemiology.

### Experimental

Experimental verification of causal mechanisms is possible using experimental methods. The main motivation behind an experiment is to hold other experimental variables constant while purposefully manipulating the variable of interest. If the experiment produces statistically significant effects as a result of only the treatment variable being manipulated, there is grounds to believe that a causal effect can be assigned to the treatment variable, assuming that other standards for experimental design have been met.

- **Quasi-Experimental:** Quasi-experimental verification of causal mechanisms is conducted when traditional experimental methods are unavailable. This may be the result of prohibitive costs of conducting an experiment, or the inherent infeasibility of conducting an experiment, especially experiments that are concerned with large systems such as economies of electoral systems, or for treatments that are considered to present a danger to the well-being of test subjects. Quasi-experiments may also occur where information is withheld for legal reasons.

## Approaches in Epidemiology

Epidemiology studies patterns of health and disease in defined populations of living beings in order to infer causes and effects. An association between an exposure to a putative risk factor and a disease may be suggestive of, but is not equivalent to causality because correlation does not imply causation. Historically, Koch's postulates have been used since the 19th century to decide if a microorganism was the cause of a disease. In the 20th century the Bradford Hill criteria, described in 1965 have been used to assess causality of variables outside microbiology, although even these criteria are not exclusive ways to determine causality. In molecular epidemiology the phenomena studied are on a molecular biology level, including genetics, where biomarkers are evidence of cause or effects. A recent trend is to identify evidence for influence of the exposure on molecular pathology within diseased tissue or cells, in the emerging interdisciplinary field of molecular pathological epidemiology (MPE). Linking the exposure to molecular pathologic signatures of the disease can help to assess causality. Considering the inherent nature of heterogeneity of a given disease, the unique disease principle, disease phenotyping and subtyping are trends in biomedical and public health sciences, exemplified as personalized medicine and precision medicine.

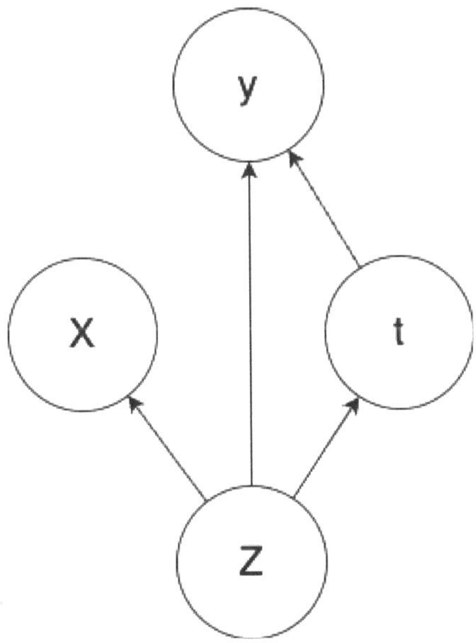


**Fig: Causal Graph where the Hidden Confounders Z have an Effect on the Observable Variables X, the Outcome y and the Choice of Treatment t**

Causal Inference has also been used for treatment effect estimation. Assuming a set of observable patient symptoms(X) caused by a set of hidden causes(Z) we can choose to give or not a treatment t. The result of the giving or not giving the treatment is the effect estimation y. If the treatment is not guaranteed to have a positive effect then the decision whether the treatment should be applied or not depends firstly on expert knowledge that encompasses the causal connections. For novel diseases, this expert knowledge may not be available. As a result, we rely solely on past treatment outcomes to make decisions.

## Approaches in Computer Science

Causal inference is an important concept in the field of causal artificial intelligence. Determination of cause and effect from joint observational data for two time-independent variables, say X and Y, has been tackled using asymmetry between evidence for some model in the directions, $X \rightarrow Y$ and $Y \rightarrow X$. The primary approaches are based on Algorithmic information theory models and noise models.

### Noise Models

Incorporate an independent noise term in the model to compare the evidences of the two directions.

Here are some of the noise models for the hypothesis Y $\rightarrow$ X with the noise E:

- **Additive Noise:** $Y = F(X) + E$
- **Linear Noise:** $Y = pX + qE$
- **Post-Nonlinear:** $Y = G(F(X) + E)$
- **Heteroskedastic Noise:** $Y = F(X) + E.G(X)$
- **Functional Noise:** $Y = F(X, E)$

The common assumption in these models are:

- There are no other causes of Y.
- X and E have no common causes.
- Distribution of cause is independent from causal mechanisms.

On an intuitive level, the idea is that the factorization of the joint distribution P(Cause, Effect) into P(Cause)*P(Effect | Cause) typically yields models of lower total complexity than the factorization into P(Effect)*P(Cause | Effect). Although the notion of "complexity" is intuitively appealing, it is not obvious how it should be precisely defined. A different family of methods attempt to discover causal "footprints" from large amounts of labeled data, and allow the prediction of more flexible causal relations.

## Approaches in Social Sciences

### Social Science

The social sciences in general have moved increasingly toward including quantitative frameworks for assessing causality. Much of this has been described as a means of providing greater rigor to social science methodology. Political science was significantly influenced by the publication of Designing Social Inquiry, by Gary King, Robert Keohane, and Sidney Verba, in 1994. King, Keohane, and Verba recommend that researchers apply both quantitative and qualitative methods and adopt the language of statistical inference to be clearer about their subjects of interest and units of analysis. Proponents of quantitative methods have also increasingly adopted the potential outcomes framework, developed by Donald Rubin, as a standard for inferring causality.

While much of the emphasis remains on statistical inference in the potential outcomes framework, social science methodologists have developed new tools to conduct causal inference with both qualitative and quantitative methods, sometimes called a "mixed methods" approach. Advocates of diverse methodological approaches argue that different methodologies are better suited to different subjects of study. Sociologist Herbert Smith and political scientists James Mahoney and Gary Goertz have cited the observation of Paul W. Holland, a statistician and author of the 1986 article "Statistics and Causal Inference", that statistical inference is most appropriate for assessing the "effects of causes" rather than the "causes of effects".

Qualitative methodologists have argued that formalized models of causation, including process tracing and fuzzy set theory, provide opportunities to infer causation through the identification of critical factors within case studies or through a process of comparison among several case studies. These methodologies are also valuable for subjects in which a limited number of potential observations or the presence of confounding variables would limit the applicability of statistical inference.

On longer timescales, persistence studies uses causal inference to link historical events to later political, economic and social outcomes.

### Economics and Political Science

In the economic sciences and political sciences causal inference is often difficult, owing to the real world complexity of economic and political realities and the inability to recreate many large-scale phenomena within controlled experiments. Causal inference in the economic and political sciences continues to see improvement in methodology and rigor, due to the increased level of technology available to social scientists, the increase in the number of social scientists and research, and improvements to causal inference methodologies throughout social sciences. Despite the difficulties inherent in determining causality in economic systems, several widely employed methods exist throughout those fields.

- **Theoretical Methods:** Economists and political scientists can use theory (often studied in theory-driven econometrics) to estimate the magnitude of supposedly causal relationships in cases where they believe a causal relationship exists. Theorists can presuppose a mechanism believed to be causal and describe the effects using data analysis to justify their proposed theory. For example, theorists can use logic to construct a model, such as theorizing that rain causes fluctuations in economic productivity but that the converse is not true. However, using purely theoretical claims that do not offer any predictive insights has been called "pre-scientific" because there is no ability to predict the impact of the supposed causal properties. It is worth reiterating that regression analysis in the social science does not inherently imply causality, as many phenomena may correlate in the short run or in particular datasets but demonstrate no correlation in other time periods or other datasets. Thus, the attribution of causality to correlative properties is premature absent a well defined and reasoned causal mechanism.

- **Instrumental Variables:** The instrumental variables (IV) technique is a method of determining causality that involves the elimination of a correlation between one of a model's explanatory variables and the model's error term. This method presumes that if a model's error term moves similarly with the variation of another variable, then the model's error term is probably an effect of variation in that explanatory variable. The elimination of this correlation through the introduction of a new instrumental variable thus reduces the error present in the model as a whole.
- **Model Specification:** Model specification is the act of selecting a model to be used in data analysis. Social scientists (and, indeed, all scientists) must determine the correct model to use because different models are good at estimating different relationships. Model specification can be useful in determining causality that is slow to emerge, where the effects of an action in one period are only felt in a later period. It is worth remembering that correlations only measure whether two variables have similar variance, not whether they affect one another in a particular direction; thus, one cannot determine the direction of a causal relation based on correlations only. Because causal acts are believed to precede causal effects, social scientists can use a model that looks specifically for the effect of one variable on another over a period of time. This leads to using the variables representing phenomena happening earlier as treatment effects, where econometric tests are used to look for later changes in data that are attributed to the effect of such treatment effects, where a meaningful difference in results following a meaningful difference in treatment effects may indicate causality between the treatment effects and the measured effects (e.g., Granger-causality tests). Such studies are examples of time-series analysis.
- **Sensitivity Analysis:** Other variables, or regressors in regression analysis, are either included or not included across various implementations of the same model to ensure that different sources of variation can be studied more separately from one another. This is a form of sensitivity analysis: it is the study of how sensitive an implementation of a model is to the addition of one or more new variables. A chief motivating concern in the use of sensitivity analysis is the pursuit of discovering

confounding variables. Confounding variables are variables that have a large impact on the results of a statistical test but are not the variable that causal inference is trying to study. Confounding variables may cause a regressor to appear to be significant in one implementation, but not in another.

- **Multi-Collinearity:** Another reason for the use of sensitivity analysis is to detect multicollinearity. Multicollinearity is the phenomenon where the correlation between two explanatory variables is very high. A high level of correlation between two such variables can dramatically affect the outcome of a statistical analysis, where small variations in highly correlated data can flip the effect of a variable from a positive direction to a negative direction, or vice versa. This is an inherent property of variance testing. Determining multicollinearity is useful in sensitivity analysis because the elimination of highly correlated variables in different model implementations can prevent the dramatic changes in results that result from the inclusion of such variables. However, there are limits to sensitivity analysis' ability to prevent the deleterious effects of multicollinearity, especially in the social sciences, where systems are complex. Because it is theoretically impossible to include or even measure all of the confounding factors in a sufficiently complex system, econometric models are susceptible to the common-cause fallacy, where causal effects are incorrectly attributed to the wrong variable because the correct variable was not captured in the original data. This is an example of the failure to account for a lurking variable.
- **Design-Based Econometrics:** Recently, improved methodology in design-based econometrics has popularized the use of both natural experiments and quasi-experimental research designs to study the causal mechanisms that such experiments are believed to identify.

## Malpractice in Causal Inference

Despite the advancements in the development of methodologies used to determine causality, significant weaknesses in determining causality remain. These weaknesses can be attributed both to the inherent difficulty of determining causal relations in complex systems but also to cases of scientific malpractice.

Separate from the difficulties of causal inference, the perception that large numbers of scholars in the social sciences engage in non-scientific methodology exists among some large groups of social scientists. Criticism of economists and social scientists as passing off descriptive studies as causal studies are rife within those fields.

### Scientific Malpractice and Flawed Methodology

In the sciences, especially in the social sciences, there is concern among scholars that scientific malpractice is widespread. As scientific study is a broad topic, there are theoretically limitless ways to have a causal inference undermined through no fault of a researcher. Nonetheless, there remain concerns among scientists that large numbers of researchers do not perform basic duties or practice sufficiently diverse methods in causal inference.

One prominent example of common non-causal methodology is the erroneous assumption of correlative properties as causal properties. There is no inherent causality in phenomena that correlate. Regression models are designed to measure variance within data relative to a theoretical model: there is nothing to suggest that data that presents high levels of covariance have any meaningful relationship (absent a proposed causal mechanism with predictive properties or a random assignment of treatment). The use of flawed methodology has been claimed to be widespread, with common examples of such malpractice being the overuse of correlative models, especially the overuse of regression models and particularly linear regression models. The presupposition that two correlated phenomena are inherently related is a logical fallacy known as spurious correlation. Some social scientists claim that widespread use of methodology that attributes causality to spurious correlations have been detrimental to the integrity of the social sciences, although improvements stemming from better methodologies have been noted.

A potential effect of scientific studies that erroneously conflate correlation with causality is an increase in the number of scientific findings whose results are not reproducible by third parties. Such non-reproducibility is a logical consequence of findings that correlation only temporarily being overgeneralized into mechanisms that have no inherent relationship, where new data does not contain the previous, idiosyncratic correlations of the original data. Debates over the effect of malpractice versus the effect of the inherent difficulties of searching for causality are ongoing. Critics of widely practiced methodologies argue that researchers have engaged statistical manipulation in order to publish articles that supposedly demonstrate evidence of causality but are actually examples of spurious correlation being touted as evidence of causality: such endeavors may be referred to as P hacking. To prevent this, some have advocated that researchers preregister their research designs prior to conducting to their studies so that they do not inadvertently overemphasize a nonreproducible finding that was not the initial subject of inquiry but was found to be statistically significant during data analysis.

## 8.2.2 The Need for Causal Inference in Explainable AI

Traditional machine learning models operate as black boxes, providing predictions without clear justifications. Feature importance methods, such as SHAP and

LIME, help shed light on model decisions, but they often fail to establish true causal relationships. For instance, a model might predict a higher probability of loan default for individuals living in certain neighborhoods, but this correlation does not necessarily mean that location causes default. Without causal inference, explanations may be misleading, reinforcing biases rather than uncovering genuine decision-making patterns.

Causal inference addresses this challenge by differentiating between mere associations and real causal links. This distinction is crucial in high-stakes applications. In healthcare, for example, an AI model diagnosing diseases must distinguish whether a symptom directly causes a condition or is merely a byproduct of another underlying cause. Without causal insights, AI models risk propagating errors and reinforcing societal biases.

### 8.2.3 Causal Inference vs. Correlation-Based Methods in XAI

A major limitation of traditional feature attribution methods in XAI is that they often rely on correlations rather than causation. These methods, while useful for approximating feature importance, do not reveal how changing one variable affects the model's outcome. Causal inference, on the other hand, provides a framework for understanding whether altering an input variable would directly influence a model's prediction.

Consider an AI system designed to predict employee performance based on multiple features, including working hours, educational background, and previous job experience. A correlation-based approach might suggest that employees who work longer hours tend to perform better. However, causal inference allows us to determine whether extended work hours actually cause better performance or if another factor, such as intrinsic motivation or task complexity, is responsible.

By incorporating causal inference into XAI, we can refine feature attribution techniques, ensuring that explanations provided by AI models are not just interpretable but also actionable. This distinction is especially important for policy-making, where decisions should be based on true causal relationships rather than spurious correlations.

### 8.2.4 Methods for Causal Inference in Explainability

Several techniques exist for incorporating causal inference into explainable AI. These methods help uncover cause-and-effect relationships within complex machine learning models, improving the reliability of AI explanations.

#### Structural Causal Models (SCMs)

Structural Causal Models (SCMs) provide a formal framework for causal inference by representing relationships between variables as directed graphs. These models distinguish between direct and indirect effects, allowing AI systems to assess how interventions impact outcomes. SCMs are particularly useful in healthcare, where understanding causal mechanisms can improve diagnosis and treatment decisions. For example, an SCM can help determine whether a specific medication causes an improvement in patient health or whether other confounding factors, such as lifestyle changes, play a role.

### Do-Calculus

Proposed by Judea Pearl, do-calculus is a mathematical framework for estimating causal effects from observational data. Unlike traditional statistical methods, which rely solely on correlations, do-calculus helps determine the consequences of interventions. This is particularly useful in AI-driven decision-making systems, where understanding the impact of policy changes, medical treatments, or financial regulations is essential.

### Counterfactual Explanations

Counterfactual reasoning is a fundamental concept in causal inference. It involves asking, "What would have happened if a certain condition had been different?" In XAI, counterfactual explanations allow users to understand how changing a single input would alter an AI model's prediction. For example, if an AI system denies a loan application, a counterfactual explanation might show that approval would have been granted if the applicant had a slightly higher credit score. This method provides actionable insights, enabling users to adjust their behavior based on clear causal relationships.

### Instrumental Variables

Instrumental variables (IV) are used in causal inference to control for confounding factors. These variables influence the treatment but do not directly affect the outcome except through the treatment. In explainability, IV methods help isolate causal effects, improving model transparency and fairness. For example, in AI-driven hiring systems, using an instrumental variable such as randomized training interventions can help distinguish whether education level truly causes better job performance or if other unobserved factors, like socio-economic background, play a role.

### Mediation Analysis

Mediation analysis helps uncover pathways through which causal effects operate. It determines whether an independent variable influences an outcome directly or through an intermediate mediator variable. In AI explainability, mediation analysis is valuable for understanding complex decision-making processes. For instance, if an AI model predicts that patients with higher incomes are more likely to recover from a disease, mediation analysis can help determine whether income itself is the causal factor or if it operates through better access to healthcare.

### 8.2.5 Applications of Causal Inference in Explainable AI

#### Healthcare and Medical AI

In healthcare, AI models assist in disease diagnosis, treatment recommendation, and patient risk assessment. However, these models must provide explanations grounded in causal reasoning rather than mere correlations. Causal inference techniques help doctors understand whether a specific drug improves patient outcomes or if external factors, such as exercise and diet, are responsible. This prevents AI models from reinforcing incorrect medical assumptions, leading to more reliable and ethical healthcare decisions.

#### Finance and Risk Assessment

Financial institutions use AI for credit scoring, fraud detection, and investment strategies. However, if these models rely on correlations rather than causal relationships, they may reinforce biases or lead to unfair outcomes. Causal inference in finance helps determine whether a feature, such as zip code, genuinely affects creditworthiness or if it is merely a proxy for socio-economic status. By incorporating causal reasoning, financial AI systems can ensure fairness and compliance with regulatory requirements.

#### Criminal Justice and Fairness

AI models used in criminal justice, such as predictive policing algorithms, must be explainable and free from bias. Causal inference techniques help identify whether certain features genuinely contribute to crime prediction or if they reflect systemic biases. For example, an AI model might associate specific neighborhoods with higher crime rates, but causal inference can help determine whether socio-economic conditions, policing practices, or historical biases drive these patterns. This ensures that AI-driven decisions do not reinforce existing inequalities.

### 8.2.6 Future Directions in Causal Explainability

The integration of causal inference in XAI is still evolving, with ongoing research focusing on improving causal discovery algorithms, developing more interpretable causal models, and applying these techniques across diverse industries. As AI becomes more embedded in critical decision-making, ensuring that models provide causal rather than correlational explanations will be essential for building trust and accountability.

One promising direction is combining causal inference with deep learning models to create inherently interpretable AI systems. By embedding causal reasoning into neural networks, AI developers can ensure that models make decisions based on meaningful cause-and-effect relationships rather than statistical artifacts. Additionally, advancements in reinforcement learning and causal discovery algorithms will further enhance explainability, making AI systems more reliable and ethical.

## 8.3 MULTI-AGENT SYSTEMS AND XAI

Explainability in Multi-Agent Systems is essential for ensuring transparency, trust, and accountability in AI-driven decision-making. By leveraging techniques such as causal inference, counterfactual reasoning, graph-based analysis, and reinforcement learning interpretation, researchers and practitioners can uncover meaningful insights into MAS behaviors. As MAS continue to shape industries ranging from healthcare to finance, developing robust XAI frameworks will be key to maximizing their potential while minimizing risks.

### 8.3.1 Understanding Multi-Agent Systems

Multi-Agent Systems consist of multiple autonomous agents that interact within an environment to achieve individual or collective goals. These agents can be cooperative, competitive, or a mix of both, depending on the system's objective. For example, in autonomous traffic management, multiple self-driving cars operate as agents, coordinating their movements to minimize congestion and avoid accidents. In financial markets, trading bots interact in a competitive environment, making independent yet interrelated decisions.

The complexity of MAS arises from emergent behaviors, where interactions between agents produce outcomes that are not explicitly programmed. This complexity necessitates explainability techniques that can shed light on why specific behaviors emerge, how agents influence one another, and whether the system adheres to predefined rules and ethical guidelines.

### 8.3.2 The Need for Explainability in Multi-Agent Systems

Explainability in MAS is crucial for several reasons. First, stakeholders, such as regulators, end-users, and developers, must understand how agents make decisions, especially in high-stakes applications like healthcare and finance. Second, explainability helps identify and mitigate biases, ensuring that MAS operate fairly and ethically. Third, transparency builds trust, which is essential for human-agent collaboration in fields like robotics and cybersecurity. Lastly, debugging and improving MAS require clear insights into agent interactions, allowing developers to fine-tune system behavior efficiently. Without explainability, MAS can exhibit unpredictable behaviors, making it difficult to diagnose errors, address unintended consequences, and ensure compliance with legal and ethical standards. XAI methods tailored to MAS provide structured explanations, offering insights into agent decision-making, system-wide dynamics, and potential risks.

### 8.3.3 Challenges of Explainability in Multi-Agent Systems

MAS pose unique challenges for explainability due to their dynamic, distributed, and interactive nature. Unlike single-agent AI systems, where explainability focuses on individual model decisions, MAS require explanations that account for interactions between multiple agents. Key challenges include:

- **Emergent Behaviors:** MAS often exhibit behaviors that arise from agent interactions rather than explicit programming. Understanding and explaining these emergent patterns can be complex.
- **Decentralized Decision-Making:** Agents in MAS operate independently, making local decisions based on partial information. Aggregating these individual decisions into a cohesive explanation is challenging.
- **Dynamic Environments:** Many MAS operate in real-time and adapt to changing environments, requiring explanations that can evolve with the system.
- **Diverse Agent Roles:** Different agents may have different objectives, strategies, and knowledge bases, making it difficult to create a single unified explanation framework.
- **Scalability:** Large-scale MAS, such as those used in swarm robotics or financial trading, involve thousands of agents, necessitating efficient and scalable XAI techniques.

### 8.3.4 Techniques for Explainability in Multi-Agent Systems

To address these challenges, several XAI techniques have been developed for MAS. These techniques focus on interpreting individual agent decisions, understanding agent interactions, and providing meaningful system-level explanations.

- **Rule-Based Explanations:** One approach to explaining MAS decisions is through rule-based methods, where agents follow predefined logical rules. By tracing agent decisions back to these rules, stakeholders can understand why specific actions were taken. This method is particularly useful in expert systems and robotic automation, where rules are explicitly programmed and can be interpreted by humans.
- **Causal Inference in MAS:** Causal inference techniques help identify cause-and-effect relationships within MAS. By analyzing how changes in one agent's behavior influence the overall system, causal inference provides insights into emergent properties and inter-agent

dependencies. This approach is valuable in financial markets, where understanding how one trading agent's decisions impact market dynamics can inform risk management strategies.

- **Counterfactual Explanations:** Counterfactual explanations describe how an outcome would change if different decisions were made. In MAS, counterfactuals can be used to assess how modifying an agent's behavior affects system performance. For example, in a multi-agent healthcare system, counterfactual reasoning can reveal how alternative treatment decisions by different AI-powered agents impact patient outcomes.
- **Graph-Based Explainability:** Since MAS involve interactions between multiple agents, graph-based methods provide a natural way to visualize and explain agent relationships. Techniques like network analysis and attention mechanisms can highlight key influencers within the system, demonstrating how information and decisions propagate across agents.
- **Reinforcement Learning-Based Explanations:** Many MAS utilize reinforcement learning (RL), where agents learn optimal strategies through trial and error. Explaining RL-based MAS requires methods like reward attribution, policy visualization, and trajectory analysis. These techniques help reveal why agents favor certain strategies over others and how rewards influence decision-making.
- **Human-Agent Interaction and Explainability:** For MAS that interact with humans, explainability must be designed to accommodate human cognitive processes. Natural language explanations, interactive dashboards, and visual storytelling techniques can bridge the gap between complex AI behaviors and human understanding. For instance, in autonomous vehicle platooning, a user-friendly interface can explain why a group of self-driving cars chose a particular route based on real-time traffic data and collective decision-making.

### 8.3.5 Applications of Explainable Multi-Agent Systems

- **Healthcare and Medical AI:** MAS are increasingly used in healthcare for patient monitoring, diagnostics, and treatment planning. In a multi-agent hospital management system, AI-driven agents coordinate patient care, allocate medical resources, and optimize workflows. Explainability ensures that doctors and nurses understand how these agents make decisions, improving trust and accountability in AI-assisted healthcare.
- **Finance and Algorithmic Trading:** Financial markets rely on MAS for algorithmic trading, fraud detection, and risk assessment. Trading bots interact in competitive environments, making split-second decisions

that influence market dynamics. XAI techniques help regulators, investors, and risk analysts understand trading strategies, detect market manipulation, and ensure compliance with financial regulations.

- **Autonomous Vehicles and Smart Transportation:** Self-driving cars operate as MAS, coordinating movements, negotiating traffic scenarios, and avoiding collisions. Explainability in autonomous transportation enhances safety by allowing human operators and regulators to understand why specific driving decisions were made. This is particularly important for accident investigations and legal accountability.
- **Cybersecurity and Threat Detection:** MAS play a critical role in cybersecurity by autonomously detecting and mitigating cyber threats. AI-driven agents monitor network traffic, identify anomalies, and coordinate defensive measures. Explainable MAS help security professionals interpret threat assessments, enabling proactive responses to cyber attacks.
- **Supply Chain and Logistics:** MAS optimize global supply chains by managing inventory, forecasting demand, and coordinating logistics. XAI ensures that supply chain decisions, such as route optimization and supplier selection, are transparent and justifiable, leading to improved efficiency and stakeholder confidence.

### 8.3.6 Future Directions in Explainable Multi-Agent Systems

As MAS continue to evolve, research in XAI must advance to address scalability, adaptability, and human interpretability. Future directions include developing hybrid explainability models that combine rule-based logic with deep learning, integrating explainability into decentralized AI architectures, and improving human-agent interaction through natural language processing and interactive visualization.

Additionally, ethical considerations in MAS explainability will play a vital role in ensuring fairness, accountability, and bias mitigation. As AI regulations become more stringent, explainability in MAS will be critical for compliance, trust-building, and responsible AI deployment.

## 8.4 HUMAN-IN-THE-LOOP EXPLAINABILITY

Human-in-the-Loop Explainability is a critical component of Explainable AI, ensuring that AI models remain transparent, interpretable, and aligned with human values. By integrating human feedback, refining model behavior, and fostering trust, HITL approaches enhance AI usability across various domains. While challenges such as scalability, cognitive load, and regulatory compliance persist, advancements in interactive AI interfaces, continuous learning, and ethical AI deployment will shape the future of HITL Explainability. As AI systems continue to evolve, maintaining a balance between automation and human oversight will be essential for responsible and effective AI implementation.

### 8.4.1 Understanding Human-in-the-Loop Explainability

HITL Explainability is based on the principle that AI systems should be designed with mechanisms that allow human users to understand, intervene in, and refine model decisions. Unlike fully automated AI systems, HITL frameworks provide iterative feedback loops where human experts can validate outputs, correct errors, and refine model behavior based on domain knowledge. The fundamental idea behind HITL Explainability is that AI should not operate as a "black box" but rather as an interactive system where users can query, interpret, and improve its decisions. This ensures that AI remains aligned with human reasoning and ethical considerations, reducing instances of bias, misinformation, and unexpected model behavior.

### 8.4.2 Key Components of HITL Explainability

- **Model Interpretability and Transparency:** A critical aspect of HITL Explainability is designing AI models that provide interpretable insights into their decision-making processes. Techniques such as feature attribution, counterfactual reasoning, and rule-based logic help translate AI decisions into a human-understandable format. When users can see why a model made a particular decision, they can provide more informed feedback and corrections, improving system reliability.
- **Human Feedback Integration:** HITL systems must be designed to incorporate human feedback at different stages of the AI lifecycle. This can be achieved through interactive interfaces, annotation tools, and active learning strategies where human users continuously refine AI predictions. For instance, in medical diagnostics, radiologists can review AI-generated scan interpretations and correct misdiagnoses, enabling the model to learn from expert feedback over time.
- **Iterative Learning and Adaptability:** A significant advantage of HITL Explainability is that it allows AI models to evolve based on human expertise. Iterative learning mechanisms ensure that AI does not just rely on static training data but improves through real-world interactions. This is particularly beneficial in rapidly changing fields like cybersecurity, where new threats emerge frequently, requiring AI models to adapt based on expert insights.

- **Ethical and Bias Mitigation Measures:** AI models are prone to biases that can lead to unfair or unethical decision-making. HITL frameworks introduce a layer of human oversight that helps detect and mitigate biases. By allowing human experts to review and correct biased predictions, HITL Explainability enhances fairness and accountability in AI-driven decision-making.
- **Trust and User Confidence:** One of the primary motivations for HITL Explainability is to build user trust in AI systems. When users understand how and why AI models generate specific outputs, they are more likely to adopt and rely on these systems. By fostering transparency and human involvement, HITL approaches reduce skepticism and resistance to AI adoption in critical sectors.

### 8.4.3 Applications of HITL Explainability

#### Healthcare and Medical Diagnosis

In healthcare, AI-assisted diagnostic systems analyze medical data to identify diseases and recommend treatments. However, without explainability, doctors may be hesitant to rely on AI-generated insights. HITL approaches ensure that medical professionals can validate AI diagnoses, adjust recommendations, and provide feedback to enhance model accuracy. For instance, an AI model analyzing MRI scans can flag potential abnormalities, which radiologists can then verify, confirm, or correct, improving diagnostic reliability.

#### Finance and Risk Assessment

Financial institutions use AI for credit scoring, fraud detection, and investment analysis. However, black-box AI models can lead to unfair loan approvals, biased credit assessments, or undetected fraudulent transactions. HITL Explainability allows financial analysts to understand AI-generated decisions, review risk assessments, and intervene in cases of anomalies. This enhances regulatory compliance and reduces biases that may disproportionately affect certain demographics.

#### Autonomous Vehicles and Transportation

Self-driving cars and autonomous transportation systems require a high level of explainability to ensure safety and regulatory compliance. HITL methods allow engineers and regulators to analyze AI-driven decisions, ensuring they align with safety protocols. For instance, if an autonomous vehicle makes an unexpected stop or lane change, human experts can review the AI's reasoning, validate its decision, or correct errors to improve future performance.

### Cybersecurity and Threat Detection

AI is widely used in cybersecurity for detecting malware, phishing attempts, and network intrusions. However, AI models may generate false positives or overlook sophisticated threats. HITL frameworks ensure that cybersecurity experts can review AI alerts, analyze patterns, and refine threat detection strategies. By incorporating human expertise, AI security systems become more robust and adaptive to emerging cyber threats.

### Legal and Criminal Justice Systems

AI is increasingly used in legal case analysis, predictive policing, and sentencing recommendations. However, concerns about bias and fairness necessitate HITL Explainability.

Human legal experts must review AI-generated recommendations to ensure compliance with legal standards and ethical guidelines. HITL approaches reduce the risk of biased decision-making and wrongful convictions by incorporating human judgment into AI-driven legal frameworks.

## 8.4.4 Challenges in Implementing HITL Explainability

### Balancing Automation and Human Intervention

One of the key challenges in HITL Explainability is finding the right balance between automation and human involvement. Too much reliance on human input can slow down AI processes, while excessive automation can lead to unchecked errors and biases. Striking a balance between efficiency and oversight is essential for effective HITL implementation.

### Cognitive Load and Human Fatigue

Human experts reviewing AI-generated outputs may experience cognitive overload, leading to decreased accuracy and decision fatigue. Designing intuitive and user-friendly interfaces, incorporating AI-driven suggestions, and prioritizing critical cases for human review can mitigate this challenge.

### Scalability of Human Involvement

As AI applications expand, ensuring sufficient human oversight can be challenging. HITL frameworks must be designed to scale effectively, utilizing crowdsourcing, expert validation, and active learning strategies to distribute human oversight efficiently across large datasets.

### Trust Calibration and User Training

While HITL Explainability fosters trust, over-reliance on AI-generated explanations can lead to blind trust in models, while excessive skepticism may result in unnecessary re-evaluations. Proper training programs for users interacting with AI models can help calibrate trust and improve decision-making effectiveness.

#### Regulatory and Ethical Considerations

HITL Explainability requires adherence to regulatory standards and ethical guidelines. Ensuring compliance with data protection laws, algorithmic transparency requirements, and fairness principles is essential for the responsible deployment of HITL AI systems.

### 8.4.5 Future Directions in HITL Explainability

#### Advancements in Interactive AI Interfaces

Future HITL systems will integrate advanced interactive AI interfaces, enabling real-time collaboration between humans and AI. Natural language processing, visualization tools, and conversational AI will enhance human-AI interaction, making explainability more intuitive.

#### AI-Assisted Human Decision-Making

Rather than AI simply providing explanations, future HITL systems will facilitate AI-assisted decision-making, where humans and AI work collaboratively to generate optimal outcomes. This shift will redefine human-AI collaboration, making AI a valuable assistant rather than just an automated tool.

#### Continuous Learning and Adaptive Explainability

AI models will incorporate continuous learning mechanisms, allowing human feedback to refine model behavior dynamically. Explainability frameworks will evolve to provide personalized explanations tailored to individual users' expertise levels and decision-making contexts.

#### Cross-Domain Applications

HITL Explainability will expand across industries, influencing AI deployment in areas such as climate modeling, scientific research, and personalized education. By integrating human oversight, AI systems will contribute to more ethical, transparent, and socially responsible decision-making processes.

# Glossary of Key Terms

**Algorithmic Transparency:** The ability to understand how an AI model processes inputs and generates outputs, ensuring clarity in decision-making.

**Attention Mechanism:** A neural network component that helps models focus on important parts of the input data, improving interpretability.

**Bias in AI:** Systematic errors in AI decision-making due to skewed training data, model architecture, or algorithmic design.

**Black-Box Model:** An AI or machine learning model whose internal workings are not easily interpretable by humans.

**Causal Inference:** The process of determining cause-and-effect relationships within data to enhance AI explanations.

**Counterfactual Explanation:** A method of explaining AI decisions by showing how outcomes would change if certain inputs were altered.

**Decision Tree:** A machine learning model that splits data into hierarchical structures, making its decision-making process more interpretable.

**Deep Learning Interpretability:** Techniques used to explain how deep neural networks arrive at their predictions.

**Explainability:** The ability to make an AI system's decision-making process understandable to humans.

**Fairness in AI:** The principle of ensuring that AI models do not discriminate against individuals or groups based on biased data.

**Feature Attribution:** A method used to determine the importance of different features in an AI model's decision-making process.

**Feature Importance Methods:** Techniques such as SHAP and LIME that assess how individual features influence an AI model's predictions.

**Glass-Box Model:** A machine learning model designed with built-in interpretability, allowing users to understand its reasoning.

**Global Explanation:** An approach to explainability that provides insights into the overall functioning of an AI model.

**Gradient-Based Explanations:** Techniques that analyze how small changes in input affect model predictions, often used in deep learning models.

**Human-in-the-Loop (HITL) Explainability:** A system where human users interact with AI to refine explanations and improve understanding.

**Interpretability:** The degree to which a human can understand an AI model's logic and reasoning.

**Justifiability:** The ability to provide logical and ethical reasoning for AI decisions.

**LIME (Local Interpretable Model-Agnostic Explanations):** A popular technique that approximates AI model behavior using simple, interpretable models.

**Local Explanation:** A method of explainability that focuses on individual AI predictions rather than overall model behavior.

**Model-Agnostic Methods:** Explainability techniques that work across various machine learning models, independent of their underlying architecture.

**Model-Specific Methods:** Explainability techniques designed for particular types of AI models, such as convolutional neural networks (CNNs).

**Multi-Agent Systems in XAI:** The study of AI explainability in environments where multiple AI agents interact.

**Neural Network Visualization:** Techniques used to visually interpret neural networks, such as heatmaps and saliency maps.

**Post-Hoc Explanation:** An explanation derived after an AI model has made predictions, rather than being built into the model from the start.

**Predictive Accuracy vs. Interpretability Trade-Off:** The challenge of balancing model performance with its ability to be understood by humans.

**Proprietary XAI Solutions:** Explainability tools and frameworks developed by private companies to enhance AI transparency.

**Prototype-Based Explanation:** A technique that explains AI decisions by comparing them to representative examples from training data.

**Rule-Based Models:** AI models that use explicit rules for decision-making, making them inherently interpretable.

**Saliency Maps:** Visualization tools that highlight which parts of an input data set contributed most to an AI model's decision.

**SHAP (SHapley Additive exPlanations):** A widely used technique that quantifies the contribution of each feature in an AI model's predictions.

**Stakeholder-Centric Explainability:** Designing AI explanations tailored to the needs of different user groups, such as regulators, developers, and end-users.

**Surrogate Models:** Simpler, interpretable models used to approximate the behavior of complex AI systems.

**Testing and Validation in XAI:** Methods for assessing whether AI explanations are reliable, accurate, and meaningful.

**Transparency in AI:** The principle of making AI operations, data, and decision-making processes accessible and understandable.

**Trust in AI:** The confidence that users have in AI systems based on their fairness, reliability, and explainability.

**Uncertainty Quantification:** Methods used to assess how confident an AI model is in its predictions.

**User-Centered Explanations:** AI explanations that are tailored to different audiences, ensuring usability and comprehension.

**Visual Explanations:** Techniques such as heatmaps, attention maps, and graphical tools that aid in AI interpretability.

**Weight-Based Interpretability:** Analysis of an AI model's internal weights to understand its decision-making logic.

**White-Box Model:** Another term for glass-box models, referring to AI models that are inherently explainable.

**XAI (Explainable AI):** The field of AI research focused on improving transparency and interpretability in machine learning models.

**XAI for Generative AI:** The study of making AI-generated content, such as images and text, more interpretable and understandable.

**XAI in Criminal Justice:** The application of AI transparency techniques to ensure fairness and accountability in legal systems.

**XAI in Education:** The use of explainable AI to enhance personalized learning experiences and decision-making in education systems.

**XAI in Finance:** The application of AI explainability in risk assessment, fraud detection, and algorithmic trading.

**XAI in Healthcare:** The integration of explainability methods in AI-driven medical diagnoses and treatment recommendations.

**XAI in Law Enforcement:** The role of explainable AI in ensuring fair and unbiased decision-making in policing and investigations.

**XAI Regulatory Compliance:** Laws and guidelines that require AI models to be interpretable and transparent to users.

**Zero-Shot Explainability:** The ability of an AI model to generate explanations for predictions without prior examples.

# Reference


Artificial Intelligence: A Modern Approach Authors: Stuart Russell and Peter Norvig Publisher: Pearson Publication Year: 2020 (4th Edition)

Artificial Intelligence: A New Synthesis Author: Nils J. Nilsson Publisher: Morgan Kaufmann Publication Year: 1998

Artificial Intelligence: Foundations of Computational Agents Authors: David L. Poole and Alan K. Mackworth Publisher: Cambridge University Press Publication Year: 2010

Artificial Intelligence: Structures and Strategies for Complex Problem Solving Author: George F. Luger Publisher: Pearson Publication Year: 2008 (6th Edition)

Artificial Intelligence: A Guide for Thinking Humans Author: Melanie Mitchell Publisher: Farrar, Straus and Giroux Publication Year: 2019

Artificial Intelligence: A Guide to Intelligent Systems Author: Michael Negnevitsky Publisher: Pearson Publication Year: 2005

Artificial Intelligence: A Systems Approach Author: M. Tim Jones Publisher: Jones & Bartlett Learning Publication Year: 2008

Artificial Intelligence: A Very Short Introduction Author: Margaret A. Boden Publisher: Oxford University Press Publication Year: 2018

Artificial Intelligence: The Basics Author: Kevin Warwick Publisher: Routledge Publication Year: 2012

Artificial Intelligence: What Everyone Needs to Know Author: Jerry Kaplan Publisher: Oxford University Press Publication Year: 2016

Biomedical Data Analysis and Processing Using Explainable (XAI) and Responsive Artificial Intelligence (RAI) Publisher: Springer Publication Year: 2022

Computer Vision: Algorithms and Applications Author: Richard Szeliski Publisher: Springer Publication Year: 2010

Deep Learning Authors: Ian Goodfellow, Yoshua Bengio, and Aaron Courville Publisher: MIT Press Publication Year: 2016

Explainable AI Recipes: Implement Solutions to Model Interpretability with Python Publisher: Apress Publication Year: 2021

Explainable Artificial Intelligence: First World Conference, xAI 2023, Lisbon, Portugal, July 26–28, 2023, Proceedings, Part I Publisher: Springer Publication Year: 2023

Explainable AI with Python: Interpretability and Explainability of Machine Learning Models and Deep Learning Neural Networks Publisher: Springer Publication Year: 2021

Explainable AI: Interpreting, Explaining and Visualizing Deep Learning Publisher: Springer Publication Year: 2019

Explainable Artificial Intelligence: An Introduction to Interpretable Machine Learning Publisher: Springer Publication Year: 2021

Explainable Artificial Intelligence: Second World Conference, xAI 2024, Valletta, Malta, July 17–19, 2024, Proceedings, Part I Publisher: Springer Publication Year: 2024

Explainable AI for Healthcare: From Black Box to Glass Box Publisher: Springer Publication Year: 2021

Explainable AI for Practitioners: A Practical Guide to Interpretable Machine Learning Publisher: O'Reilly Media Publication Year: 2021

Explainable AI in Health Informatics Publisher: Springer Publication Year: 2023

Explainable AI within the Digital Transformation and Cyber-Physical Systems Publisher: Springer Publication Year: 2021

Explainable AI: Foundations, Methodologies and Applications Publisher: Springer Publication Year: 2022

Explainable AI: Interpreting, Explaining and Visualizing Deep Learning Publisher: Springer Publication Year: 2019

Explainable Artificial Intelligence: A Comprehensive Review Publisher: Springer Publication Year: 2021

Explainable Artificial Intelligence: An Applied Perspective Publisher: Springer Publication Year: 2023

Explainable Artificial Intelligence: What Do You Need to Know? Publisher: Springer Publication Year: 2020

Exploring Explainable AI: A Bibliometric Analysis Publisher: Springer Publication Year: 2024

Human Compatible: Artificial Intelligence and the Problem of Control Author: Stuart Russell Publisher: Viking Publication Year: 2019

Interpretable Machine Learning with Python: Learn to Build Explainable AI using Python Publisher: Packt Publishing Publication Year: 2020

Interpretable Machine Learning: A Guide for Making Black Box Models Explainable Publisher: Springer Publication Year: 2022

Introduction to Explainable AI Publisher: Springer Publication Year: 2023

Life 3.0: Being Human in the Age of Artificial Intelligence Author: Max Tegmark Publisher: Knopf Publication Year: 2017

Machine Learning: A Probabilistic Perspective Author: Kevin P. Murphy Publisher: MIT Press Publication Year: 2012

Natural Language Processing with Python Authors: Steven Bird, Ewan Klein, and Edward Loper Publisher: O'Reilly Media Publication Year: 2009

Pattern Recognition and Machine L earning Author: Christopher M. Bishop Publisher: Springer Publication Year: 2006

Probabilistic Graphical Models: Principles and Techniques Author: Daphne Koller and Nir Friedman Publisher: MIT Press Publication Year: 2009

Reinforcement Learning: An Introduction Authors: Richard S. Sutton and Andrew G. Barto Publisher: MIT Press Publication Year: 2018 (2nd Edition)

Robust Explainable AI Publisher: Springer Publication Year: 2023

Speec h and Language Processing Au thors: Daniel Jurafsky and James H. Martin Publisher: Pearson Publication Year: 2008 (2nd Edition)

Super intelligence: Paths, Dangers , Strategies Author: Nick Bostrom Publisher: Oxford University Press Publication Year: 2014

The Quest for Artificial Intelligence: A History of Ideas and Achievements Author: Nils J. Nilsson Publisher: Cambridge University Press Publication Year: 2009

# Index

www.ingramcontent.com/pod-product-compliance
Lightning Source LLC
LaVergne TN
LVHW071244210926
848486LV00008B/344
* 9 7 8 1 7 8 7 1 5 6 1 0 4 *